'*Finding Your Way with Your Bab*
based on years of clinical work an
authors' own experiences of paren
who tell their stories, coupled with
the realities of the business of parenting. As well as
the wonders of caring for small babies, what makes the book distinctive is that it tackles more difficult experiences that are rarely discussed in parenting books, but which nevertheless are common and deeply felt – such as fear and uncertainty, ambivalence and jealously, not just in the parent–infant relationship, but in relations between parents themselves. These can be frightening feelings that we would rather block off, yet, as the authors show, they may have negative consequences if we do not acknowledge them. The great strength of the book is that such experiences are taken seriously and treated sympathetically; clear and convincing accounts are provided for why they might occur, thereby lessening their power to be distressing, especially if they can be discussed with someone else. This book will be an enormous source of support for parents of young babies.'

– **Lynne Murray**, Professor of Developmental Psychology at the University of Reading and author of *The Psychology of Babies*

FINDING YOUR WAY WITH YOUR BABY

Finding Your Way with Your Baby explores the emotional experience of the baby in the first year, and that of the mother, father and other significant adults. It does so in a way that is deeply informed by psychoanalytic understandings, infant observation, developmental science and decades of clinical experience.

Combining the wisdom of many years' work with the freshness of up-to-date knowledge, Dilys Daws and Alexandra de Rementeria engage with the most difficult emotional experiences that are often glossed over in parenting books such as pregnancy, through birth into bonding, ambivalence about the baby, depression and the emotional turmoil so often brought to the surface by being a new parent. Acknowledgement and understanding of this darker side of family life offers a sense of relief that can allow parents to harness the power of knowing, owning and sharing feelings to transform situations and break negative cycles and old ways of relating. With real-life examples, references to current thinking and a calm and simple writing style, they also provide new insights into the more commonly covered issues such as weaning, sleeping and crying.

Finding Your Way with Your Baby is primarily aimed at parents but it will be a helpful resource for all those working with parents and babies including health visitors, midwives, social workers, GPs, paediatricians and childcare workers. It will appeal to parents and professionals who are interested in ideas from psychoanalytic clinical practice and the latest research in developmental psychology and neuroscience.

Dilys Daws is Honorary Consultant Child Psychotherapist at the Tavistock and Portman NHS Foundation Trust, London, and continues to practise at a baby clinic at the James Wigg Practice, Kentish Town. She was Founding Chair of the Association for Infant Mental Health, UK, and was Chair of the Association of Child Psychotherapists. She has fifty years of clinical and teaching experience, much of that on work with parents and babies, and has lectured on infant mental health widely in the UK and abroad.

Alexandra de Rementeria is on the doctoral training programme for child psychotherapy at the Tavistock and Portman NHS Foundation Trust and works at Lewisham Child and Adolescent Mental Health Services. She taught Early Years for five years prior to having her family and moving into mental health. She is the author of numerous articles for publications including the *Journal of Psychodynamic Practice* and the *Journal of Infant Observation.*

WITHDRAWN

FINDING YOUR WAY WITH YOUR BABY

The emotional life of parents and babies

Dilys Daws
and
Alexandra de Rementeria

LONDON AND NEW YORK

First published 2015
by Routledge
27 Church Road, Hove, East Sussex, BN3 2FA

and by Routledge
711 Third Avenue, New York, NY 10017

Routledge is an imprint of the Taylor & Francis Group, an informa business

© 2015 Dilys Daws and Alexandra de Rementeria

The right of Dilys Daws and Alexandra de Rementeria to be identified as authors of this work has been asserted by them in accordance with sections 77 and 78 of the Copyright, Designs and Patents Act 1988.

All rights reserved. No part of this book may be reprinted or reproduced or utilised in any form or by any electronic, mechanical, or other means, now known or hereafter invented, including photocopying and recording, or in any information storage or retrieval system, without permission in writing from the publishers.

Trademark notice: Product or corporate names may be trademarks or registered trademarks, and are used only for identification and explanation without intent to infringe.

British Library Cataloguing in Publication Data
A catalogue record for this book is available from the British Library

Library of Congress Cataloging in Publication Data
Daws, Dilys.
Finding your way with your baby: the emotional life of parents and babies/Dilys Daws and Alexandra de Rementeria.
pages cm
1. Parent and infant. 2. Parenting. 3. Parenthood—Psychological aspects. 4. Infants—Development. 5. Infant psychology. I. Title.
HQ755.84.D39 2015
649′.1—dc23
2014033287

ISBN: 978-1-138-78705-6 (hbk)
ISBN: 978-1-138-78706-3 (pbk)
ISBN: 978-1-315-76440-5 (ebk)

Typeset in Sabon
by Florence Production Ltd, Stoodleigh, Devon, UK

Printed and bound in the United States of America by Publishers Graphics, LLC on sustainably sourced paper.

To Health Visitors, the emotional safety-net
for all parents and babies.

To James, Amaia and Frankie and
to Ethan, Noa, Rosie, Tess, Polly and Conrad,
and to the memory of Nancy.

CONTENTS

A NOTE ON THE AUTHORS

Dilys Daws

This book is written by two child psychotherapists from different generations. I, Dilys Daws, qualified fifty years ago, have worked for over thirty years with parents and infants in a baby clinic and I am a grandmother. The other, Alex de Rementeria, still in doctoral training, was previously a teacher and is the mother of a baby and a toddler. We hope that we combine some wisdom of long experience with the freshness of up-to-date knowledge of child development research and recent experience of day-to-day life with babies.

When I had my own two children in the 1960s, there were times when I struggled with all the emotions of being a new mother. There were few books, but one charismatic one, *Baby and Child Care* by Dr Spock (first published in 1946), had a lovely tone to it, respectful of both mother and baby. Fathers were less often mentioned in those days. My copy, still lovingly kept, falls open at 'Crying in the early weeks'. It didn't stop my baby crying in the night, but it was comforting to read it while he did! I was lucky to meet Dr Spock in the 1980s, to chair a talk that he gave and to get him to sign my precious book. As well as reading the book, as a child psychotherapist, I had colleagues and friends to talk with about my feelings. At the time I wondered how other people managed. When I went back to work at the Child Guidance Training Centre and then the Tavistock Clinic, I decided to set up a service for parents who needed to talk about their new baby. In 1976 I started to work one morning a week at the Baby Clinic of the James Wigg Practice in Kentish Town, and am still there. I also helped develop the Under 5s Counselling Service at the Tavistock Clinic and have had much support from colleagues there.

My role in the Baby Clinic is to see parents referred by their health visitor or GP, who come, often distressed, with problems around feeding, sleeping or excessive crying, or with worries about bonding with their baby or with post-natal depression. These are parents for whom common-sense advice is not enough. Very often we find a relationship problem between parents and baby and surprisingly often there has been a separation or serious loss in the parents' own lives that makes it hard for them to sort out their baby's problem. This is not parent-blaming; thinking about the cause of a problem strengthens people's ability to solve it. My role is not to provide solutions, but to help parents to find their own and it is surprising how quickly these problems often get resolved. This reflects the style of Donald Winnicott, often quoted in this book. He was a paediatrician and psychoanalyst who popularised psychoanalytic thinking about mothers and their babies. His series of radio talks, starting in 1943, had an astonishingly direct way of talking about the feelings mothers have for their babies. These talks had passion, and mischievous humour. He encouraged mothers to trust their instincts, not to rely on others' advice (Winnicott, 1947). Anne Karpf has recently collated the talks in BBC4's *Archive on 4*. If you are interested in the work of child psychotherapists working with babies and their families today, *What Can the Matter Be* (Emanuel and Bradley, 2008) describes some work of my colleagues and me at the Tavistock, and Tessa Baradon's book *The Practice of Psychoanalytic Parent Infant Psychotherapy: Claiming the Baby* (2005) describes some of the excellent work undertaken at the Anna Freud Centre.

Alexandra de Rementeria

I was in the right place at the right time. I met Dilys while doing my pre-clinical masters, a course involving infant observation, child development research and psychoanalytic theory. I was lucky enough to have Dilys as my infant observation seminar leader and benefited personally, and in my learning, from her warmth and lightness of touch. When she first gave me a draft to read, I was delighted to find these qualities in her writing and feel sure you will benefit from them too.

I became pregnant with my first child in the last year of my masters and Dilys noted that I had recently read all the latest research on babies, was about to find out a few things for myself, and would have access to other new mums. I went back to my textbooks and added much of what is in the 'research' boxes and then to my friends and neighbours who populate the 'from parents' quotes. (I have also mixed in some of my own experiences with theirs, in order to afford my family some anonymity.) My children were very young when I started work on the book. I don't yet have the rose-tinted perspective of looking back on parenting that people tend to develop, so my main influence has probably been emphasising ambivalence as a normal part of parenting. I am now working part time as a trainee child psychotherapist at Lewisham Child and Adolescent Mental Health Services.

ACKNOWLEDGEMENTS

'It takes a village to raise a child.' Our respective 'villages' helped us greatly in writing this book – our families, friends, neighbours and patients. Also, our communities of the Tavistock Clinic, our child psychotherapy and other colleagues, and for Dilys, the James Wigg Practice and its Baby Clinic, Aimh-UK and Waimh. For Alex, it has been my mother who has made my involvement possible – she provided childcare so that I could write and her powers as a reader and editor to improve what I wrote.

Those who have inspired and encouraged us along the way, and those who have read the book at many stages (or both!) include Eric Rayner, Juliet Hopkins, Janine Sternberg, Eileen Orford, Mary-Sue Moore, Antoine Guedeney, Frances Thomson Salo, Campbell Paul, Astrid Berg, Rachael Davenhill, Louise Emanuel, Margaret Rustin, Susanna Rustin, Louise Greenberg, Miranda Passey, Rebecca Swift, Anna South, Graham Music, Eilis Kennedy, Ben Barnaby, Leila Bargawi, Louise O'Dwyer, Simon Corscaden, Adele O'Hanlon, Lynette Aitken, James Alexander, Hilary-Ann Salinger, Fanny Lena, Claire Gold, Georgia Law, Mollie Cooke, Barbara Dinham, Ursula Main, Imogen Kretzschmar, Linda Ashken, Vinita Joseph, Dawn de Freitas and Josh Garson.

Thanks to all at Routledge – to Joanne Forshaw for believing in this book, to Kirsten Buchanan, Katharine Atherton and Janice Baiton for their friendly partnership, and Sarah Steele and Susan Park for the finishing touches.

We do not wish to name all those who were so generous in providing anecdotes, in order to afford them anonymity, but we are very grateful to them for both their candour and their humour which have made their contributions such an important part of the book.

As well as providing the wonderful illustrations, Ros Asquith helped us reflect on the book's content and what was missing.

ACKNOWLEDGEMENTS

We would like to thank Anne Stevenson for permission to use her 'Poem for a daughter' from Anne Stevenson, *Poems 1955–2005* (Bloodaxe Books 2005) and Margaret Drabble for permission to use quotations from *The Millstone* (Penguin Books 1965).

INTRODUCTION

Why another baby book?

There is a wealth of interesting and useful information available in books, newspapers, magazines and online but it is not always easy to know how to make the most of what is out there. Busy parents are likely to skim or dip into things. As a result, much of what is written takes specific issues and deals with them in isolation. When a particular problem arises, such as sleeplessness or endless crying, parents will scan these texts for solutions. This will certainly be a help and Penelope Leach's *The Essential First Year* (2010) is a particularly good book of this kind. It starts at this point but goes further and looks at the context of emotions and relationships. We go further still. We know that 'advice' cannot take into account the specific story of a particular baby and his family. We are also aware that parents who are already in the throes of such painful family dramas are in no position to reflect on the context of events and relationships that might help to explain the problems they are experiencing. We feel there is a real danger that your baby, the real baby, might get pushed out of the picture by a bombardment of advice based on generalisations about babies. We invite you to reflect on your own baby and your own feelings and to find your own solutions.

What this book aims to do

This is the baby book that does not tell you what to do. We hope that it will encourage you to observe your baby, to really attend to the detail of what is happening in the moment and the feelings being aroused in you. We are not 'teasing' you by withholding knowledge of what to do when there are problems. You know your own baby better than we can, and might be strengthened to find your own solutions. The book describes the emotions involved in having a baby and watching his development. In becoming a parent you develop too. Perhaps nothing else in your life changes you so much.

This book is about knowledge, but it is also about not-knowing – about bearing uncertainty, conflicts and inconsistency, and about learning from your baby. The poet Keats created the phrase 'negative capability' which, rather confusingly, means bearing the negative. We talk, as do many books, about problems, we also talk more than most about negative feelings. This is not just because psychotherapists can see trouble everywhere. It is because we believe that negative feelings are an ordinary part of the human condition and that not being in touch with them can actually make your life more difficult. Understanding the origin of your feelings can help you manage them now.

Our intention is an optimistic one – that people who have had difficult childhoods or other hard times themselves need not feel this is bound to be passed on to their own baby. Remembering and thinking about your experiences can help you work out how to be different for your baby now, especially if you have support. Sometimes just reading the book and recognising your own situation will be helpful and give you a fresh view of how to cope. A key theme, however, is that talking to someone about any difficulties – putting thoughts into words, often for the first time – can bring great relief. It can enable people to have new thoughts and move on. It may help parents talk to each other about their feelings as well as about problem-solving. This is not about pathologising ordinary problems, it is about frank acknowledgement of the struggling that is inherent in ordinary development. We often suggest talking to a friend, or a professional, such as a health visitor or counsellor. Forgive the repetition! We believe so much that talking can help that we wanted to be sure that if you just dipped into the book there it would be.

The first section of the book deals with issues that might arise for you on becoming a parent. Some of the ideas discussed here may be unsettling. If you are reading this before your baby is born, you may find that it all sounds a bit too intense. The powerful emotional and biochemical changes described might feel threatening, but it is worth remembering that once the baby arrives, everything has its own momentum and logic and you will likely take these changes in your stride. The second section goes on to look at each aspect of life with your baby, such as sleeping or weaning, roughly in the order that it might take centre stage. This section also looks at play and how you come to know your baby's emerging personality. In the final section the focus will expand to look at your new family in the wider context of extended family and work. We will encourage you to reflect on your own experiences, views and expectations and to stay focused on what your baby seems to be experiencing. Research, theory and practice from various fields will be presented, with references where appropriate. You will decide whether to follow up or ignore these ideas depending on whether they have any resonance for you and whether you have the time!

Two of the themes that weave through the book are worth highlighting. The first is the way in which, for all of us, our own experience of being parented informs the way we parent. This is true at a conscious level when we try to avoid or emulate aspects of our parents' parenting (from fondly remembered bedtime routines to dreaded phrases you swear never to use). However, much of what determines the way we behave as parents happens at an unconscious level. The second theme is linked to this. It is about helping you to harness the power of knowing, owning and sharing your feelings, especially the dark and difficult feelings, to transform situations and break negative cycles. It is easy to become trapped in negative cycles in specific interactions with loved ones and through generations in a family. This time in your life, when there is so much change, when the plates are shifting and stirring up all sorts in the deep, presents a wonderful opportunity to break with old ways of relating and forge a new landscape for yourself and your family.

Who is this book for?

Understandably, at times, parents want to be told what to do. We all long for certainty and the feeling that we can trust in an authority figure when we are troubled with doubt. However, in turning to a voice of certainty you may limit your capacity to entertain different possibilities and so miss out on the chance to work out creative solutions that really work for you and your family. Rather than telling you what to do, we hope to support you to do the thinking that might free you up to enjoy life with your baby.

A note on culture

Since the 1960s, research in the fields of anthropology and ethnography has shown that differences in parenting practices across cultures reflect the different expectations each culture has of its adult members. Parenting is adapted to create the kinds of adult individuals that a society values. Western child-rearing practices tend to produce individualistic people well adapted to the relatively 'atomised' existence of those of us living in wealthy capitalist economies. Many Eastern cultures are noted for placing more value on interdependence and their parenting practices prepare people to be dependable within large close-knit extended families. In fact many of the parents we talked to when researching this book found themselves torn between the maternal and the paternal families' traditions, which often differed in the degree to which they had been influenced by such ideas. With the recent birth of a royal baby, it has been reported that Princess Diana broke with Windsor traditions by using *The Continuum Concept* (Liedloff, 1975). This book popularised the idea that Western child-rearing practices had become detrimental to the needs of children and communities and recommended that Western parents take up the practices Liedloff (1975) had observed when living with traditional South American Indians in a Venezuelan jungle. It might be fascinating to speculate on Diana's personal and political motivations: perhaps she wanted to rebel against and rescue her children from the culture of 'a stiff upper-lip', a culture personified by her mother-in-law and one that had propelled the British Empire. However, perhaps what is more helpful is to note how complex and heterogeneous contemporary, post-colonial families and societies tend to be. They are also ever-changing. China is now home to the fastest growing middle class and presumably this will impact on the parenting styles there. Ethnic difference does not presuppose cultural difference, and explanations about differences in parenting based on ethnic or cultural differences may or may not be helpful when talking about particular families but are likely to be unhelpful when talking in generalities, which is what this book must often do. We do not claim that this book is about everybody but we do hope that it might be useful to anybody.

We work in inner-city clinics serving communities with complex, mostly peaceful social and ethnic mixes. We enjoy diverse heritages ourselves, Russian–Jewish and Chilean/Basque respectively, but would probably be identified as white and middle class. As such we are honoured to be taken seriously by families very different in origin from ourselves. However, who we are and where we come from does position the book within a particular, albeit complex, set of norms and assumptions and it is important to acknowledge this. Graham Music (2011) describes the difficulty of accepting that there may be alternative and radically different ways of parenting that are good enough and the best fit for a particular culture, when one's own beliefs feel as if they have a moral certainty about them. He cites research by Heidi Keller to illustrate this. She showed Nso mothers (rural Cameroons) videos of German mothers trying to comfort their babies without breastfeeding them. Typical Nso responses were to question if these were in fact the real mothers or to wonder if it was forbidden in German culture to hold your baby. They were shocked to see videos of German babies sleeping alone. Conversely, German mothers watching videos of vigorous bodily stimulation massage, common practice in many cultures, were very concerned about this being intrusive and not taking account of the babies' own tempo. Of course it is not possible or helpful to take an entirely relativist position because there is a need to draw a line somewhere in order to protect children from mistreatment. Yet we endeavour, and inevitably fail sometimes, to acknowledge that we are mostly thinking about culturally prescribed norms rather than universal truths.

A note on research

The ideas and experiences that inform this book are varied. The 'knowledge' compiled here has been gained in many different arenas. Knowledge is never absolute truth. It is something generated and each kind of 'knowledge' has its own claims to validity.

Most of the research cited in outlined boxes comes from the fields of neuroscience and developmental psychology. The former is a 'hard science' and follows the principles of objectivity. This is the most effective approach for gathering accurate information about the physical world and, quite rightly, scientific validity is highly valued in our society. This is why much of the research undertaken in developmental psychology tries to emulate the experimental model which has been able to provide persuasive evidence for formulations about how minds develop. There are, however, limitations to such an approach to studying human experience and human interactions. The main problem is the sheer complexity of the phenomena of minds. The most sensitive equipment for picking up and analysing such subtlety and nuance is an individual's experience of a situation. However, if subjective experience is admitted as a source of information then, many people feel, claims to scientific objectivity are compromised.

We would urge you to read the 'from research' boxes with as critical an eye as you would read anything else, in this book or elsewhere. The ideas described there have been included because they are the findings of peer-reviewed research. The ideas have earned the status of being worthy of consideration, or of being thought reasonable explanations, but they are not irrefutable facts. All research methods from naturalistic observation to laboratory experiments have inherent weaknesses, which should be held in mind when considering the findings they produce. Graham Music's book *Nurturing Natures* (2011) is wonderful in many ways and we refer to it many times in this book. It brings together and brings to life the findings of much varied research in the fields of child development but does so with a constant and thoughtful commentary on the research methods used and their relative strengths and weaknesses. This book is less formal and we excuse ourselves from such academic rigor in the name of staying conversational but we recommend his book if you are interested in research methods.

Psychoanalytic theory has been developed using the subjective experience of analysts and therapists. Ideas about how the mind works are generated and tested, discarded and developed based on a loose consensus about what best describes what happens in therapeutic encounters. These ideas have been helping people to overcome psychological and emotional difficulty very effectively for many decades. The wise and humorous former Archbishop of Canterbury Rowan Williams said that the history of the Anglican Church was a 'history of discarded solutions'. In your journey with your baby you may discard many solutions as you move on; it doesn't mean they were not right at the time.

The anecdotes from parents in italics can only speak of each specific experience described. By most measures for evaluating the validity of knowledge this does not rate highly, yet they will probably speak most directly to your own experience. We hope that they will help to illustrate some of the other ideas.

Between us the authors have considerable experience in chatting to parents and babies and reading and evaluating research from various fields. Dilys has had a long career in which to test the usefulness of ideas in her therapeutic practice. However, we do not want you to take our word for anything written in the boxes. By using differentiated boxes to delineate different kinds of knowledge and by explaining a little about how that knowledge was generated, we leave it to you to decide whether what is said has enough authority to influence you.

Part I

BECOMING A PARENT

These first six chapters are about the process of becoming a parent. Your own experiences, particularly of being parented, will all inform the kind of parent you will become. This section explores the biochemical changes that pregnancy and bonding can trigger in both parents and the inevitable changes to identity that ensue. If this is all sounding rather pre-determined and making you feel uncomfortable about a loss of control, then you might be relieved to know that those uncomfortable feelings, and many others, are part of what we explore here.

1

LIFE WILL NEVER BE THE SAME AGAIN

Creating a new life

Apart from being born oneself, having a baby is probably the most momentous event in any mother's life and usually in the father's too. You are creating new life. Then you will be responsible for that life, for keeping a dependent little human being alive. You will also become officially part of the adult/parent generation.

You are bound to have mixed feelings about all this. On the one hand is the excitement, perhaps the feeling that this is the crux of all worthwhile creativity; on the other hand is the loss of independence and of identity. These mixed feelings do not mean you will be a 'bad' parent. In fact you are more likely to be a good parent if you can 'own' all these feelings. Your baby needs parents who are not set upon being perfect (see Chapter 4). If you don't have too fixed an idea about how you should be, you can be spontaneous and follow your instincts, and your baby will have real people to respond to.

In pregnancy you may feel like the star of the show. This might feel like a privilege at times, a burden at others. Perhaps you feel overlooked – just a vessel for the all-important baby. It may seem like your body is enhanced by the new life growing inside you, or that you have a little alien eating up your resources.

From parents . . .

> *'I felt besieged from within by the baby and from without where suddenly I was public property.'*

> *'I loved being pregnant. I felt like a queen, honoured by the world for my services to humanity – being given a seat on*

> *the bus, my husband having to put my shoes on, but also joining the human race – being claimed by strangers from different communities who would never usually talk to me at a bus stop.'*
>
> *'I felt potent and powerful and I loved the feeling. I wanted to do it all over again almost straight away – it felt addictive and I remember thinking: no wonder men want to conquer countries – they're just trying to get this feeling.'*

Having a baby is of course different for each of you. Mothers have the direct responsibility of 'growing' the baby and giving birth. A father's contribution, beyond the physiological one of impregnating the mother with his sperm, is the enjoyable unselfishness of looking after both mother and the developing foetus. This can be equally heroic but is often less well acknowledged.

However you feel about it, there will be many physical changes and much hormonal upheaval. You probably knew all this was likely. What can be more surprising is the way that at times you feel like a baby yourself, especially in the company of your own mother. The feelings aroused by having to look after the little baby inside you can stir up infantile feelings of needing to be looked after. These ordinary feelings can be indulged in if your mother is available. It can be a particularly sad time if you haven't got such a relationship. How you, as an expectant mother, feed the baby inside depends

From research on the physiological 'tugs of war' of pregnancy . . .

While the common fantasy of being host to an alien may seem fanciful, Graham Music describes the physiology of pregnancy in such a way as to show that it isn't actually that far off the mark: 'The foetus sends hormones into the mother's blood steam that can raise maternal blood pressure, sometimes giving rise to symptoms ranging in seriousness from swollen calves to preeclampsia, all to increase its own supply of nutrients. The foetus re-models the mother's arteries so that she can no longer constrict the vessels that supply the embryo without starving herself. In effect the foetus establishes control of the territory and can then start to grow' (2011: 15).

partly on your relationship with your mother and how you feel about the way you were nourished as a child. If you felt physically and emotionally well fed by your mother, it is often easier to take pleasure in what you eat now in order to help your baby grow inside you.

Pregnancy can be a time of hope but also great anxiety. Fear of miscarriage, especially if you have already experienced this loss, can be quite powerful at the beginning. Routine ante-natal testing can bring fears for the baby's health to a peak twice during this period but it usually leaves couples reassured and able to move into later pregnancy more confidently, although some continue to worry about their capacity to produce a healthy baby.

Pregnancy can be a scary but exciting time for other reasons too. You and your partner are having to re-evaluate your relationship. This may be the moment for committing yourselves to each other in a major way. Women may worry about their partner leaving at this point. It can be hard to believe that he will happily adjust from the romantic twosome that you may have previously enjoyed or that your changing body will still be attractive. These are ordinary thoughts and perhaps they serve as a warning to the mother about not getting too privately absorbed into thoughts about the baby, thus shutting her partner out. Men may well feel tempted to escape to the familiar world outside. The challenge is to pull together at this stage and support each other through all that is new and uncertain.

From parents . . .

> *'My husband and I do not have big confrontations but the night before I was due to do a pregnancy test I picked a fight with him, pulling at all the loose threads in our relationship and finally storming off to sleep on the sofa. He was utterly bemused and actually so was I. In the morning we took the test and were delighted to discover that I was pregnant. Perhaps I was just scared and looking for an excuse to bolt.'*

With unexpected pregnancies, parents who have not yet committed themselves to be partners may have a difficult task of deciding whether or not to get together permanently. They can feel trapped by the baby or relieved to have a reason to stay together but complicated feelings may linger after the decision is made. Unmarried fathers in an accidental pregnancy are often treated as 'naughty boys'. The woman who decides to go ahead with the pregnancy may mature in the process. The young man may have no one pay attention to him, or tell him he is important and needed. He has no help in growing into a responsible father. If he and the mother can agree on him being involved, even if not wanting to continue their own relationship, he may become a valuable support to mother and baby. He may then find his self-respect increase as a result.

The personal dreams and worries, and the memories of childhood that flood in, need to be shared. Talking about this is part of shaping your lives together, and how you will co-operate as parents. It helps to start this before the hard work of parenting bombards you. Worries about the responsibility for the baby, about giving up freedom, the mother's concerns about losing control of her body, are all important things to share. Trusting your partner with your deepest feelings is the first stage of trusting him or her to be the co-parent of your baby. These need not be gloomy conversations – humour can help get to the essence of your feelings.

Remembering the past

Pregnancy is a time of looking backwards as well as forwards. Many mothers-to-be find themselves remembering all sorts of strange things that they have not thought of for years. Some describe the experience as a sort of 'stock-taking' of life up to now. For others it is more difficult, they find themselves trawling through painful or embarrassing times that they would prefer not to remember. Two friends in conversation came up with an interesting theory to explain this experience.

Friend 1: 'I keep thinking of all the stupid things I've ever done, you know, every humiliation relived. It's awful.'
Friend 2: 'I know exactly what you mean, I call it rummaging around in the shit cupboard, I can spend a whole afternoon in there!'
Friend 1: 'Yeah, maybe that's it. Maybe it's like a spring clean of the mind, you know, so everything's all cleared out and ready for the baby.'

Revisiting your childhoods

Most prospective parents find themselves remembering and thinking about their own childhood, with pleasure, with resentments, probably both. These memories are important, they are part of the information about how to be parents with your own baby.

You may still be going through a necessary time of growing away from your own parents. You need to think for yourself, to work out your own values and philosophy, otherwise each generation would be clones of the last one. It can then be difficult to give up this questioning and get back in touch with the positive in what you learnt from your parents. Having said that, many people find they have a sort of 'reconciliation' with their parents at this time.

It is more difficult if you had an unhappy childhood or were actually neglected or badly treated. In fact if you can remember and think about this, it can be easier than if it is all a blank. Telling someone you trust can help you recover from its effects and get it into perspective. You then have a better chance of a happy relationship with your own baby (see Chapter 4).

Being pregnant can feel like its own state, divorced from the reality of the coming baby. 'Not many parents realise they'll get a baby as a result,' said a health visitor running ante-natal classes.

Coming to the end

It is fortunate that pregnancy usually takes nine months – there is so much to do in the time. Not only is it a growing period, physically and emotionally, but also a time for conflicting feelings to be reconciled. Pregnancy means two parents having to learn to get together about an inescapable responsibility. There are two families with different histories converging about their shared hopes for the future. It is not just the baby that you will need to take on after conception, you have also created prospective grandparents to the baby and they may feel strongly involved.

Childbirth and after the birth

After nine months you finally get to the birth. This is a time of excitement, fear and huge emotions. Preparing for the birth involves making lots of decisions and managing your own hopes and fears. If you are informed and have thought through the choices, you have a better chance of keeping some control over the process. You may, however, have to 'let go' and trust that the medical team will make sure that you and your baby will be OK. One doula said that she recommends women write a birth plan, mean it and then burn it so that they can meet the actual birth with an informed but open mind.

Talking over your feelings and fears about the labour, with your partner, a friend or with a helpful professional, is part of the preparation for birth. Most women probably feel as they start to give birth, 'Help, I'm not ready yet,' and wish this was the rehearsal, not the real thing – but if you have seriously ambivalent feelings, and haven't let anyone else know about them, it may be harder to go through the birth in an uncomplicated way. It would be foolish to suggest that difficult births are all psychologically based – but how a woman responds to difficulties can depend on her emotional state. The loss of control over what is happening to her body and who gets access to it during labour can be particularly difficult for anybody who has suffered physical or sexual abuse in the past.

Giving birth is a very strange time – it is both an end and a beginning – the end of the time when you and your baby had a unique, almost secret relationship. She was inside you, and only you. As she comes out, the rest of the world can see her. She belongs to her father, the rest of the family, and you can see her as herself, as an individual.

From parents . . .

> *'Sometimes, when I greet my own adult children a wave of memory will come over me and a disbelief that their large persons were once tucked inside me. It's hard to imagine it now, but impossible to forget.'*

So, the labour is the end of this special relationship with the baby. Mothers can have a strong feeling of loss of the baby inside; the outside visible baby can feel to be somehow less special.

If the baby is premature, there may be feelings of upset at not having 'kept hold' of the baby inside for longer. There will be fears, sometimes for good reasons, that the baby was not really ready for the world and is vulnerable.

Of course it is harder for anyone who has had late miscarriages, or has reason to think something may be wrong with the baby, to go through the birth process optimistically. But there is something about pregnancy and birth that can carry optimism with it.

Fathers and the birth

It really matters that fathers are not marginalised out of this significant moment in the history of their family.

From fathers . . .

> *'It was a traumatic birth and I felt so helpless, but I kept telling myself how important it was for my wife, myself and our baby that I should be there and stand it.'*

> *'The midwife was brilliant and boosted our confidence. We phoned her at the beginning of labour and she left me responsible for monitoring when to call her to the house. When it got under way, I felt my role was to just be around and to be encouraging but at times I didn't know what to say. It was dreadful to witness her pain. I kept feeling like bursting into tears. Then there was the elation of her birth. It is a real privilege to be in a position to grapple with life and death. Although come the second stage my wife was more fixed onto the midwife than me.'*

> *'When I heard her making noises that I recognised from the late stages of our first daughter's birth I phoned the*

> *midwife, then 999 to say we needed an ambulance. Meanwhile my wife tried to climb into the pool, which at this stage only had about one inch of scaldingly hot water in it. She swore at me like a docker. As I described the situation to the guy on the phone it became apparent that the baby was coming. The next thing I remember is seeing my daughter's whole head appear. I told my wife to give one more push and then I was holding my daughter. The guy on the phone heard her cry and said: "It sounds like you've done it. Congratulations!" We all shuffled over to sit on the sofa in a daze of laughing and crying. Then the ambulance crew all steamed in saying "Right, so your waters have broken . . . oh I see we're a bit late!"'*

It shouldn't take events as extraordinary as those just described for fathers' relevance and competence to be realised. However, there does also seem to be a special point in having another woman present at the birth. It may be sufficient for this to be the midwife, especially if she has become known and trusted during the ante-natal period as in the 'one-to-one' midwifery care system. Many women find that to have a woman who has had a baby – mother, sister or friend – can be particularly supportive in the hours leading up to the birth. Something about women's experience through the generations perhaps gets handed on. It is vital, however, that this does not hustle out the father and make him feel he is in the way. He really does belong in there.

Talking aloud about what is going on during the birth is important and this is where fathers are essential, in listening to mothers and making sure that the professionals are keeping you both informed. Afterwards good midwives and doctors will want to help you de-brief and get the process of the birth into perspective by exchanging recollections. You may then want to tell whoever will be looking after you and your baby's health, usually your GP and health visitor, about your experience. Having them know about the birth is the best way to start a long-term, professional relationship with them and can help you recover sooner from any traumatic aspects of the birth. These different stages of talking are enjoyable in their own right, and help ensure that a difficult birth does not turn into a difficult start for your relationship with your baby.

A magical moment

The moment when the baby comes out is unforgettable. Many parents feel that they know their baby's character at once, and that perhaps the baby knows them too (see Chapter 7). Parents describe every sort of reaction from awe and wonder right through to confusion or shock.

From parents . . .

> *'This little creature that we created actually exists and that means we are parents now!'*
>
> *'The euphoria and elation in the moments and hours after birth were amazing! I remember having the insane thought that I wanted another one, next week!'*
>
> *'Our midwife was amazing and we had a doula who had taught my husband massage techniques to help control the pain. I was really well supported and had an amazing birth but during transition I still went to a really dark place and for that time I hated them all, including my husband and the baby and I bitterly regretted my situation but then once she was born the euphoria and elation kicked in.'*
>
> *'The birth was awful. Once she was born I wanted to know that she was ok but to be honest I didn't really want to be with her for a little while. I was shaking horribly from the adrenalin and could not focus. Within half an hour I was all moony eyed, poring over her perfect little face, awash with love.'*
>
> *'My wife had a caesarean and after the event came the quiet. I was concerned about my wife's condition but I also felt tremendous things, wishes, hopes – wanting to almost worship my wife and her body and this baby, our daughter. I did also need to distance myself from the awfulness of the operating theatre and stepped out for a moment to remove my gown. I could hear her saying: "What is your daddy doing? He's putting his clothes back on." I caught myself wondering who this man "daddy" was, even thought some other man was in there with them. Then I realised she was talking to our baby about me. I didn't yet recognise myself as "daddy".'*

> *'The labour was protracted and the birth not at all as I had wanted but when she was born it was lovely. We were just so thrilled with her and wanted to make her as comfortable as possible. I loved the feeling of her naked body against mine. My husband put our clothes over the lamps to dim the lighting, we felt the light must have seemed so harsh to her. We were completely focused on her and her experience. When the time came to move to the ward I was really reluctant to dress her. You don't put nappies on perfect little creatures who just popped out naked! I just wanted to hold her like that for ever.'*

For the parents of a baby with a disability there can be even more complicated and conflicting feelings to work through. This is movingly expressed in the quote below from the mother of a baby with Down's syndrome. In later chapters we will return to their story to hear about how their bond developed in time.

> As I became more fully conscious a wave of euphoria came over me, I experienced an overwhelming sense of joy that our son, the one I had hoped for, had been born. Then they told me he was to be physically and mentally handicapped for life. I don't remember any more words, just the awful feeling, a kind of sickness and blankness – a candle flickering and spluttering and finally going out.
>
> (Wyllie 2012: 19)

There are many reactions to birth for many reasons. It can be particularly difficult if the birth doesn't go according to plan. If you had an unexpected caesarean, or an epidural when you'd decided not to, you can feel disappointed or even like a failure. Anaesthesia can make you sleepy and not ready to take an interest in your baby yet. Your baby may similarly be feeling drowsy. Also, some mothers feel 'detached' after a traumatic birth. For whatever reasons, after the birth you might feel as if your baby is simply getting in the way of your own needs, then the last thing you want to do is cuddle him or her. Give yourself time.

It does help to think that even if the big moment after birth falls rather flat, *your* moment of discovery and excitement may come in your own time, a day to two later.

From research on establishing a bond . . .

Graham Music pulls together research showing that encouraging contact between infants and mothers at risk of parenting disorders reduces the risk of abandonment. Also: 'if an infant's lips touched it's mother's nipple within the first hour of life, it increased the time mothers kept her infant with her by one hundred minutes a day' (2011: 24). You don't need to have fireworks between you or be breastfeeding from the off, but you and your baby do need the chance to get to know one another, physically and emotionally.

After the birth

If you are spending just a couple of days in hospital, a lot will be crowding in to a very short time – but time is relative and this is one of the most eventful bits of your whole life. The nurses may be very helpful in letting you have the space just to get to know your baby by looking after you and leaving you free to care for your own baby. This allows you to feel your baby is safe under their expert eyes. If it's not like that, at least you know you'll soon be out. But don't let anyone bully you into making decisions you don't want to

From psychoanalytic theory and clinical practice . . .

The paediatrician and psychoanalyst Winnicott noticed that in order to become 'well enough attuned' (see Chapter 4) to the baby to be able to 'feel' his needs and respond to them, mothers must: 'reach a heightened state of sensitivity . . . which enables them to adapt delicately and sensitively to the infant's needs . . . to become preoccupied with their own infant to the exclusion of other interests' (Winnicott 1956: 2). He named this state 'primary maternal preoccupation' and described the way in which a mother's thoughts attention and energy are pulled towards her baby, skewing her perspective and even her perception of reality. A baby requires an extra-ordinary feat of altruism in his carer in order that he be kept safe and have his physical and emotional needs met. Maternal preoccupation seems to be nature's way of making sure parents can orientate to this monumental task.

make. For instance, breastfeeding can be hard going at first – but you don't have to get it right straight away. You've got a couple of days' breathing space before your milk properly comes in and the baby can coast along till then. A few hours can seem like an eternity, but it isn't. Don't be cheated out of the chance to breastfeed just to rescue you from a difficult few days.

Primary maternal preoccupation

I, Dilys, remember general well-founded fears about a nuclear war at the end of my first pregnancy and thinking, 'They must all know the world can't be going to blow up, because I'm about to have my baby.' A somewhat grandiose thought! Yet, it seems that this sort of loss of perspective is quite common.

From parents . . .

> *'On returning home from hospital I was embarrassed to remember that I had "thoughtfully" drawn the curtain around my baby, whilst on the ward, so as to save the other mothers from having to look upon his superior beauty!'*
>
> *'A day or two after my caesarean I made it to my feet and went to the loo. It was the first time I had left my baby and I was on my way back to my bed when I saw a man trying to leave the ward with a baby in his arms. I found myself hobbling towards him at speed before intercepting him and asking him in a friendly but firm voice: "Is that your baby? What's his name?" (I'd catch him out!). He was, of course, the father of the baby in the next bed.'*
>
> *'I was on such a high leaving the hospital, so proud of our daughter that I thought it quite natural that strangers in the street would be staring at us, admiring her and envying me. Later I realised that the car seat we were carrying her in was facing backwards, so that none of these people could in fact see her. They were probably staring at me because of the wildly smug smile on my face.'*
>
> *'A few hours after the birth I got into a pleasurably aggressive attitude towards the ward sister who did not want me to have my baby in bed with me overnight. I shrank away from her when she offered to hold my daughter while I went to the loo. Although it was awkward*

> *I managed to use the loo with my baby gripped to my chest. I felt strangely alert and potent. It was delicious to know that I had access to all the power of animal aggression usually so well repressed in my biddable nature. I can now look back and have some sympathy for the ward sister but at the time nothing was going to come between me and my baby.'*

It is interesting that, in hindsight, these women are able to see that their thinking had not been reasonable. Each describes a temporary loosening of her grip on reality. They may be slightly embarrassed to recall these stories but they are also proud of them. They seem to understand that this strange state is appropriate to this special time.

Intensive care

If your baby has to be in intensive care, try to be with her as much as possible. She certainly needs the technology and expert medical and nursing care to keep her alive and develop physically but she also needs her parents to help her develop emotionally. You need to be able to watch her, to be there with your presence and, as much as is feasible, to touch or even hold her. Your feeling of empty arms if you don't hold her is instinctive information; that's where your baby really belongs. Don't be put off by the skill and expertise of the medical staff. Your baby also needs your thoughts about her and needs, when possible, to start learning about the feel and smell of your body and the sound of your voice. Whenever it is safe to do so, she could be getting to know you in this way. Premature babies may need to curl up, as they would have done if they were still in the womb. You can help your baby snuggle up to you, holding her in this curled up position.

Having your baby admitted to the neonatal intensive care unit can be an extremely stressful time. Parents are obviously very worried about their baby's immediate health and the prognosis. Furthermore, they can feel guilty if there are other children at home, whom they are seeing less of, because they are spending a great deal of time on the unit. McFayden (1994) and Mendelsohn (2005) have written about their experiences of working with parents in neonatal intensive care units. They found that the admission on the unit 'tends to constrain [parents' abilities] rather than promote them' (McFayden 1994: 169), as parents can feel exposed in front of professionals. Mendelsohn points out that because the nurses are so competent, mothers find it hard to believe that their baby is truly theirs, or needs them. She says that many parents of babies in neonatal intensive care units have been traumatised by their experiences of birth, which was not the birth that they had planned for or anticipated. The developing relationship between the parent and infant is then complicated when the infant is admitted to a neonatal unit. Issues of closeness and distance can be difficult to regulate, as some parents, seeing no stimulation for the infant, will try to redress the balance and over stimulate their babies, whereas other parents will feel their infant is too fragile for any stimulation and will become distant.

From research on Kangaroo Care . . .

Kangaroo Care means taking the baby out of the incubator and placing her naked, tucked inside mother or father's top, for a few hours a day. Genesoni et al. (2008) describe how the heat of the parent's body regulates the baby's temperature, which means they can act as 'natural incubators' for the baby. Skin-to-skin contact reproduces, if only partially, the sense of 'oneness' mothers feel when their baby is still in utero. It can help relieve the sense of loss experienced at birth – due to the baby's admission to the special care baby unit – through the re-establishment of the mother–infant unit. It can trigger parenting behaviours that may stay dormant if there are no such opportunities for affectionate touch and stroking of the baby, gazing at the baby's face, 'motherese' vocalisations, positive maternal affect, and the co-ordination of the mother's or father's behaviour to the infant's state and signals.

Kangaroo Care also allows the immature preterm infant to recover at least some aspects of the prenatal environment. The feel of her body against another body which moves and breathes, the gradual adjustment of her body on her mother's chest requires her to continue to develop her proprioceptive sense as she would in utero. The change of position from horizontal to vertical similarly stimulates the vestibular sense and proximity means she can smell her mother and hear the familiar sound of her mother's heartbeat and voice. These experiences give her back some of her experience in the womb but also introduce the preterm baby to the experience of a nurturing, contingent, stable and predictable caregiver.

Skin contact promotes the physiological growth of the baby and her autonomic nervous system maturation. Specifically, Kangaroo Care improves arousal regulation, increases the infant capacity to habituate to and cope with external stimulation, stabilises the heart rate, optimises breastfeeding and fosters motor organisation by minimising purposeless movements. Moreover, it provides a natural protection from the often abrupt sensory stimulation of a special care baby unit, such as lights and sounds.

Researchers have reported that parents who provided Kangaroo Care to their babies were more focused and confident in meeting the needs of their infants, felt more comfortable with the surroundings and had greater self-esteem. In particular parents' confidence increases regardless of the infant's health status, from a state of feeling nervous and scared to feelings of 'being needed' by the child and the nursing staff.

From parents . . .

'It was an enormous wrench when they were delivered by emergency c-section. I felt I'd let them down badly by not keeping them safe and nurtured inside me. I was so sad to have lost my pregnancy bump and all the excitement and anticipation of the rest of the pregnancy. I was tortured by 'what ifs' – maybe if I'd rested more . . . I wanted to turn the clock back so much so that I dreaded the thought of returning home from the hospital, fearing that I'd be overwhelmed with longing to have the babies back inside me. I also wanted to be near them all the time and the prospect of leaving them behind in hospital seemed terrible.

One thing that I didn't quite expect was the incredible strength of the connection we both felt as parents towards the babies. Despite all the machines, the doctors and nurses, the worry, it was as if their suffering drew us even closer to them. Although fragile and painfully small, their distinct personalities shone through. They had a whole range of expressions from frowns and looking perplexed to smiles of contentment and pleasure. We both got to know them very early in their existence and looking back I wonder if this was something positive that came out of the experience, not the prematurity obviously, but that sense of closeness has stayed with us.

The anxiety is hard to bear. There is the immediate anxiety of the babies being connected to monitors that are constantly going off and the worry that they might suddenly deteriorate and then the longer-term anxiety about the impact of the prematurity on their overall development. Some nursing staff were sensitive and seemed to have the knack of fostering our developing relationship with the babies. Others appeared to be inured to the anxiety generated by the high-tech medical environment and parental worries were readily dismissed. I feel quite sore about being made to feel an "anxious mother" now that I've had a full-term baby that I wasn't anxious about taking home. The paediatric doctors were careful to temper any optimism on our part with caution about the long-term consequences of prematurity. On the other hand, friends and family members tended to be eager to reassure us that everything was just fine. It could be frustrating at times trying to navigate a middle course, realistic about likely problems yet positive about our children's potential.

It's demanding to look after a baby in such a setting. One of the other mothers used to refer to the experience as "neonatal boot camp". Right from the start you are encouraged to express breast milk every three hours over a twenty-four-hour period using a large hospital-grade electric pump. It was very easy to become obsessed with the quality and quantity of breast milk as cartons of milk accumulated in the fridge. When our baby daughter was born a couple of years later I couldn't quite believe that instinctively she could competently feed from the moment of birth.'

2

BRINGING YOUR BABY HOME

After getting used to the idea of a pregnancy, and managing the birth, what next? Nothing can really prepare you for what it's like to have a new little being, which the two of you created, there in your home. It is wonderful and exhilarating but may be surprisingly scary. If you had your baby in hospital, you may have felt looked after, watched over by the experienced staff. Even if it felt too busy and noisy and at times you felt intruded on, you will probably have felt relieved that you didn't have to be totally in charge.

You may feel immensely excited and proud about starting life together at home as a family but the responsibility that you as mother and father now have for keeping this new little person alive can be overwhelming. All the decisions are now yours to make. You may find you miss not just the hospital staff but the institution of the hospital. We all have a tendency to 'regress', to go back to childlike dependency when we are in a 'caring' place, and can find it hard to pull back into being our adult selves. How much more when you now have a totally dependent being, who needs you to be the adult in charge. It can be hard to know what is 'right' or 'normal' in this strange new world.

From parents . . .

> *'Trying to keep my daughter's tiny, delicate little body supported as I lowered her into the car seat seemed impossible. She sensed my anxiety and started to cry. It seemed so wrong that I actually considered walking the four miles home from the hospital despite a broken coccyx, just so that I could keep her in my arms.'*
>
> *'We brought him into the living room in his car-seat and thought, "Where do we put him?" "What do we do now?" Even having prepared a space for him didn't prepare us for the feelings when we brought home the actual baby.'*

It can also feel very flat.

From parents . . .

> *'Is this all? Is what I thought when we got back home.'*
>
> *'I got home and even though we had newly decorated and cleaned in preparation for the baby, I just felt trapped by those bright, new walls.'*

Among the many changes in your way of life, you can't even pop out of your home by yourself for a few moments.

There is so much to do and so much to get used to. The existence of a new member of the family, and one who has so many needs in the first few days, can be a shattering experience.

From parents . . .

> *'You get home and everything's changed. We were all over the place; the first few weeks are like a dream. But that doesn't go on for ever, thankfully.'*

> *'The first time I was left alone with our firstborn was particularly memorable. My wife was having a bath. I was left in deep peace watching over our daughter, hardly daring to breathe, certainly not leaving her alone (what would happen?). It really hit me: "I am now a responsible adult – like it or not – but no one's told me what to do!"'*

Adjusting to family life

If the mother or father of one of you, or another relative, is able to be around, you may feel very fortunate and enjoy being cosseted; or you may feel that your adultness is in danger and find yourself becoming like a complaining small child. Some parents find that, after proudly showing the baby to their parents, they need to have some time together in the first few days, to sort out the complexities of being a threesome, and after that grandparents are invaluable. If you have made your parents grandparents for the first time, they also will be adjusting to a new role.

From parents . . .

> *'My mother and I are very close but perhaps because of that I found that I needed to keep her at a distance for a time after the birth of my first daughter. It was not a particularly conscious decision but looking back I can see that I did need the space to discover who I was going to be as a mother. This didn't take long and then I wanted and needed my mum around. My children are both very close to their grandmother and see her most days and, indeed, by the time my second daughter was born it was a real pleasure to have my mum with us right from the moment we left hospital.'*

The exhaustion of this first period is of course from the full-time effort of feeding and of broken nights. It is also the effort of adjusting to the full-time responsibility of the baby. There is no let-up, no going back.

For mothers, as your milk comes in and you get to grips with all the unknowns of feeding, you can find yourself getting very emotional. For fathers, you have your own emotions to deal with as well as looking after mother and baby, and doing your best to sort out the tearful, messy chaos around you. It can be hard to believe that this tiny person takes up all the time and energy of two adults.

Time seems to go in slow motion, with a relentless bombardment of feeds, nappy changes, washing, always the next thing to cope with. Bathing the baby may seem like a pleasure – handling this tiny miracle of a body; or a terrifying ordeal. 'What if I drop him?' might seem like a cliché, but it's a graphic way for a new parent to describe their uncertainty about how to hold on safely to this little scrap of dependency.

As well as the baby himself, there are so many other people to deal with. If you were in hospital only briefly, then the local midwife will come to attend to you and the baby. If you were longer in hospital, then the first professional will be the health visitor, coming to meet you at ten days or so.

There are also all the other visitors, family and friends. Are they coming to congratulate you? Or to claim the baby as belonging to the family, not just to you? They can be a huge support, or get in the way, making you feel jangled and wishing you could be on your own with the baby. Sometimes it feels as though nothing is right – the baby seems like a monster if you're on your own with him, but it's just as bad when you've got company and the visitors eat up your space. In other moods this can feel like a time of perfect happiness with your own beautiful baby, and you can feel that your pleasure radiates out to include all the visitors.

Keeping the world simple

It is best for baby and parents if the world can be kept simple. Ideally, this means that the potentially overwhelming barrage of new experiences is sifted out so that the baby is exposed to only a small sample of the environment. In some cultures there is a 'taboo' period when mother and baby stay cloistered at home for up to a month; in our culture there used to be an ideal of a 'confinement', with middle-class mothers staying in bed for two weeks after giving birth. Luckily for both physical and mental health, mothers are now up and about once they feel ready but some privacy and protected space still matters. Fathers can be central in helping to provide this.

From parents . . .

> *'The first time I put her in the buggy and took her to the supermarket I became confused by all the little things competing for my attention – other shoppers, my list, and the food on the shelves. At home she had been all I'd had to think about, but here I momentarily forgot her and must have assumed that it was a trolley I was pushing. I picked up a sack of potatoes and almost put them on top of the baby! I suddenly realised why my husband had been doing the shopping for the first two weeks.'*

> *'Crossing the road seemed terribly dangerous at first. It's bizarre that the most precious thing, the baby, is pushed out into the road first.'*

Some mothers may feel the urge to get back out into the world immediately. This might be a wish to deny the enormity of the changes to life the new baby is going to bring. It might reflect a wish to prove to oneself and the world that you are 'coping' and are taking it all in your stride.

From parents . . .

> *'I was left very weak after a difficult birth and could not venture out of the house for several weeks. When my sister-in-law told me she and her baby had visited a museum on day five I felt devastated. I thought that this must be "normal" or some sort of ideal that I couldn't attain. With my second I didn't have that doubt. I took great pleasure in staying in my pyjamas for two weeks.'*

Your changing relationship as a couple

How do parents adjust to each other, no longer just partners, but with this third person to care for jointly? This is perhaps the biggest test of 'grown-upness' that can be devised. Babies are literally another mouth to feed. Partners have had to get used to sharing with each other and now they have to do it all over again to accommodate this new being, who can sometimes feel like a parasite.

More prosaically, it is also the time to work out how to share the chores. At present you may feel rather like two well-intentioned siblings, trying very hard to share everything equally. This can work very well even during pregnancy, but may not seem relevant when the baby arrives and equality becomes rather complicated. What is not equal is a woman's capacity to be the one to be pregnant, to physically 'grow' the baby, to give birth and to breastfeed. Each may be jealous of the other, a man of the woman's creativity, the woman of the man's freedom from all this.

It is too easy for parents-to-be to focus on the birth and not think enough about life after birth, life as a parent. Having a baby is the start of a new you. It changes you. If you carefully shared out the domestic tasks, including earning money, then the inescapable gender differences in parenting tasks may be more troublesome for you to accommodate to.

From parents . . .

> *'When I fell pregnant with our first I was earning twice what my husband was, I then had to watch his career soar while mine flatlined. I would watch him sleep while I was up with the baby and I hated him. Neither of us really valued what I was doing. Now we have three children and everything has changed. He is much more involved in their care and this "work" has higher status in both our minds now. We've both changed a lot.'*

> *'Our daughter had a cleft palate which meant that it took the two of us six weeks, in bed with her and the feeding equipment, working to keep her nourished. I could not have done it without him and his role as co-parent was established. We have approached parenting as a team since then. When one of us works, the other cares for our daughter and we share all the other duties around the house, although I do have to point out what needs doing sometimes!'*

> *'We both had to travel for work so as a couple we were often apart and then meeting up, having missed each other. It was exciting and romantic. Suddenly we were together all the time, stuck indoors, the sex had gone out the window. Then my partner went back to work and we started playing the blame game, competing about who it was harder for. I felt so isolated, bored and lonely. He was overworked and tired.'*

'After a particularly bad night with a sick baby my husband was on his way back to bed for a bit but he decided to load the dishwasher first. Later he was woken from his sleep by a horrible dream in which I tripped on the open door of the dishwasher and impaled myself on a knife! I think a part of him wanted me to be punished for the terrible night he'd had. But then I only think that because I have equally violent thoughts when sleep deprived and feel myself to be hard-done-by.'

Of course it's good to remember that you are both on the same side and to avoid becoming competitive about who is the most hard-done-by but there may be times when you need someone to blame. It is difficult to own such angry and resentful feelings towards the baby (see Chapter 4) and perhaps we need to let ourselves be the villain in our partner's mind, temporarily, so that we can stay well disposed towards the baby.

Responding to your baby's cues

Really the best tutor to consult on being a parent is your baby. If you are feeling well and strong enough to notice and bide your time, your baby will give you very big clues as to what he needs. These clues are biologically programmed to keep you near to him, attending to him and from the to-and-fro of this grows attachment (see Chapter 7). It will be amazing how your world becomes centred on the sight, sound and feel of this tiny creature; all your feelings about yourself become tangled up in your hopes for him.

Organising a routine

Mothers vary in whether they like a routine or not. You may want to get the baby into a routine of say three-hourly feeds. This might make you feel more comfortable because you can keep tabs on what is going on, be sure that the baby is feeding enough. You might feel it is worth making an effort to keep the home tidy, and that this tidiness will help you keep your doubts about being a good parent under control.

Or it may be the opposite. You want at first just to be there for your baby, and feed him at any time he feels like it. You will probably be rather untidy, perhaps not making it out of your dressing-gown very often. Your way of coping is to take your lead from your baby and to follow his cues.

Both these ways of starting out with a baby have something to offer – but an extreme version of either can lead to difficulties. If it means too much to you to be in control, then you may feel it is a battle between you and the baby if he cries to be fed when the clock says it's too soon. You may feel you have to 'train' him to wait. Perhaps this is the wrong battle at the wrong time and the priority should be responding to your baby's cues while he is still very little. Later he will be able to accommodate himself to your timetable. Similarly if tidiness in the home, or getting yourself carefully dressed with your make-up on, is imperative, perhaps the surface look of things has got rather out of hand. Are you trying to protect yourself and the baby from the emotional messiness that usually ensues when two human beings get really close?

However, while a baby does need to be attended to, the extreme of too much wallowing in being an 'earth mother' can ignore the fact that some settling into a timetable and sorting out day from night can also help him learn about structure. Untidiness can in the first place be a sign of spontaneity. Too much can be a sign of depression, or indeed lead to depression.

Fathers may have a difficult time sorting out what all this means. Should you be more worried if you find a tidy home and immaculate partner, or a disorganised home and a dishevelled partner? Probably a balance of these is the happiest state to be in. Either way, it takes time to gain confidence in how to be a parent. The more that you handle the baby, the more 'positive' and 'negative' feedback you will get; that is to say, the more you will learn about what your baby needs. Allowing yourselves at first to get into the baby's rhythm, sleeping when he does, can be the most restful way to start. It is important that fathers do this finding out directly for yourselves; finding out directly for yourselves what you feel is best, rather than just taking instruction. Chapters 8 and 9 will look at how to negotiate with the baby, to get into more predictable routines of feeding and sleeping.

From parents . . .

> *'My son was really hard to settle at first. Child-centred care and breastfeeding was messy, intimate and alien to my husband but it was how I wanted to do it. He tried to reconcile this with his own wish for order and structure by*

drawing up complex spreadsheets charting when baby fed and from which breast, what time he peed or pooed and when he slept. The idea was that as a pattern emerged, a routine could be built upon it. He was honouring my wish to "listen to the baby" and his own wish to impose order on chaos. But then the chart got rather complicated and I ended up lobbing it at him. We did find a way together. My husband helped me to see that I had got a bit obsessive about trying to meet the baby's every need perfectly and I was able to show him that the baby was not being manipulative, just communicative.'

'I remember going to dinner when I was pregnant, with friends who had a newborn. They were "training" her into "the routine". She was not due a feed for three hours and this was supposed to be a sleep period, so they turned the monitor down and the music up. This all seemed very reasonable to me at the time, and it certainly allowed us to have an uninterrupted meal, but now it really upsets me to think about that night. Her cries fell on deaf ears. When our daughter was born I immediately knew that when she cried nothing would stop me from going to her. I now have two happy children aged two and four but I still can't leave them to settle themselves. I know in some cultures that would be normal so I don't worry about it too much but I often don't sleep next to my partner and that does make me sad.'

From psychoanalytic theory and clinical practice . . .

The psychoanalyst Joan Raphael-Leff (1993) has worked extensively with pregnant women and mothers. In her practice she observed a range of approaches to babycare routines, which can be understood as fitting somewhere on a spectrum and reflecting aspects of the parent's identification with the baby. At one extreme is the 'regulator', who expects the baby to make a passive adaptation to her lead. This is usually because, at some level, she fears the baby will greedily take control if not kept in line. It is complicated because she also identifies with the 'greedy baby' and feels like she is keeping an unruly part of herself in check too. Taking the opposite approach, a mother becomes a mere 'facilitator' for meeting the needs of her idealised baby. Such apparent altruism is actually only thought possible because this time the mother is in identification with an idealised part of herself that is represented by the baby. In the long run either of these extremes is problematic for the relationship and for the baby's development. There is a third way that allows for mother and baby to negotiate within a reciprocal relationship. The 'reciprocator' can tolerate ambivalence. The baby is both greedily demanding and deserving. She represents both the idealised and the denigrated self. It is possible to 'hear' and take account of the baby's needs and desires but they do not become law. The 'reciprocator' can say 'no' to her baby. If you or your partner find yourselves pulled to either extreme, it may be worth thinking about why that might be so.

3

BONDING

Bonding is about you and your baby getting to know each other and falling in love. It can feel like a magical process, some parents are struck, all of a sudden and soon after the birth, but bonding is not just about a flash of lightning between you and your baby. It will mostly come from the constant intimate interplay, from the routine of attending to your baby's needs. As you hold her to feed, the two of you get to know each other. You get into each other's sensory awareness. 'I've got you under my skin' is a pretty accurate way to describe it. For your new baby, being enfolded in your arms, coming to know the feel, smell and sound of you is the major part of her life.

From parents . . .

> *'I remember at the beginning she did almost nothing but then that was just right because all I wanted to do was gaze at her doing nothing . . . taking her in, the detail of her fingernails and the smell from her head that could make my tummy somersault. At times I felt we were suspended in time and motion. I felt so alert and yet we were so calm and still.'*
>
> *'I was completely bowled over by her perfectness when she was a newborn. I couldn't imagine anything better, until she started to hold my gaze. What a thrill! Later came her first smile and I accepted that that must be the peak but then came better smiles, more personal, more charming as the weeks passed. Then came giggling and tickling and other games and the passion became something more bold and robust but also more ordinary.'*
>
> *'It was like being bewitched at the beginning.'*

After the initial disappointment of discovering her son had Down's syndrome, one mother described how he started to claim her: 'His head, which seemed flattened out at first, had become round and was covered in blonde fuzz. His small slanted eyes were still puffy and Mongolian-looking but he had such a sweet, cheery demeanor it was easy to love him' (Wyllie 2012: 40).

What bonding is

Our relationships with other people are the foundations of our lives, our health and happiness. The kinds of relationships we have throughout life depend, in the first place, on the kind of bond we had with our own parents. These bonds are not formed overnight. The psychiatrist Betty Tilden talked about: 'the hard work of daily loving'. While bonding can be highly enjoyable it is also a very serious business that can be said to have three broad functions. The first may seem rather obvious but it cannot be taken for granted. Bonding improves the baby's chance of survival by making it more likely that her adult carer will keep her close, fed and safe. From an evolutionary perspective, a human baby is a great drain on material and emotional resources because she is born with an immature body and brain (compared to all other animals), making her dependent for a long time. Shocking though it may sound, good bonding between carer and baby helps to ameliorate the high risk of abandonment that such a 'resource expensive' offspring carries with it. The second function of bonding is to initiate the baby into the particular social world she is born into and to set a template for future relationships. The third is to finish cooking the brain. The human brain doubles in weight over the first year and whole regions are inactive and unconnected at birth. The last areas to get wired up are those areas that only humans have. You could say that the process of becoming human happens after birth and, increasingly, neuroscientists are showing that this brain growth depends on experiences with an adult carer: on the kind of bonding that occurs.

From parents . . .

> *'At four months my daughter was sat happily on my mother's lap opposite me while I composed a difficult and absorbing email. On clicking "send" my mind returned to the room and I looked at my baby with a big smile. She was looking away so I called her name. She glanced up at*

me with a frighteningly flat expression and looked immediately away. I took her on to my lap and cuddled her, but she was unresponsive. I felt like I did not exist! It took me a while to win her back. There was something about my being present but indifferent to her that was worse than being absent. At some very primitive level I think she thought that she had ceased to exist for me and that therefore her survival was under threat. Unable to cope with such a scary idea, she just sort of cut herself off from the experience and from me.'

From research on how babies deal with stress . . .

In *Why Love Matters*, Sue Gerhardt explains that: 'babies' resources are so limited that they cannot keep themselves alive, so it is very stressful if the mother is not there or does not respond quickly' (Gerhardt 2004: 38). At some basic level they respond to inattention as a threat to life. Given their dependence on their carer for survival, this is understandable. This kind of stress is manifested in the brain as an overproduction of the hormone cortisol. We need cortisol for everyday 'get-up-and-go'. In moderation it provides energy but in high-stress situations we produce too much of it which interferes with brain functioning and, in infants, the growth and development of the brain.

Bowlby (1982) compared human and animal bonding, or attachment as he called it. He showed that all mammal young share instinctive behaviours such as sucking, clinging, following and crying which serve the function of bonding the offspring to the mother and getting protection and nurturance in return. Human babies also smile and make eye contact so that once proximity is secured, emotional closeness can ensue. Babies cannot regulate their own stress response but they do have all these ways of eliciting adult attention. The amazing thing is that the right kind of adult attention does have the power to regulate the baby's stress response and return the baby to biochemical equilibrium. The human baby is highly dependent but not passive. Her 'proximity seeking' behaviour is profoundly important as it elicits the parental behaviour that creates the bond that her survival and maturation depends on.

We do not mean to say that mothers should not write emails or that babies are damaged by such experiences. Inevitably all babies will experience moments of stress around attachment like this and they may respond by cutting off emotionally or becoming angry and demanding. This is a normal part of life and not in itself a problem. However, if a baby experiences high levels of such stress on a regular basis, these responses crystallise into what is known as an 'internal working model'.

From research on internal working models and attachment styles . . .

Bowlby (1944) had observed a link between delinquency in boys and maternal deprivation. He argued that children developed an 'internal working model' of their experience of an attachment figure. This is an unconscious set of expectations about what relationships will be like. The individual is not aware of the model and might not have any memory of the experiences that informed it but it does determine the way a person feels and acts in a given situation, especially in a stressful situation. In this way a baby becomes adapted to the particular social environment in which she is growing up. This adaptability has enabled humans to develop ever more complex co-operative social groups. However, an infant can have a maladaptive response. That is to say she may develop an internal working model which enables her to make the best of, or survive, difficult early attachment relationships, but this may not equip her well for the wider social environment she must move into as she matures. Different kinds of 'internal working model' have been identified and categorised. We will return to these 'attachment styles', as they are now known, in the next chapter.

The role of bonding from a broader evolutionary perspective

You might wonder what the relevance of all this is to the daily business of bonding with your baby but perhaps it is rather exciting to think about the profound importance of what is happening between you both, in the wider context of the history of our species. The findings of neuroscience, evolutionary psychology and attachment research converge to support three linked ideas. Humans, like all other higher mammals, survive by being able to work together in teams. This has led to increasingly complex societies. These complex social groups rely on sophisticated individual brains. However, these brains only reach their potential after birth as they develop and grow within relationships. They get wired-up in the way that best helps them to cope in the particular social environment they find themselves in. This adaptability can become a burden when the brain adapts to a hostile environment, becoming warped and then 'malfunctioning'. The human brain's plasticity is our crowning glory and our Achilles' heel.

We will now look more closely at *how* bonding happens in other aspects of your relationship with your baby. We will be focusing on what parent and baby do, the feelings they experience and how this is all manifested in the brain biochemically.

Getting a head start: bonding during pregnancy

Bonding with your baby can start before birth, though it doesn't work for everyone. In pregnancy you can daydream about your baby, you may connect the real foetus now with the baby you imagined in your own childhood. As the actual foetus grows, moves and kicks inside your womb, you can feel her, and the baby's father can share in it too. The baby becomes more real, responding to your body, to your movements, as well as initiating her own activity. Mothers start to recognise patterns; both mother and baby are responding to each other's personalities and are already having a relationship.

From parents . . .

> *'I loved pressing on my wife's abdomen, and feeling the baby's answering kick. I noticed the girls were different. Even in the womb they had their own timing and vigour, their own personalities.'*
>
> *'I noticed their movements in the womb were similar to their way of moving about after birth. I could feel the first baby moving constantly and stretching from her toes to her fingers inside me and I would think there isn't room. After she came out, she stretched her body in the same expansive way, she remained active, her lively mind and body always on the go. The second baby had her own characteristic patterns with calmer, wide movements; when she stretched I felt her bottom sticking into my ribs. After she was born, she would arch her back like a cat, bottom sticking out. She was a responsive baby; at six weeks old, when she smiled and "mouthed" at me, her arms waved about but her rhythm was slower than my first daughter's.'*
>
> *'The first time I saw his face was on Christmas Eve, ten days before he was born. The scan just happened to catch his face perfectly, and that is the same face I see when I watch him sleeping now. I remember thinking "I'm your mummy and you're my baby. Hi."'*

Birth bonding

The birth itself is a part of the bonding process, an adventure that you and your baby embark on together. Fathers who are there can just as much share in the excitement or the trauma.

From parents . . .

> *'I, his father, saw him first! And that special moment of seeing him come out enhanced our bond.'*
>
> *'We know she recognised us as soon as she came out. At the moment of birth she started to cry but the minute she heard our voices she stilled. We felt she recognised our faces. She looked at one of us, then the other, and we felt she knew we were her parents. It is a moment we'll never forget.'*
>
> *'She was put straight on my belly, all slippery with stuff, but she did not root. I think we had both been wiped out by the birth. They took her to check her over and then put her in my arms. She looked at me briefly and I was thrilled but did not get the feeling she knew me. Then my husband spoke and she definitely tried to find him with her eyes. That was when I started to believe that she knew us.'*

From research on biochemical aspects of birth . . .

The physical process of birth is orchestrated by biochemicals, triggering each event from waters breaking to the urge to push. Oxytocin is such a key player that artificial oxytocin is given to speed up deliveries. It also plays an important role in how the birth is experienced by mother and baby. Oxytocin reduces the experience of pain and makes you feel good in yourself and good about others. In this way it supports the mother–infant bond. Oxytocin levels also increase when you feel cared for. It is likely, then, that emotional support for mothers during labour would support bonding. Bad birth experiences are certainly associated with bonding difficulties (Ayers et al. 2006: 389).

Bonding is about getting emotionally close. To do that, you have to be physically close. Parents and babies get to know each other by touch, smell and looking at each other from very near. Babies used to be whisked away to be cleaned up before their mothers were allowed to hold them; now they are often put straight on to their mother's abdomen with the warm animal smell of bodily fluids still on them. It can feel as though your baby still has your imprint on her. In the first hour after the birth, mothers are usually in what is called a maternal sensitive period and they and their baby may be alert and receptive to each other. When you are able to hold the baby so immediately and look at her, you may find she has her eyes open and wants to take you in.

The benefits of medication during labour are great, although large amounts can leave mother and baby still very drowsy so that they partly miss out on this first encounter. This does not mean that mothers need to try to manage without medication in a painful labour! Such heroism is not necessary and getting through the birth reasonably comfortably is a priority for you and the baby. The effects of most ordinary doses will have worn off by the moment of delivery. We must also put this in perspective. The bonding process can indeed get a good head start in the first few hours after birth but this is not the only time it can begin. If your baby has to be taken away to an incubator for a few hours, you might feel cheated of this special time but you need not feel it stopped you bonding with your baby.

Difficult births can make for a more complicated start between mother and baby, and can affect how the mother is able to influence the baby's physiological processes, their feeding and sleep–wake rhythms. One mother said, 'We started off on the wrong foot.' It is really important that mothers get a chance to talk about such a birth and the feelings it leaves them with. This can make a big difference to how they get on with their baby.

From parents . . .

> *'Bonding the second time was impacted by really bad piles. Sounds silly I know but I'd had to have stitches through them due to tearing and I was in a lot of pain. It got me down and made it hard for me to be completely available to her.'*
>
> *'It had been a terrible birth, very badly managed (official complaint to hospital upheld), and when they put him in my arms he looked up and gave me a dirty look. But do you know I didn't blame him. I would have given me a dirty look too. I felt we were on the same side and had both got a rough deal. It just made me more determined to protect him from that sort of trauma in the future. I wanted to make it up to him.'*

Fathers and bonding

Men's bodies can change biochemically to support bonding in similar ways to women's bodies but only if there is enough physical contact and interaction to trigger it. Excluding men from childcare on the basis that they are not cut out for it is a self-fulfilling prophecy.

From research on biochemical changes in fathers . . .

Prolactin increases feelings of protectiveness and concern and this goes up in men who are living with their partners during pregnancy. Their testosterone also goes down after birth, which is likely to reduce sex drive. If men have the right social experiences – involvement and intimacy with their partner and child – then their bodies change to support the new role (Storey et al. 2000).

From mothers . . .

> *'After a caesarean my baby and I were completely dependent on my husband to bring us together. He had to pass her to me so that I could feed her. It was not that he was "involved" or "included". He was an essential part of keeping baby alive. Unlike some fathers he had the enormity of the change hit him just as hard as it hit me. He became a father straight away, he had to, and their bond still has the magic of those first hours and days.'*

From fathers . . .

> *'I remember feeling like a completely different person after the birth of our first child. The change seemed less seismic after the second, like I'd already been reprogrammed.'*
>
> *'I make a point of doing bath time and changing nappies because I can't do the breastfeeding. I know I need opportunities for that physical closeness.'*
>
> *'There wasn't really a moment when I felt we'd connected. I was confident that she must know me, or would in time because she belonged to me. I guess because I wasn't anxiously waiting for the moment, I didn't really notice when it happened.'*

Fathers describe the same awe and wonder, or shock, as mothers when talking about the birth of their children, perhaps more if they have been witness to it.

From fathers . . .

> *'Another miracle has happened.'*
>
> *'I would gaze at my son and think about him in the future, wondering about how much continuity there would be, what would be passed on from grandparents, and parents to this baby.'*
>
> *'I felt so proud that we'd got her out, so lucky that she was so pretty. When the nurses took her off to check her out under bright lights and she started yelling I was proud of her for that too. I told her about her name, that it means she can be anything she wants. It was so good to meet her after all that time of trying to get to know her and assigning her characteristics on the basis of how she behaved in the womb.'*
>
> *'I did cry, it was moving to meet her but then it was also relief. Childbirth is such a portal between life and death.'*

Feeding and bonding

Mothers are likely to put the baby to their breast as part of this first mutual discovery. The feel of her mouth on your nipple is another way of learning about each other. This first getting-together can also dispel your fears about your ability to breastfeed. If you have held your baby to your breast, even briefly, you may feel you can do it.

Breastfeeding soon after birth is not the only way to start, however. You may feel too exhausted, in pain or drowsy after labour even to hold, let alone try to feed your baby. Or you may feel you really need a bit of time to yourself, to sort out your own feelings about the delivery before you can remember that the whole point of it was to have a baby. You may even feel angry or resentful with the baby about what you have been through. This certainly doesn't mean you won't be able to bond with your baby when things have calmed down.

From research on biochemical aspects of feeding . . .

Breastfeeding releases oxytocin, vasopresin and prolactin. Together these hormones produce loving feelings, elation, calm and protectiveness in the mother. This does a great deal to support bonding by augmenting the mother's capacity to become emotionally involved with her baby. The baby's oxytocin levels also increase, which helps to set his biochemical clock. The more oxytocin-releasing experiences he has, the more likely he is to produce and process it effectively in the future, setting a virtuous cycle in motion (Music 2011).

From parents . . .

> *'Having a caesarean is not a process. One minute you don't have a baby and the next you do. It took me a while to catch up with events. When they first put him in my arms my compass had not been reset. I was still fairly concerned with whether my hair looked alright and things like that but after a few hours of having him lying next to me everything had changed. I suddenly realised I wanted to feed him but did not want to disturb him so I wriggled down the bed to get into position. The only way that worked left my backside hanging off the bed in a most undignified manner but when a male nurse came in I wasn't in the slightest bit concerned about how I looked. Or rather I was confident that I looked like a mother doing what she must, and I felt happy with that. That was when the bond began and that's when I became a mother.'*

Holding and bonding

Physical intimacy is one of the most important aspects of bonding. By holding your baby you come to know the pleasure that it can bring. It is self-perpetuating, drawing you both together for more good experiences and cementing your bond. Cuddling also releases oxytocin in both adult and baby. When held skin to skin, a baby's body will be kept at the optimum temperature. Relaxed arms provide just the right amount of support to feel safe, the right amount of give to feel comfortable. Babies' breathing deepens and their heart rate has been shown to synchronise with the adult holding them. This very primitive form of communication or communion between people can seem at odds with our modern world with its complex social norms.

From parents . . .

> *'My wife and I knew we wanted her to have as much skin-to-skin contact with both of us as possible in the first few hours, so I had my top off as we took it in turns to cuddle her. Suddenly a nurse marched in abruptly turning on all the lights and shattering our intimate moment, I stalked off into the ward in protest, still wearing no top, and she made it very clear that I needed to be properly dressed in the ward at all times.'*

Looking, listening and bonding

We are all familiar with the idea of a mother gazing at and cooing to her baby but it is not always realised that the baby is also actively engaging his mother. There are subtle clues that even very young babies respond conversationally to people who talk to them. With close attention we can pick up on these clues. As described in Chapter 2, new mothers usually have a heightened sensitivity to such communications (Winnicott's 'maternal preoccupation'). Later Trevarthen (2001) captured the minutiae of these exchanges in exquisite detail when he filmed and slowed down recordings of ordinary mothers responding to tiny signals from their baby. This use of technology enabled researchers to observe the signals that the mothers had picked up on without even noticing. When asked after filming, the mothers were quite unaware of what they had been doing, confirming Winnicott's observation that when mothers 'recover' from maternal preoccupation, they are unable to recall what it was like. For this reason we have included third-person descriptions of conversations between babies and their mothers (see p. 47).

These quotes are from MA students who observe a baby at home for two years using a psychoanalytic frame. In the scene below, the baby would see his mother's pupils dilate and her face lift into a smile. His body would read these signs of her aroused sympathetic system and his would begin to be pleasurably aroused also. Indeed the observer finds herself drawn into their playfulness and laughs. The biochemical manifestation of this interpersonal joy promotes connections between brain regions, connections that need to be made in infancy for the adult brain to develop optimally.

From psychoanalytic observations of parents and babies . . .

She returns to the room and pulls over the baby bouncer so they face each other. Baby regains a relaxed body and open face. She is repeating phrases, all have a similar pattern of intonation – dipping and rising like a swift. Her lively face predictably matches the phrases. After a few moments the pair go up a gear. Baby begins to open his mouth and expose his gums. It is not quite a smile, but there is something expansive about it and it makes me smile. His forefingers are curled into a grip while his little fingers are extended; they suggest anticipation somehow. After his mother's contributions his arms shoot out, accompanied by a widening of his eyes and mouth and a small explosive noise. Mother also seems to be getting more animated, moving in and out with her whole body. When there is a very obvious correspondence between their contributions, I laugh out loud at the 'game'.

From research on the neuroscience of interactions with your baby . . .

When baby and carer are in sync, matching each other's level of excitement, acting and anticipating the other's reaction, a biochemical reaction is set off in both of them. Beta-endorphin is released into the orbitofrontal cortex. As an opioid it will be experienced as pleasure but it also stimulates neuron growth by regulating glucose and insulin. For the infant this will support connectivity in this late developing 'higher brain' (Gerhardt 2004). Pally describes the similar role played by dopamine: 'these high arousal states specifically induce the sprouting of dopamine-releasing axon terminals, which grow upwards from their cell bodies located in the midbrain [limbic], to sites deep in the prefrontal cortex. The increased release of dopamine into prefrontal areas, in turn, promotes a growth spurt of synapses and glial cells in this region' (Pally 2000: 10). These events, working bottom up from our more primitive brain to stimulate the higher brain, pave or strengthen neural pathways that will enable top-down affect regulation in the future. Only with these experiences will reason blossom and come to be able to curtail desire, rein in rage and temper sadness. This enables the infant to fulfil his potential by becoming an effective member of his social group.

From research on mirror neurons . . .

Mirror neurons were discovered accidentally. A scientist having his lunch was being watched by the macaque monkey he was experimenting on (Rizzolatti 2005). The monkey was wired up so that it was possible to see which neurons fired when he grasped for something. To their great surprise, the machinery showed that the same neurons were activated when the monkey saw the man reach for his sandwich as would have activated if the monkey had reached for it. In the limbic region, which processes emotion, an emotion observed in another will cause neural networks to fire in a similar way to when an emotion is felt spontaneously by a person. 'Mirror neurons provide evidence of the human capacity to form powerful connections between people, as they allow one person to understand from the inside what another is experiencing' (Music 2011: 54).

For the baby in the interaction described on the previous page, his mother's expressive face and voice set off a firework display of emotions in his mind. As he mirrors her experience, he comes to know about the range of human feelings he has the potential to experience. Perhaps more importantly, when she matches his feelings in her behaviour, he comes to know that his feelings can be understood.

Daniel Stern (1985) uses the phrase 'affect attunement' to describe the way in which adult and baby get onto the same wavelength emotionally together. It starts as mirroring, but he points out that it quickly becomes much more complex than reflecting the same thing back. Parents attune to their baby by behaving in a way that expresses a shared feeling state rather than actually imitating the exact actions and expressions. In this way the feelings can be expanded upon or changed between the pair. If we think of adult experiences of empathy in conversation, we feel better understood if someone describes their own similar experience than if they just wear an appropriate or 'well-attuned' expression on their face.

Twins and bonding

Most parents of twins enjoy all the same thrills of bonding as parents of single birth babies. However, they do face additional challenges to bonding. The babies are likely to be premature and so fragile, tiny and less responsive. Also, as Piontelli discovered in her research with twins: 'Relating to two is quite different from relating to one . . . To try to be impartial mothers often held one twin whilst looking at the other. Gazing, facial expression, hand movements, talking, breastfeeding, rocking, cuddling and stroking were all frequently dissociated . . . Individual attention was characterised by its brevity and continuous oscillation from one baby to the other' (Piontelli 2004: 88). It would seem that twin babies arrive slightly less well equipped to make sense of the world and then find themselves in a more confusing world too. However, the quote from a mother below shows that, with support, it is still be possible to give twins the experiences they need.

From parents . . .

> *'I was advised to feed my twins simultaneously, told I would do nothing but feed all day otherwise, but it didn't feel right. We quickly noticed how different their feeding styles were. She has a light touch, apparently confident that the milk will come, her bow lips reach out to the nipple and it looks unhurried and delicate. He comes to it with gusto, pawing at the breast with his little hand apparently trying to get as much as possible into the toothless chewing of his mouth. He feeds with both urgency and abandon. It was such an important part of getting to know them that I wanted to give them my full attention as they fed. I guess I had the luxury to make that decision, my husband was happy to do everything else and my father comes to help out each afternoon, being local and retired.'*

Not always love at first sight

'Falling in love' does not come easily to all parents. You can feel quite untouched by any enthusiasm at first, even an 'Is this all?' sort of feeling. Depression will be addressed in Chapter 6 but you don't have to be actually depressed to have the feeling, in the first few days, that all the excitement is somehow eluding you. In time, however, the interplay with the baby can start to make things develop emotionally between you. The way your baby looks at you when you feed her, the fleeting first smiles you may get even if you weren't feeling like smiling first, does something to you.

From parents . . .

> *'I knew I liked him because I made him, he was part of me and my husband, but I didn't feel very much. Other mothers seemed to have overwhelming feelings but I didn't. I was able to look after him though, and the feelings just seemed to come after about two weeks.'*
>
> *'I knew I had a baby inside but I couldn't quite believe it. Holding the baby in the first few days after the birth helped. Cradling her I got the special hot, sweet newborn smell. Looking into her eyes, the world was blotted out.'*
>
> *'Now when she grips my little finger as she feeds I feel all protective.'*
>
> *'I don't know if it's because I've spent too much time around my cats but I get the urge to clean the baby's head and it's an expression of affection. I do feel more aware of being a mammal than I did before.'*
>
> *'I was immediately bowled over by my first child, with the second it took longer. I don't know that there really was a bonding moment. I was doing all the same things as I had done with my first and in time it just felt a little less false, until I realised that we had bonded.'*

Your baby will have her own way of letting you know how much you matter. You might be moved by the way she stops crying as you come into the room, or even starts crying when you appear. You may have a particular moment, a powerful experience of some kind, or lots of little signs that help you build up a feeling that you have a central importance to your baby. However it gets going, building up your baby's attachment to you is also building up her brain and her template for future relationships.

4

BEING A GOOD PARENT

You may find yourself worrying about whether you're a good parent. In fact worrying, within reason, thinking about yourself in connection with your baby, is probably a sign that you *are* a 'good' parent. You know your baby better than anyone. If you can trust your instincts and your capacity to become attuned to her, she will be the best person to tell you how well you are doing. However, every parent experiences doubt, anxiety and other difficult feelings in relation to their baby. This chapter will explore some of the uncomfortable feelings we all have and address more serious worries about being a 'bad' parent.

You don't have to be perfect

It is hard to remember this when the stakes are so high. The way that you parent will impact on your baby's developing personality. Yet, hoping to attain perfection in parenting is not only impossible, it is not actually desirable. Winnicott (1958) coined the phrase 'the good enough mother' – a brilliantly helpful concept that applies to fathers too. 'Good enough' means just that – able to be reliably there for your baby, but a fallible human being, with your own needs, bad days and irritable moods. If you make mistakes, you can learn from them and so can your baby. Early on the baby's whole experience is of her parents and she needs some introduction to the normal frustrations of life, having to wait a little sometimes, or of having to deal with a parent who isn't in tune with her in that moment. The need for the baby to make allowances for her parents, as well as them usually adjusting to her, helps her develop in her thinking and her ability to empathise with others. A baby of a few weeks can't yet think, 'Why's she in a bad mood today?' – but she can start to register a face that isn't the usual one smiling and waiting for her to smile back. It gives her more experience of the ordinary range of emotions and requires her to develop the resources to cope. This inevitable, ordinary experience of things not being 'perfect' is, of course, quite different from 'teasing' her or even training her by making her wait unnecessarily.

From parents . . .

> *'My parents split up when I was two. I know what a shadow early experiences can cast, so I can get a bit overwhelmed by the responsibility of parenting. But then I worry about a friend who seems to have given up on herself and only invests in her children. I worry they will grow up with the burden of being completely responsible for her happiness.'*

So what does make a good (enough) parent?

If you were well-enough parented yourself, it's probably all fairly easy: you have memories inside yourself, conscious and unconscious, to draw on. You will not escape having mixed, even hostile feelings towards your baby but you will be able to keep them in perspective and not let that interfere with caring for and loving your baby.

From psychoanalytic theory and clinical practice . . .

Winnicott (the paediatrician and psychoanalyst) spent a lot of time in the company of mothers and their babies. He observed that babies and children who had been too well attuned to, who never experienced a gap between what they wished for and what the world could provide, were not properly prepared for the world. Hopkins, a child psychotherapist (1996), developed her ideas in a paper called 'The dangers and deprivations of too-good mothering'. She argues that if a baby never has the need to cry out in frustration, she has been deprived of the opportunity to learn that she can express herself effectively and elicit a response. This will hamper the development of a sense of agency and the capacity to negotiate. It inhibits the development of the capacity for concern and the wish to make amends. In short, too-good mothering produces children in a state of arrested development.

If you can manage, often enough, to respond to your baby when she needs it, just as your parents responded to you, you will be able to give your baby the space to be more separate when she needs it. Importantly, you will be able to forgive yourself when you make mistakes. You have a basic feeling of 'I know how to do this, well enough.' Indeed, as Hopkins (1996) suggests, sometimes a mother or father may feel they had 'too much' good parenting. They feel rather stifled and need to get away from the influence of it. Trying to be different from your own parents may be essential for you to feel like an individual now, but it may leave you rather at sea on how to go about it, or in danger of doing the opposite just to assert yourself. If you had unhappy experiences, then you may have more to fear from becoming like your own parents.

From parents . . .

> *'In the early weeks there were nights when she would just cry and cry in my arms and I couldn't make it better for her. It was so hard to bear and yet I knew that I could bear it. I planted my feet to the floor in the darkness of our bedroom and swayed, singing lullabies. My mind was shattered but deep inside I felt solid.'*

> *'Parenting doesn't come from the intellectual self, where the bright light of reason shines; it emerges from a dark forgotten place and is full of surprises, some good and some bad.'*

> *'I was smacked a lot as a child and I worry that I will find myself smacking my children.'*

> *'When I hear myself say these things I think I've become my mother.'*

> *'I think my mother was bullied by her father when he returned a "changed man" after the war and then she, in turn, bullied me as a teenager. At times I fear I will repeat the pattern. I was worried that I would be a very bad mother. My husband and I have discussed it and if I begin to sound like my mother when talking to our daughter he tells me. He knows I don't want to do it.'*

> *'Sometimes I hear in my tone of voice some attitude that is not mine, it is from my mother. But I rejected all of that, decided I wasn't going to be like that. So where the hell does it creep out from?'*

If your memories are unhappy, then remembering your childhood will be painful, but it does seem that telling someone else about your past can really help you to avoid patterns being repeated. Therapists working with parents and their babies know that parents who have bad experiences jostling around inside them are more likely to find themselves lashing out at their own children or reluctant to really engage with them for fear they will damage them. Talking about what has happened to you, remembering the feelings you had, not just the actual events, can help to change things for the better. It is easy to grasp why this might be, in a common-sense sort of way, and the clinical experience of therapists, over the years, has borne out this idea. Now the findings of various linked experiments and pieces of research, conducted over the last thirty years, converge to tell the same story.

From research on attachment styles . . .

The researcher Mary Ainsworth (1985) used observations of infant behaviour in an experimental 'strange situation' to help understand the different strategies children use to help them cope in a stressful situation. This has revealed the different kinds of attachment or bonds parents and babies develop. Reunions of mother and infant, after organised brief absences and after interactions with a friendly stranger, were analysed and categorised. 'Securely attached' infants show adaptive strategies for coping with the stress of the strange situation: they seek and receive comfort from a reliable caregiver on reunion. Insecurely attached infants display a range of behaviours that have been grouped into the following classifications. 'Avoidant' – those who cope with a sense that there is no reliable caregiver by denying their need of one and pretending they don't want or need their carer. 'Ambivalent' describes those who become angry and demanding in the face of unreliable parenting. Those children who have had very bad experiences with their carers are likely to have a 'disorganised attachment', which means they do not have any one coherent strategy for coping with stressful situations. It is important to note that one child can have different attachment styles with different caregivers. For example, a child might be securely attached to his father but insecurely attached to his mother.

The adult attachment interview: reflecting and talking really can make a difference

It is known that such relationship problems get passed through generations. However, some further research revealed an important ameliorating factor. An 'adult attachment interview' which classified adults' recollections of their childhoods was given to a group of pregnant women. The women's responses were not grouped according to how positive or negative what had happened to them was but rather the manner in which they recalled it. Some described awful memories but showed no emotional involvement in their own stories. Others claimed to have had happy childhoods but went on to refer to bad experiences and were then dismissive about their significance. Others became very distressed, as though they were reliving the bad experiences with the same intensity as when they had first happened. The researchers were able to accurately predict the insecure attachment status of their unborn children at eighteen months. More encouragingly, there was a fourth category of women who had also had bad experiences but were able to talk about them and describe how they had felt then and now. These women were much more likely to have toddlers classified as 'securely attached' when put in the 'strange situation'. Those mothers who were able to recall the detail and know about the pain were less likely to find themselves caught up in their past and reliving the pain. They were also less likely to become cut-off from their past and their own feelings in the past or present (Bowlby 1982; Ainsworth 1985; Main et al. 1985).

It seems that those parents who could talk coherently about their difficult childhoods were less trapped by them; they had cut themselves loose and were able to live fully in the present, free to respond to their children's needs unhampered by the past, but without denying what had happened. Such is the power of being in touch with your feelings and being able to articulate them. Talking about your experiences can halt their intergenerational transmission. Although people might worry that they will be thought to be an unfit parent and that their baby will be taken away if they seek help and are honest about their feelings, it is more likely that people will respect you for your courage and strive to work with you to make the changes you want.

Worries about being a bad parent

It is really wretched when you feel you are a bad parent, yet feeling guilty and worrying about what you do is an ordinary part of parenting. However, it is worth exploring where these guilty feelings come from. The short answer is that they are a response to the very common hostile feelings that most parents experience towards their children. It is a difficult notion to accept but we hope to show that 'maternal ambivalence' is common and not something to worry about. There are some elements of love and hate, empathy and anger in all ordinary relationships, and normally this is fluid, the force of feelings comes and goes. We can usually recognise that all relationships involve good and bad feelings yet, probably because of their unique vulnerability and dependence, we tend to think that relationships with babies are the exception. The truth is that they are not. Caring for your baby requires putting her needs before your own most of the time. We might marvel at the fact that most parents do usually manage this. Every day with your baby requires a new feat of altruism and to imagine that this would not cause feelings of resentment is naïve. As a society we pretend that there are good parents who only have loving feelings towards their babies and then there are bad parents who hate their children. In fact we all experience both.

Many parents don't become conscious of hostile feelings until their baby becomes a toddler and begins to challenge them directly. For others the mixed nature of parental love is closer to the surface earlier on. The mother quoted below describes a realisation about her own ambivalence that might seem quite shocking.

From parents . . .

> *'Lying on the sofa poring over my lovely baby I would suddenly get scared that when I got up from the sofa I would lose my balance and her tiny delicate head would hit the sharp corner of my glass coffee table. I only had these thoughts when I was tired and I thought it was a rational fear about sleep deprivation causing clumsiness, tinged with the lurid potency of maternal protectiveness. Reading about maternal ambivalence helped me to realise that it was, in fact, a murderous fantasy of my own. Of course I was alarmed that I could think such a thing but it was strangely reassuring once I let myself accept that a part of me might want to harm her. I knew that her incessant neediness could push me to the edge but I also knew I would never actually hurt her. This meant I knew I was in control. The fear subsided.'*

You may find that you redirect any unconscious hate out into the wider world, onto bossy or unhelpful professionals or family members. While this might be a fairly benign and common way of dealing with difficult feelings, it might also isolate you. Unconscious ambivalence can also lead to debilitating doubt, a lack of confidence in your judgement about what is best for baby. For some parents these feelings manifest in a dismissive attitude to their baby's needs. So often you hear an adult say, 'they're just attention seeking' – as though attention were an indulgent luxury rather than a basic need for a baby or child.

When you are stuck with hatred, it can be very hard to acknowledge it to yourself or others, but if you are able to be honest with yourself and your partner, they are likely to remain just that: difficult but manageable feelings. Humour can provide an outlet for dark feelings and there can be great relief in saying the 'unsayable'. This is different from a dismissive kind of joking that keeps feelings at bay. If the feelings do become too much, you are more likely to act on them and this may put your relationship with your baby at risk. You may find that getting to know your baby is enough to help you to discover that you can respond to her and her needs despite the bad feelings and this can be enough to pull you through it. (Chapter 3 on bonding and Chapter 6 on depression look at this in more detail.) If you find that good experiences with your baby are not enough to make the bad feelings manageable, you may need to seek professional help.

From psychoanalytic theory and clinical practice . . .

The psychotherapist Rozsika Parker has written extensively on maternal ambivalence. She explains that it is an ordinary and inescapable part of parenting but makes the distinction between manageable and unmanageable feelings of hate. When hate is manageable, we can resist the impulse to act on it and instead it can actually intensify our feelings of concern for the baby. She gives the example of a mother trying to comfort an inconsolable baby: 'part of her wishes to shut the baby up at almost any cost but another part of her passionately wants to make it better for the baby'. Hate and anger can keep us from becoming cut-off from the baby's feelings and our own. Although it is counter-intuitive, the experience, tolerance and acknowledgement of ambivalence, Parker argues, can be a creative force promoting engagement, reflection and concern. However, when hate overpowers love, the balance has been tipped. Overwhelmed by hate, a mother is more likely 'act on violent impulses' or 'succumb to helpless despair' (Parker 2005: 117).

Managing difficult feelings

Letting yourself know what you are feeling is the first step. Next is to tell someone else.

From parents . . .

> *'I was talking to a couple of mothers at a playgroup about how an inconsolable baby can make you feel. One said that*

> *she had been standing next to the cot rocking her baby in her arms and murmuring words of comfort and reassurance into his ear while staring at a blank spot on the wall opposite for some time when suddenly a flash of anger ripped through her. At this point the other mother interrupted to say: "And you wanted to smash his head against that spot on the wall." The three of us froze for a moment, perhaps expecting there to be some fall-out from the awful thing that had just been said. Yet it was a great relief to acknowledge those feelings together.'*

> *'I meet up with a group of mothers who are fun and friendly but they will not tolerate talk of bad days or aggressive feelings towards the baby. When I tried to open up myself they immediately asked if I was suffering from post-natal depression. I didn't feel it was genuine concern but more an attempt to draw a line between mothers who have bad thoughts and feelings and those that do not.'*

> *'Finding things difficult can feel humiliating and the longer I didn't talk about it the longer those difficulties felt humiliating.'*

Many parents describe being surprised and alarmed by how quickly they can feel out of control, the intensity of feeling being unfamiliar in adult life. The mother who described anger 'ripping through her body' as she held her inconsolable baby had been 'murmuring words of comfort and reassurance'. Although she had been imagining herself into his shoes, trying to make sense of his experience using empathy, perhaps the misfit between her empathy and her anger communicated itself to the baby and added to his distress. The baby's distress is raw. He has not the experience to temper his response, no sense that 'things will look better in the morning' or that the wind in his tummy will pass. In identifying with her baby in these moments, she exposes herself to the full impact of his unprocessed emotions. It is possible that this may have put this mother in touch with long-forgotten infantile emotions and caused her own confusion and distress.

From parents . . .

> *'I think until you have children you are not prepared for the fact that they experience their emotions at a different level of intensity. They have a different emotional reality*

> *and when you are exposed to it your repressed capacity to experience emotions at full throttle is drawn out, you find yourself pounding your fist on the car bonnet over putting a pair of gloves on the child! You lose your adult perspective.'*

From psychoanalytic theory and clinical practice . . .

Various psychoanalysts have described the special state that mothers of young infants ordinarily go into. Bion talked of 'reverie' and Winnicott of 'maternal preoccupation'. What each description has in common is a receptiveness to the baby's emotional communications, a sort of hyper-empathy in which the mother's sense of well-being is completely bound up with the baby's experience. Freud (1957) argued that this is made possible by a narcissistic identification. That is to say that it is actually the mother's own infant self she sees in her baby and wants to protect from distress or discomfort. It is not that she treats his needs as though they were her own: at an unconscious level she actually experiences his needs as her own. This idea might go some way to explain how the wellspring of altruistic parental love gets replenished; if the giver is also the receiver at some level. However, such an intense identification is also thought to be the reason that mothers are put in touch with their own infantile neediness. When this meets with the external reality of having many of her adult needs frustrated by the task of parenting, the outcome is disturbing. 'Sudden dips into intense rage' (Parker 2005: 226) is the phrase used by Parker to describe the stories told her by mothers in therapy with her.

From parents . . .

> *'Somebody had pulled my life, my identity out from under my feet when I had a baby. I had no identity and no reality, the only thing that seemed real any more was this baby, and so I had to hold on to her, she needed me but I also needed her. I had lost my lifestyle, my career, in the second that she was born she had taken away everything that made me feel secure and made me "me". She was all I had now, I held on to her like if you took her away from me I would cease to exist.'*

Anne Stevenson's 'Poem for a daughter' describes beautifully the way in which becoming a parent is both negating of a previous sense of self and, at the same time, lends a profound sense of meaning and belonging.

> A woman's life is her own
> until it is taken away
> by a particular first cry.
> Then she is not alone
> but part of the premises
> of everything there is.
>
> (Stevenson 1983: 38)

Dealing with difficult feelings, your own and the baby's, is one of the most important tasks in parenting a baby. If you can, when holding your crying baby, bear her feelings, you have done a great deal. If you have resisted being dismissive, absenting yourself emotionally or physically, if you have not been overwhelmed, becoming helpless or lashing out, then you are being a good parent when it's hardest. You have kept in touch with enough of your adult mind to try to think through what might be wrong or indeed accept that you might not be able to find out. Sometimes accepting that you can't make it all better right now but still sticking it out, staying close and sharing the bad times together is what being a good parent looks like.

There is no shame in asking for professional help if your feelings are too much for you. It is easier to work out what is in your mind, if you have someone there to say it to. They are not likely to be shocked at the things you want to say. Parents who feel unmanageable hostility towards their babies may keep a distance from them, thinking this will protect the baby. They may refrain from looking at the baby fearing their expression might damage her. However, your baby needs you to be emotionally available. Once you start to feel understood by someone, perhaps your health visitor or a counsellor, you may be freer to get close to your baby, and to respond to what she needs. You may be less filled with internal preoccupations and feelings towards her that get in the way of noticing her, the actual baby. If the origin of your problems is with your own parents, you may need someone to talk to, and keep you in mind. When you feel sufficiently looked after, you will be more emotionally available to your baby.

Factors that might impact on your parenting

There are many reasons why you might have these feelings of hate towards your baby. One of the most powerful is if you felt that your parents hated you. You are then repeating with your baby what you know from your own experience. Being faced with your baby's vulnerability puts you in touch with your own vulnerability as a child. If you were well cared for then your baby's dependence will bring out the protecting, caring part of you. If you were not well cared for you may have felt you could not afford to be needy. You might now find yourself despising vulnerability in your baby as a weakness that needs to be punished and driven out. If you were often criticised and blamed as a child, you might find yourself blaming the baby.

Other factors that might lead to overwhelming feelings are an unplanned pregnancy, a difficult birth, a baby who cries a great deal or has feeding or sleeping difficulties. If you are depressed after the birth, if your relationship with your partner is unhappy, or if you are lonely, you are likely to find this will have an effect on what you feel about your baby. You may be feeling active anger or perhaps you are aloof and distant, not wanting to have anything to do with the baby. It is important to try to sort out cause and effect. You may feel that this is a 'bad' baby and the cause of your unhappiness.

An unwanted pregnancy can be particularly difficult these days when termination is an option. If you have gone ahead with an unplanned pregnancy, perhaps you had very mixed feelings about what you wanted to do. You might have made your decision in deference to other people's views and feel it could have been different. Most mothers have quite complex feelings anyway about their pregnancy, and usually giving birth resolves most of these. It is much harder if you are left, after the birth, still feeling that you would not have wanted this baby. Even if you do now genuinely want the baby, there can be feelings of guilt about the time of not wanting her, worries that your womb was not a loving place and this could have harmed her.

Problems may arise from before the baby was born. If you and your partner were getting on badly, a baby may be a focus – someone to love – or alternatively she might represent the worst of what is already happening in your life and find herself in the middle of an existing battle. You may feel the baby has come at the wrong time in your life and robbed you of other opportunities; that she has come when you didn't have the resources to care for her; that you needed to be looked after better yourself, before you could look after a baby. One immigrant mother, expecting a baby, said: 'I have nothing to give her.'

Sometimes problems stem from unresolved difficulties in the family you grew up in. You may have a baby who reminds you of a brother or sister that you had problems with. The baby may come in the same position in the family, or have a strong resemblance to them.

Babies with disabilities

When babies are born with any kind of disability or illness, it *is* an enormous shock to parents and it takes real qualities of heroism to manage these feelings and the extra burdens of care that the baby needs. Many parents find the baby's vulnerability brings out special qualities of love and tenderness and ability to care. Others cannot easily get over the shock and worry that it will affect their feelings towards the baby in a negative way. Parents of babies with disabilities often feel marginalised, excluded from the universal world of babyhood. We hope that much of this book is relevant to you and we list specialist literature written by knowledgeable professionals and parents to help with where your concerns are different.

Making sure you are not lonely

Most worries about being a good parent are much less dire than those discussed in the previous couple of pages, but all parents have moments of feeling quite inadequate. One problem can be mother and baby shut up together at home for most of the day. It may be ideal for mothers and babies to be able to spend much of the first weeks with time and space to get to know each other. But that doesn't mean being in a sort of two-person solitary confinement.

The organisation of women and children at home, separate from the rest of the community and its work, is fairly recent in history. It is also not how things are done in many non-industrialised parts of the world today (Liedloff, 1975). While not romanticising the past, for most of our history women would have shared the care of their children with their mothers and sisters. In hunter-gatherer communities all work is usually undertaken communally. A mother can leave her baby between breastfeeds while she works in some other capacity, she is part of a group with a shared purpose.

Mothering does not lead to isolation nor do women lose their function in society beyond being a mother.

From parents . . .

> *'The things that I miss about work are not just to do with the stimulation of the job but about the status it conferred, the respect and acknowledgement of skills from other adults, but also the pretty clothes and the flirting, just being an adult in my prime in the world of adults.'*

Your baby can be great company right from the beginning (see Chapter 3), but she cannot meet all your needs as an adult. Anyone who is feeling fed up, tired or bad tempered, needs another adult to talk to and a change of scene. Staying home alone with a baby when you are feeling like that can leave you stuck with a low mood. Good enough parents let themselves get it into perspective with enjoyable company and interesting things to do. However, if in company you feel that you are boring and that no one will want to talk to you, or that they are boring and you don't want to talk to them, this perhaps means that your depression is hard to lift and you might need more help.

The quotes below are from parents of toddlers and so aggressive feelings are to the fore. For parents of babies it may be low mood and listlessness that being with other adults helps to keep at bay.

From parents . . .

> *'I think play-dates are so important. I'm a better parent when there's another adult there. I'm more attentive and less irritable. You could say we have a sort of policing effect on each other.'*
>
> *'I'm definitely nicer when I'm with other mums. Although I do understand that the way I am with my children is really important to their development, stuff just seems to count more in front of other adults. It's hard to remember that what you're doing is important when you seem so unimportant to the rest of the world.'*
>
> *'Being responded to by an adult is different to being responded to by a baby. They are, and should be, completely egocentric but that makes being with them annihilating at times. It's not that I stop myself from being*

> *bad tempered in front of other adults; I just don't find myself getting so bored and frustrated.'*
>
> *'Apparently almost two-thirds of mothers responding to a survey on "netmums.com" admitted to deliberately giving other mums the impression that they were coping better than they really felt they were. Some specified bedtimes and the amount of time spent playing with their children as areas they felt tempted to fib about. The same mothers said they felt other mums were doing better than them. We should be supporting each other, not making it worse!'*

Here again, letting yourself know about and talking about your difficult feelings makes them less potent. You are less likely to act on them and their power to haunt you with a sense of non-specific guilt and low mood is diffused. Generally happy parents make good parents so don't be hard on yourself and be honest with other parents. It'll do you, them and all your babies good.

Your identity as a parent

Some have always known that they wanted to become parents. They anticipate growing into a part of themselves that has been there waiting to bloom. This will usually be a part of your 'self' built on a positive identification with your own parents. For mothers in particular it can be very gratifying to have such a clear biological function and sometimes fathers describe having a new-found sense of purpose and drive in their work now that they are a provider. For others it is more complicated. If you do not have a positive model from your parents, you may feel like you are stepping into the dark. There will be much that is unknown and some fear about what you might discover.

From parents . . .

> *'I had a bad relationship with my mother and consequently a fairly negative image of motherhood as something dull, done by moany people with saggy bottoms and ugly clothes. I hated pushing a pushchair around, felt chained by it, labelled by it, weighed down literally and metaphorically.'*
>
> *'I remember being elated by the sudden but absolute conviction that I had finally discovered my purpose and*

> *now life had meaning: this is what I'm for; to look after this being! After a couple of years I refound myself. Although my life is unrecognisable and completely structured around the kids now, as the intensity ebbed away some of "me" has come back.'*

Often mothers have lost their everyday work friends, and haven't made new ones. It matters who your friends are, and you may feel you're not going to make friends with just any woman pushing a buggy in the neighbourhood. If you are still a bit unsure that you wanted to find yourself in this situation, stuck with a baby, and rather wishing you were back in your old life, will making friends with other mothers trap you even more? It can seem as though the best solution is to get back to work as soon as possible, leave the baby to an 'expert' carer and leave behind worries about being a good mother. There may be other practical reasons for a mother having to go back to work and for some mothers it may be essential, but if an early panic about loneliness becomes the deciding factor, you might rob yourself of the chance to explore this new life. There may be an opportunity to develop a part of yourself that might have gone underground as you were consolidating your career. Paradoxically, it can be unnecessarily high standards for being a 'good mother' that causes some women to give up and escape into returning to work. If you do give yourself the chance, and try to stick it out for a few weeks, you may find you discover your own creative fun with your baby and the people around.

Valuing what you do as a parent

Our wider culture also impacts on how parents feel about themselves. As a society, we have traditionally had a split attitude to those who care for children, at once idealising and dismissing. Trying to be perfect is not only not best for your baby but also you are likely to feel set up to fail. Idealisation is not helpful but some women may find they have taken on dismissive attitudes about the importance of child rearing as part of their identifying as professionals.

From parents . . .

> *'While shopping for a pushchair in late pregnancy I became aware of being rather lacklustre about it. This confused me.*

> *It was a big buy, and not only in terms of expense, it was the very emblem of motherhood. Then I realised that that was the problem. There was to be no soaring pride in my first identification with motherhood. I wanted to mother a baby but I did not want to be a Mother.'*

> *'I don't always tell people straight away that I have children. Some of the associations people have aren't true of me so I prefer people to get to know me a bit first. But then I don't always tell people I'm a lawyer straight away for the same reason.'*

Perhaps part of the problem with developing a positive identity as a parent is that it is hard to quantify the 'work' of parenting. Most paid work has a system of targets and evaluation. Satisfaction in completing a task competently usually depends on how much skill the task requires, or is thought to require. Stadlen in *What Mothers Do: Especially When It Looks Like Nothing* identifies a serious problem with regard to the lack of discreet, achievable tasks in parenting: '[mother] has tried to be patient but he looks cross and tired. Where has all her mothering gone?' (2004: 84). Stadlen identifies aspects of parenting that are often overlooked, like mediating the physical and social world for your baby; the work of constantly imagining yourself into her mind and thinking about what she might make of every new situation. With regard to how parents feel about what they do all day, she finds parents tend to be self-deprecating and dissatisfied: 'doing nothing . . . bored . . . lonely . . . invisible and unimportant' (2004: 2).

From parents . . .

> *'I have found myself letting the baby whinge while I finish wiping the kitchen surfaces down. I know that having a clean surface right that minute is not as important as being available to her but sometimes I just long for the pleasing feel of a job well done. Even if the job is a small boring one at least it is demonstrably finished and does not leave me with a lingering sense of doubt about whether I'm doing it right.'*

Actually, even this mother who feels that she is neglecting her baby when wiping down the surfaces is also actually showing the baby that chaos can be put into order – an important lesson.

From psychoanalytic theory and clinical practice . . .

Bion's theory of containment describes the importance of what is happening in the mind of a parent holding a distressed baby. First, the intolerable anxiety experienced by babies is projected out. If the carer is able to 'contain' this anxiety, she takes it in, makes it tolerable and it can then be taken back in by the baby. To make the anxiety tolerable the mother demonstrates that she can bear it and not be overwhelmed. She also uses her adult capacity for logic and reason to try to marshal the mass of unruly feelings into something she can make sense of and describe in words. She may possibly even alleviate his distress by making changes in the external situation. Crucial to the baby's development is that the function of containment – the capacity to modify anxiety – is also taken in from the carer, thus providing for his future mental health as he learns to regulate his own feeling states.

Parents joke about sleep deprivation but it is gallows humour. The feat of remaining reasonable, patient and receptive when sleep deprived is no laughing matter. It is worth remembering that sleep deprivation is used as torture to break a person's will. Part of the 'work' of parenting is to endure while keeping a grip on yourself.

This challenging work is often thought of as passive and unskilled. Yet, in the worlds of neuroscience, developmental psychology and psychoanalytic theory, a great deal is known about what is happening when an adult comforts a crying baby. It is complicated, difficult and crucially important to the future happiness of the baby.

So, quite unaware of what you are doing, you might start by reflecting his feelings, frowning and making pained noises yourself. Slowly you will bring him down to a simmer with you by becoming calmer and more positive yourself. Finally you will think aloud with him about what might be wrong, showing that thinking can help with feelings. On the following page is a description of how this all gets manifested at the biochemical level.

This is recognisably the same phenomenon as that described as 'containment' but in the research discussed here it is babies' cortisol (stress biochemical), heart rate and adrenalin that are measured and thought about in relation to a body of knowledge about the

From research on how experience in relationships shapes body and brain development . . .

The adult structure of the brain will be decided by the way our genes and environment (the care we receive) interact during infancy. Parasympathetic and sympathetic responses are innate. All babies are born with this primitive nervous system which enables the psychological experiences of avoidance (pretending not to feel or pretending not to be there) or a dopamine-fuelled fight-or-flight response. These automatic responses have been essential for survival in more physically hazardous times. However, these states can quickly become maladaptive and need to be regulated. An adult, who can acknowledge and remain calm in the face of the infant's distress, acts directly on the infant's nervous system by influencing the balance of hormones being released and processed. This in turn will determine what that infant's baseline or set-to-normal balance of biochemicals is. Once set this is very hard to change in later life and will determine automatic physiological and emotional responses to stress situations. There is, of course, innate variation in the way each brain creates and uses different biochemicals, leading to innate temperament, but adult care at this highly plastic time can redress the balance when someone is dealt a bad hand by their genes or ruin the game for someone who had a good hand to start. This regulation by the adult is no more or less than remaining receptive to your baby's pain, even when it feels unbearable (Schore 2001; Gerhardt 2004).

brain and body as well as our understanding of minds and behaviour. Again what we see is that the person 'left holding the baby' has the unfolding shape of a human brain in their hands. It is profoundly important work.

Handling and touching your baby

This does link with a serious problem for parents today. Now that there is so much knowledge about sexual abuse, parents can feel concerned about touching their babies. It would be a great shame for parents and babies to miss out on the ordinary pleasure of physical contact. In fact physical affection and the intimacy of care routines are essential experiences that your baby needs for her emotional and intellectual development (see Chapter 3 on bonding). What confuses people is that part of this pleasure is a kind of sexual feeling. You can also see the excitement babies quite naturally have from the feel of their own bodies, touching their own genitals with enjoyment and baby boys having erections in the bath or elsewhere.

From parents . . .

> *'Changing my newborn son in front of the health visitor, I found myself trying to "convey" disinterested efficiency in the way that I handled and cleaned his penis. But I do love his little penis. I guess it's a bit sad that I feel I have to pretend not to in case it is misinterpreted as sexual interest.'*

> *'I've been really disturbed a couple of times while enjoying handling my baby by the graphic descriptions of sexual abuse so rife in the media. I've spoken to a couple of other mums who have said the same. None of us were abused but it's just sort of there in your mind sometimes and it's really upsetting.'*

It is important to think about boundaries and not to touch babies or older children intrusively. It can be difficult for parents who were themselves seductively caressed and told this was 'alright' to be able to discriminate now as to what is right. If you can talk about it, it will be less confusing. Adults who were actually abused themselves really do need help in talking about this. If you can sort out your feelings about these experiences, you will have less worry about mishandling your baby or the opposite of keeping too much distance.

Worries about baby's illnesses

In this book we concentrate on emotional issues and the way that how you feel affects how you look after your baby. This still applies when there is a question of illness, or worry that there is something wrong with the baby. Parents do, of course, have to watch their children for signs of sudden illness, but it is usually quite obvious when a baby is not herself, has a fever or severe pain. When in doubt, it is always better to consult a doctor, but if you find that you have had more than one or two false alarms, it is worth thinking about why your assessment has gone wrong. How is it that you have become so anxious?

From psychoanalytic theory and clinical practice . . .

In my work consulting to GPs, I heard about a mother who kept on calling out the doctor whenever her baby had a slight cold or other ailments. At first the doctor was bothered by these frequent consultations. Then she remembered that the mother had had a still birth before the birth of this baby, and her sister had also lost a baby. So she was right to feel anxious, any small illness could trigger off fears of a serious loss. The doctor talked sympathetically about this with her, and although she continued to have these underlying memories, it helped to recognise the origins of some of her anxieties.

Anyone who has had miscarriages or lost a baby may feel that they just can't take a chance, and become reluctant to rely on their own judgement. Similarly, if a tragic event has happened in your family, or with friends, it may make you feel how risky everything is. If the birth of your baby was difficult, it can leave you much more aware of danger. It can be helpful to talk about these fears to make them more manageable. It is then worth practising your powers of observation, so that you can exercise your own judgement about whether your baby is well. It is important for your baby's sake to try not to become phobic of too many situations. A partner can be very helpful in reassuring the other parent, but this reassurance needs to be truthful, and not come from impatience with the fears.

Nappy changing

Changing your baby's nappy can be very pleasurable – the look of relief or even delight on her face at the feeling of the clean nappy. There is the feeling of co-operation as your baby lets you move her to put the nappy on, or the irritation as she thwarts your attempts. There is the shared pleasure as you stroke her bare bottom and the smiles and the looks you exchange. However, there can be anger that you are the one that has to clean up the mess of a soiled nappy.

Parents have many different feelings about having to change nappies. While babies are breastfed it may feel that even their poo is an extension of yourself. This changes when the baby has solids, the smell then becomes alien. Changing nappies is one of the topics most frequently joked about by parents. In fact, having to deal with a baby's excrement is a real problem for some parents, especially if, when you were a baby, you were made to feel that bodily products were dirty and shouldn't be handled. Babies are not disgusted by faeces and, in fact, are rather curious about their own as the first thing that they produce. It may be that your own baby-pleasure in these products was frowned on and you were made to feel you were a nasty, messy child. It's hard to get over these sorts of feelings, though you have most likely forgotten about them. One result can be that your child's bottom is a rather worrying area, and keeping it clean fraught with some anxiety. If there then is a problem and your baby has nappy rash, it can stir up feelings that your nasty dirty habits have been exposed. You might find that you project this on to the baby – that they are nasty and messy in having dirty nappies. If you are already feeling low, you might sometimes avoid changing the nappies, which can make the nappy rash worse. You might feel embarrassed to tell the doctor or health visitor about it and feel stuck with the mess. In reality, this is a very common problem and they will be able to tell you how to solve it.

Hospital stays

If your baby has to be in hospital, that is the time she needs you most. You will probably be invited to stay in with her, and if not, you might have to insist. It used to be thought that parents visiting 'upset' their babies. Hospital staff often mistakenly thought they were quiet because they had 'settled'. The ground-breaking films by James and Joyce Robertson (1967–75) showed that unvisited babies felt abandoned and lapsed into apathy. These films changed social policy. If you do have to leave her at times, saying goodbye and telling her you are coming back, even if she is preverbal, will help her to manage. When a baby, or any young child, has an operation or any procedure requiring an anaesthetic, it is essential for a parent or someone close to be there beforehand and as the child starts to drift back into consciousness. They may seem not to notice you are there but they would know if you weren't.

In 1965 not all hospitals were observing the new rules about allowing parents to visit their children. In Margaret Drabble's *The Millstone*, published in that year, she describes how a mother experiences her instinctual knowledge that she should not be separated from her infant. Although this is a fictional account, we recognise in the ferocity of the mother the sheer animal instinct in mothers to protect their young.

'We went to the hospital and I handed her over, and she smiled at me. Then cried when they took her away. The world had contracted to the small size of her face, and her clenching, waving hands.' After the operation the mother tries to visit the baby but is refused. 'The lady in white embarked upon a long explanation about upsetting children, upsetting mothers, upsetting other children, upsetting other mothers, justice to all, disturbing the nurses' routine and such topics.' The Sister tries to reassure the mother that she'd be amazed by how quickly they settle but the mother is alarmed: 'I didn't like the sound of that word "settle".' She tries to insist on access to her baby and when she is still prevented she begins to scream: 'All the time I was thinking I must go on with this until they let me see her . . . I remember the clearness of my consciousness and the ferocity of my emotion' (Drabble 1965: 13).

Thankfully you should not experience anything like this now but it is a salutary reminder that we must take full advantage of that which was once fought for. There are still some who will describe apathy as evidence of contentment in a baby.

If your baby needs to be in a neonatal intensive care unit, it's important to make sure the staff get you there, in a wheelchair if necessary, to be with her as much as you are able. She needs you just as much as she needs the technology and care of the unit and as much as you need to be with her. Ask the staff how much you can actually hold her, as well as touching, looking at and talking to her (see the section on intensive care in Chapter 1).

If you have to be in hospital yourself, you might want to see if the baby can come to visit you, unless you are too ill to respond to her normally and think it would be more worrying for her than not seeing you at all. The best people to look after her at home, if possible, are of course her other parent and other family members. If she is old enough, they will be able to talk to her about you and show her photographs of you. This will help her not to think you have disappeared off the face of the earth.

Managing on your own

When two parents are together they tend to complement each other's qualities, as one can make up for what the other is less good at. Mothers may be more openly caring and fathers firmer in their attitude, but if this is too strongly divided, it becomes gender stereotyping, and in good relationships it is usually fluid. If parents are able to co-operate with each other, a mother can enable the father to constructively back up her authority rather than either having all the authority herself or handing it all over to him. Same-sex couples do not offer such obvious gender contrasts but they do afford the complexity of relating to two people of different personalities.

In a single parent family, it is harder to give your baby the experience of an alternative perspective to your own and hers. She will need opportunities to be the third person in a relationship, the one looking on or sometimes to have her interactions with you observed by a third. These issues may not seem as pressing as the more obvious difficulties of single parenthood: always having to cope without a supportive partner, not having breaks from constantly being with the baby, lack of adult company in the evenings and a shortage of money. However, this experience of 'triangulation' is important to her developing sense of self and how to relate to others, it is also thought to be an important aspect of learning how to develop abstract thinking (Fivaz-Depeursinge, 2014).

There are many fathers who are the main or sole carer for their children and most of what follows will be relevant for single fathers too. However, the majority of single parents are women and some of what is discussed reflects this.

Single parents often feel they have regained some control in ending the relationship but others feel that the authority and strength has all walked out with the other parent, especially if they were the one who left. The one left behind can find herself being inexplicably helpless, and without her own natural authority, perhaps unconsciously leaving a space for the missing person to come back. To the baby it can feel as though no one is really in charge.

From parents . . .

> *'As a university graduate, used to a comfortable lifestyle, I never imagined that I would find myself alone and receiving no financial, practical or emotional support. For a time we were living in a tower block and I was dependent on social security. At the end of the week I would have to choose between taking them to the children's activities at the Arts Centre or having a proper Sunday lunch.'*

> *'Many of my single parent friends were constantly chasing their exes for money owed, which was stressful, humiliating and exhausting. For me, this was more of an issue*

when we had been together. We were poor now but I was in control. He did not have the power to disappoint us any more.'

'In leaving my husband I took control and regained my strength and authority. Although I knew that it had been the right decision for my children and me, I couldn't help feeling guilty at having deprived my children of their father. Later on I realised that I had leant on my eldest, let her be the "other adult" that was missing in our family.'

If you are separated or divorced, there are a variety of feelings you might have about being on your own. You may feel deserted and unfairly left to do it all, or relief that anger or violence has come to an end. Either way it can feel like the last straw that your baby, quite independently of your feelings, is missing her father or mother. Sometimes the baby may resemble the absent parent and be vulnerable to being identified with the 'bad parent' in the other parent's mind.

There are increasing numbers of women choosing to become single parents. In some social groups it is young mothers who do not seem to have an expectation that fathers will be involved in daily family life. For many women it is a choice made later in life when the hoped-for couple with children set-up is looking less and less likely.

From parents . . .

'At thirty-six my long-term partner left me weeks before we were due to be married. At thirty-eight I had recovered from the shock and disappointment but realised that if I waited to be sure (again!) with another man I would probably miss my chance of conceiving, so I decided to do it by myself. There are advantages to being older and single. I have a good support network of friends and family that I know I can rely on and I am financially secure. Our situation is actually very secure and stable compared to many two-parent families.'

If you have chosen to embark on single parenthood from the beginning, you may need to give some thought to how your baby experiences the assumption that the other parent, and perhaps the other gender, can be dispensed with.

Nurturing both you and your baby

Loneliness can be a problem for single parents and one aspect can be the need for emotional reassurance from your baby as much as she needs it from you. You will probably sleep with your baby, as indeed many two-parent families also do, but perhaps finding it harder to recognise the moment when she is ready for a bit more independence and might like to be in her own cot or own room.

As much for your baby as for you, you need to have action going on in your own life. She can then see that you have a busy and fruitful life, otherwise she may feel she has to be responsible on her own for keeping you going. She needs to meet other people, the real-life experience of having to share you sometimes as well as having you to herself at other times.

From parents . . .

> *'As a single parent I know how important friends and family are as a support network for my son and I. I make a point of looking after those relationships in the same way married friends nurture their marriage. I know we both need other people.'*

Your baby also needs contact with men who are important to you, your family and friends, but if you are 'dating', remember that your home is also your baby's home and that her privacy matters. Jealousy is much more painful to a child when the man that her mother is interested in is not especially concerned for that child's feelings, as a father might be. If having a new partner becomes the spur to putting your child in her own room, this is also likely to exacerbate the child's feelings of rejection.

Where possible, babies should have contact with both parents

When parents are separated there is often a loss of contact with the other parent. A large number of fathers lose contact with their children within two years. Sometimes the departing parent has been violent or abusive, and does not seem to be able to learn to be different. But, most often, both parents have a great deal to offer their children, even if the father and mother cannot manage to live together. The majority of estranged parents are fathers, so it is worth stressing that fathers matter to their children. Children who do not have contact with their fathers risk having less confidence and lower self-esteem. However, this is a complicated subject. In the box below, Penelope Leach (2010) and Graham Music (2011) cite important research into the impact of paternal involvement. It seems that positive father figures confer advantages but antisocial fathers are a risk to their children's development.

When the missing parent has died, you can keep the memory alive with photographs and talking about them to their child. A baby who loses a parent so early may not have conscious memories, but she can get the feel of the character of her parent from these stories. She can also get the feel of the quality of the relationship within which she was conceived and born.

From research on the impact of paternal involvement . . .

'When thousands of babies were followed into adulthood, for example, those with closely involved father figures had higher levels of education and more close friends of both sexes and were less likely to smoke or to have had trouble with the police. Similarly, women who had had good relationships with their fathers at the age of sixteen grew up to have better relationships with their husbands and a greater sense of mental and physical well-being' (Leach 2010: 166). Music makes the point that because antisocial fathers are less likely to be present, this skews the statistics on how beneficial paternal presence is per se. He looks more closely at what happens when less nurturing fathers are present: 'Fathers with antisocial tendencies were less likely to be highly involved with their infants, to be living at home with them, or to have married the mother. Striking a blow against the idea that two-parent families are always best, when antisocial fathers were living at home then the children were much more likely to show behavioural difficulties than if such fathers were absent. Some but not all fathers foster children's development . . . Generally when fathers are nurturing, playful and encouraging, advantages are conferred' (Music 2011: 177–8).

5

FIGURING OUT FATHERHOOD

'What are fathers for? To be the other parent.' Said the psychiatrist Sebastian Kraemer (2005). The wise simplicity of this statement takes us into the essential creativity and complexity of the role that this 'other parent' performs. It is not about being an additional or spare parent but about being able to offer a particular relationship to the baby and to the mother-and-baby-couple, offering a third position. We hoped that most chapters would speak, to a greater or lesser degree, to both parents. However, it became clear that a, perhaps necessary, emphasis on mothers persisted and so this chapter aims to redress the balance and focus on the particular role of a father. Of course, it need not be the biological father, or even a man who fulfils this role, although there are obvious reasons why it usually is. Also, what fathers do varies massively across and within cultures and over time. We do not claim to base what is said about fathers here on what is 'natural' or universal, only what is common within the culture and timeframe in which the authors live and work. While we will talk about 'fathers', it is worth reiterating that this role can be taken on by others – a supporting family member, a step-parent or the partner in a gay relationship.

Becoming a father

There is evidence to suggest (see Chapter 3) that fathers undergo biochemical changes during their baby's gestation and after the birth, but only if they are living with the mother during her pregnancy and have hands-on experience of caring for the baby after the birth. You have the innate capacity to make this change into parenthood, but your body needs certain social and emotional experiences to activate the biochemistry. Again, you cannot rely on being swept along by it all but need to actively take up your role.

From research on outcomes for children of gay couples . . .

Research comparing outcomes for children of lesbian and heterosexual couples showed that school performance, emotional adjustment, peer relationships and substance use were comparable in the two groups. Difficulties for adolescents were related to emotional functioning within each family rather than family 'type' (Patterson and Wainright 2007).

From parents . . .

> *'One unexpected (and seemingly permanent) consequence has been a heightened sentimentality, crying at books and TV programmes that would have left me cold before, coupled with an awareness of time passing.'*
>
> *'He's a fully modern father, took full paternity leave plus holiday so that he was around for those first few weeks and getting the skin-to-skin time he knew was so important. He's totally had his daddy-switch turned on and it's him that gets broody over other babies now.'*

A mother cannot escape the physicality of pregnancy and birth and the hormonal changes these processes trigger. Most will also be physically and emotionally bound up with their baby over feeding. There is a bodily reality to mothering that cannot be opted out of. She will find herself thrust into her new role by a biochemical tsunami (see Chapter 3). By contrast, a father has to opt in to his role. Having said that, fathers have just as much a conscious and unconscious wish to have children as mothers do, and the drive to procreate cannot be underestimated. After the conception comes the time to embrace the awesome responsibility for the baby, to bear the disquieting stirring of memories and emotions from one's own childhood; to step up to all this requires courage. There will be a constant need for decisions about where to place yourself in relation to mother, baby and the rest of the world. You will need, especially at the beginning, to be a protective barrier between the world and the mother-and-baby-couple, creating the conditions they need to get really locked into one another. You will also need to establish your bond with your baby before you are pulled back out into the world.

Bye, baby Bunting,
Daddy's gone a-hunting,
Gone to get a rabbit skin
To wrap the baby Bunting in.

This old nursery rhyme evokes the traditional function of the father as provider and protector, and this is still pertinent but he does not need to be the sole breadwinner to do this. There are many ways for a father to enable family life. This might involve taking more responsibility for providing financially in order to free mother up to care for the baby, equally it might take the form of negotiating the best paternity leave you can in order to foster your own bond with your baby and to support mother and baby in person.

From parents . . .

> *'My feelings about being at work were different from before. Although I enjoyed an absorbing job, I was pulled towards the drama at home. Work was not my main focus any more. It served to provide for home life. The whole feeling of what home was had changed, and with a mother and baby to go back to, it seemed much cosier. In spite of being short of sleep I left work feeling full of energy, which I did need in order to help out with the baby when I got in. My masculine identity grew stronger as I grappled with all these new responsibilities.'*

> *'My husband looked after me so that I could look after the baby. All I did was feed her and sleep. I guess I must have been eating and he must have made those meals but I was so absorbed by her that I don't remember even speaking to him around that time.'*

Driving your partner in labour to the hospital, and driving her and the precious new baby home again, are events that become part of a family's history. Having the house ready for them to return to after the birth is a way of taking care of everyone that some fathers relish. If the birth is at home, you will similarly be the best person to manage the setting for mother, baby and midwife. Whatever you find yourself *doing*, your presence is what really counts, your proximity that will enable your bond with your baby and establish your role in relation to mother and baby.

You are needed at home

The first week or so of your baby's life is like no other time. You are within your rights to make a fuss at work to see how much paternity leave is possible. Few families have more than two children these days. A couple of weeks' paternity leave for each child will probably only take a month out of your whole working life. The value to you, your baby and your partner of you being there at the start is incomparable.

Bridge to the outside world

You will usually be the one to telephone the news to grandparents and others and to hear the first tearful delighted reactions. You may find yourself welcoming or fending off visits as appropriate. It is important for you as a father to make yourself known to the health visitor when she first comes to visit. The mother, of course, needs special attention after giving birth, but you are one half of the baby's parents.

From parents . . .

> *'At our last check-up the health visitor introduced herself to my wife and daughter but not to me!'*

Your feelings about being a new father will influence the baby as much as his mother's, and your childhood experiences, as well as your genes, will have as great an effect on your baby as do your partner's. You may find you need to talk about your childhood to make sense of becoming a father.

Changes to your identity and priorities

From fathers . . .

> *'I recall thinking a lot about my parents and how they must have felt about us (and still do?), their children. Your own childhood becomes more vivid and some things start to make more sense. It made me think about my own character – what made me what I am – and how my children would experience my parenting. Very deep waters.'*

> *'I suddenly became more aware of other fathers, had a new interest in them as people and a new-found respect for the role of a father. I even started identifying with different characters in dramas. I guess I had switched from the 'adolescent' archetype to the 'father' archetype. Your position in society changes, I relate differently to the world now and something's changed internally too.'*

Sharing the babycare

Men nowadays are often more actively involved with their babies than their own fathers were with them. So you might not have a role model for this particular job. It can be difficult to be the first generation to try out a new way of doing things.

From fathers . . .

> *'My father was really involved in our lives and looked after us a lot but I still remember being surprised and disappointed to discover one evening that he didn't know which toothbrush was mine. I knew I wanted to be around a lot but also be the kind of dad that knows about the toothbrush.'*

From research on paternal sensitivity . . .

Music collates evidence showing that 'fathers are biologically no less sensitive potentially to infant signals than mothers. Given the right circumstances they interact and imitate in much the same way as mothers, are equally as able to identify their children by touch as mothers when blindfolded and not able to use smell, and have been shown to be as sensitive as mothers in (bottle) feeding, allowing appropriate pauses and recovery time' (Music 2011: 175).

You might think that mothers know what to do instinctively. It is true that as children they were more likely to have been playing at putting their dolls to bed and imagining themselves in the role of mother, but parenting doesn't necessarily come easier to either one of you. Studies show that fathers experience the same physiological response to a baby's crying as mothers do. It is nearness to a baby that releases knowledge of what to do. A baby's cry is itself instinctively driven, and so is the response. The sound of the cry tells us that they are in need and that we must stay near to work it out. Mothers can quickly become experts in this because, especially if they are breastfeeding, they are often already near by. If as a father you also interact with your child, regularly changing his nappies, picking him up if he cries, you will have an equal chance to understand the baby's needs. You may worry about damaging this tiny creature. If so, the best thing you can do is try holding him anyway. You will pick up from his signals information about how he likes to be held.

From lesbian parents . . .

> *'I breastfed our baby until fourteen months but I remember when my partner gave him his first bottle. She sat there with tears streaming down her face. She had never wanted to carry our baby but this was such an important moment for us. Since then their relationship has really blossomed, they're really playful together and I guess that was the beginning of her claiming her own separate relationship with him.'*

A note to mums: the perils of gate keeping

For mothers it can be lovely to have the father there to share the early dreaming time of being with the baby. But if father is also good at it, does that mean that mother is no longer the expert? It can be too easy for mothers to get into the habit of criticising a father for doing things differently. In fact, babies need to experience their two parents' own natural styles of handling them, so that they can get to know them as real people.

From mothers . . .

> *'At the beginning I wanted him to be a substitute mum, and then I'd be critical because he wasn't doing things exactly the same as me. In fact I wanted more from him. When he used the sling I felt annoyed that he wasn't holding her in his arms, like he was cutting corners. I did not trust that he had really made the transition into parenthood like I had had to. There was one time when she was crying really badly and he wanted to make a sandwich before going to her. I remember feeling such rage that he still thought his hunger came first. We now have three children and he is a really involved dad and I can appreciate that he is so much more than a substitute for me but he became that, over time.'*

> *'When I couldn't calm the baby, my husband would take her into the other room, turn up the Old-School Ska and dance her to sleep. It was beautiful but a part of me thought "I want to be doing it".'*

> *'At the beginning we would have the witching hour in the evenings. I just could not comfort her and we got into a bit of a state together. It was such a relief when my husband came home and took her from me. It would break the spell and she'd calm right down with him, after a break she and I could come back together again in a less fraught way and then she could go to sleep. I was grateful and pleased to see them together but I felt jealous too. I had a greedy wish to be everything to her, all that she needed.'*

Your baby needs *you*

As these quotes from parents show, a mother-and-baby-couple might sometimes need a third person to break into the tyranny of a twosome. Just as they will need you to hold the world at bay so that they can get lost in each other, they may also need you to rescue them from each other and show them the riches you have to offer. As Sebastian Kraemer explains: 'Fathers are just as important to their children as mothers are. This is not so much related to the level of involvement that a father has with his child, as to the child's imagined link to him. Men and women become fathers and mothers when their offspring is conceived, creating both biological and psychological systems, and the setting for a family drama' (Kraemer 2005: 1).

Babies can appreciate the difference between their mother and father. They can discern the different feel of bodies, the different experience of being held, talked to, looked at by two distinct characters. If they hear a male voice as well as a female one, it makes the world a more interesting place. Babies can identify with the parent of the same sex, so that a girl can imagine being like her mother, and a boy like his father, and at the same time have their first opportunity to be with the other sex.

From parents . . .

> *'I did find that I was slightly less careful than my wife and, being less careful, actually enabled things to move on sometimes. I was more willing to take chances. It was partly because I was less tired, partly because of my character but it is also about the binary nature of parenting. You can't get the whole world from one person – a 3D picture needs two vanishing points.'*

> *'On the Tube our very young baby started to cry and my wife felt panicky about it. She wanted to get off the Tube and feed her there and then, even though we were only one stop from home. I felt that our daughter was able to manage and we agreed to stay on the train and get home. My wife was so in tune with our daughter's feelings it could prevent her from thinking, being external to that, I could see what our daughter might be able to tolerate.'*

Your baby ideally needs two parents who are each closely involved with him, and with each other. While being harmonious together, they may still have different views from each other. The complexity of the threesome is his first introduction to the complexities of the world outside.

From psychoanalytic theory and clinical practice . . .

A baby's experience of interacting with one while having the other in mind, in parenthesis, is how his mind will become structured for complex thought, preparing it for life in that complex world. These ideas are explored in Fivaz-Depeursinge's (2008) 'Infants in triangular communication in "two for one" versus "two against one", family triangles'. This idea of a triangle is also important in terms of your baby's emerging sense of self. If the link between the parents – perceived in love and hate – can be tolerated in the child's mind, it allows a third position where the baby is a witness, not a participant. If he can observe, he can also envisage being observed. As Ronald Britton explains: 'This provides us with a capacity for seeing ourselves in interaction with others, for entertaining another point of view while retaining our own, for reflecting on ourselves while being ourselves' (1991: 87).

You are likely to provide different experiences for your baby. It sometimes seems that a mother has a feel for a baby's current needs while a father may have more of a vision of what the baby is capable of, and bring in the excitement of the new. It is not just a cliché that mothers hold babies protectively in their arms, while fathers are the ones to throw the baby up in the air, to offer challenging exciting play that includes mastery over fear.

From parents . . .

> *'His father started the scary play – chasing, hiding, pouncing and tickles. I do it too, now that I've seen the reaction, the shrieks and the giggles. But then that's only been since he got older. As a tiny baby it was me that really got him, I was more receptive to those tiny signs that he wanted to communicate with us.'*
>
> *'My husband is a quiet and still man. I do the roughhousing in our house because I have a more boisterous personality. He is really good at watching and following her interests. As she plays he makes discreet, almost silent interventions that show her that he understands what she's trying to do with a toy, but this only started once she was playing with things.'*

> *'It felt as though my wife had a nine-month head start in terms of her relationship with our daughter. I would search for ways of helping her sleep when she woke up, or ways of comforting her when she cried and through this and through spending time with her and playing I developed my own relationship with her and saw different things in her to my wife. We developed different ways of being with her and that difference was important because it allowed different sides of her personality to evolve.'*

As a father, you will also probably be lucky enough to get out of the house. Many fathers volunteer to do the shopping, to get away from the claustrophobic emotions at home. Perhaps these moments of release enable a father to fulfil certain functions of being the 'other parent', of bringing a fresh point of view back into the house, or of taking over from a tired mother. A tactful father can make mother and baby feel that he can look after them both without undermining an exhausted mother's authority.

A mother who is so in the thick of it, giving herself over to her newborn's needs day and night, might make a father feel that he has no authority to question how things are being done. Once again it will be down to you to assert yourself and the value of your insights as 'the other parent' with a different perspective. It is precisely because you have some distance and are still plugged into the outside world that you have something different to offer. You free her up to enter a state of primary maternal preoccupation (see

Chapter 4) but it is your job to keep perspective for the family, and in time to broaden their view again. It may also fall to you to be the defender of the parental couple's relationship, the one who can keep the link between those two points in the triangle strong.

From parents . . .

> *'I felt it was easier for me to bear our relationship in mind because my wife was involved in such a complex and consuming relationship with our daughter. So, when we went out for a meal on our own it was often me who would say, "Let's not talk about our daughter for a few hours, let's just have some time for ourselves."'*

This important work to nurture the couple relationship is easily overlooked when it feels like all the energies of the two parents are absorbed in meeting the needs of the baby. However, neglecting it might also be a way of avoiding the triangle and the jealousy it entails. As Maureen Marks puts it, 'Essentially, the task for the mother, father and infant involves tolerating the link between two people they desire and which excludes them. This situation cannot be harmonious' (2002: 95).

From parents . . .

> *'I came back to bed one Sunday morning to find my two-year-old son squealing "dump daddy, dump daddy" rather excitedly. My wife explained that she'd been telling him about our planned trip to the dump and he'd got rather excited about the possibilities of such a place!'*

Coping with jealousy

Some mothers feel resentment about the big smiles and excited response daddy gets on his return when it is she who has done the hard work of caring for baby all day. In other households things are more complicated.

From parents . . .

> *'When he gets in of an evening he might start checking his emails or wants to talk to me and I have to remind him that the baby will be going to bed soon. He always responds well to being reminded but she takes a while to warm up to him*

> *when they've been apart all day, so I guess it does take more effort for him, and he's tired after work.'*

This mother went on to comment that she felt guilty about her daughter being a 'mummy's girl'. When asked why she felt guilty, she confessed that it was because she did feel gratified by her daughter's preference for mummy, despite her outward attempts to bring baby and father together. This serves as a reminder of just how complicated things can get between three. This mother realises that she has mixed feelings about father coming between mother and baby and developing their own bond. She is both baby's advocate in the world and jealous keeper of the baby. Jealousy is a painful emotion; it includes a feeling of being left out. It also has its positive side, in that the jealousy is about something of value. Mothers may be reluctant to let father, and others, into their intimate twosome. Mothers may be envious of a father's freedom from childbearing and childcare – that he can enjoy his family without ever having to be pregnant or stop working.

From parents . . .

> *'I used to think about him at work getting a whole hour's lunch break while I ate something boring that I could prepare with one hand.'*
>
> *'I felt really annoyed that he could just pop in and buy a shirt on his way back from work but for me it would mean planning an expedition or arranging childcare.'*
>
> *'My husband's face has aged since we had children because he's shared the burden of the sleepless nights, but his body hasn't, not like mine has. Everyone comments that I got my figure back nicely, and I am slim but when I lie on my side the loose skin on my tummy looks like a scrotum. Having children just doesn't cost men physically in the same way at all.'*

However, the reverse is also true and it can be rather embarrassing for a father to realise that he is jealous either of his wife's ability to have babies, or of the closeness between her and the baby. Paradoxically, often the most conscientious fathers, who are very much involved with their babies, can feel this the most strongly. Perhaps those who are less involved are less affected because they have responded to these difficult feelings by becoming more detached. It is also no accident that fathers of young babies are said to work longer hours than men of the same age who either have no children or, equally significantly, have older children. It would seem that supporting the family is not the only motive for long hours of work; staying out of the house in order to avoid the family might be! If a man has a sense of certainty and competence at work, then being there may help to counter feelings of uncertainty about his new role at home. Action can seem a great salve to an agitated soul.

More painfully, some men are more likely to have affairs when there is a young baby in the house. This may be about escape from the pressures of family life or a wish to have some intimacy for himself if he feels excluded by the mother and baby's intimacy. A father may feel that the baby has displaced him as the mother's object of love because she is less interested in sex. Curiously, the more that a father is closely involved with the baby, the more he may put sex on the backburner. Sex is about excitement, physical pleasure, thrills, being in tune with another person, release from tension and you can have all those experiences just being around a baby. It is, of course, more directly fulfilling for the mother, who has had the physical exhilaration of the birth and the physical pleasures of breastfeeding. She also has the exhaustion of this and the very real feeling that her body isn't her own and that she can't manage anything more. (And, of course, until the six-week postnatal examination, sexual intercourse is not recommended.) Of course, many fathers, far from feeling jealous, are full of admiration for their wives in going through the birth and breastfeeding and are thrilled at being able to help. Perhaps such generosity is inspired when fathers are unconsciously put in touch with memories of having their infantile needs met by their own mother.

If a father does feel left out at this stage, the best way to diffuse jealous feelings is not to retreat but to become more involved. If you are making the timeless discovery of this new little character, trying to understand the meaning of his cries, you will not feel peripheral.

It is worth thinking about the past when jealousies are strong. Does it stir up memories of your mother devoting herself to younger siblings? Or alternatively, of your parents immersed in each other and leaving you out? The feeling you have now might stem from these childhood hurts. Spotting the origin of them makes the present more manageable.

Post-natal depression

Fathers are also vulnerable to post-natal depression (see Chapter 6). It is more common, however, for mothers to become depressed and for fathers to find themselves coping with the fall-out. It can be very scary if your partner becomes depressed after the baby's birth. She stops being the person you thought you knew, and the mutual looking after you have done for each other may stop abruptly from her side; it becomes very one-sided and you feel everything is up to you. She may be very critical and rejecting of you and this can feel very unfair. You may start to feel overwhelmed or angry yourself. She is badly in need of emotional understanding – she does need you to know how she feels. Once she believes you have really got it, she may be able to start to recover. If she gets stuck in the complaining stage of things, it is not unreasonable for you to point out that you are equally hurt by her reproaches. Just as at other crucial moments in a marriage, a bit of honest anger with each other may be needed; a good row to let each other know what you feel, before you are both ready to move on.

If, however, she is seriously depressed for a while, you can be a lifesaver for both her and the baby, getting professional help for her and letting her know that you can manage to keep the family going without becoming too upset yourself. You can get help from friends or family where necessary and interact with the baby, keeping vitality in his life until his mother is able to respond happily to him.

6

BABY BLUES AND POST-NATAL DEPRESSION

Having a baby is supposed to be a joyful occasion. How do you cope if that's not how you feel? If you are miserable, or perhaps even worse, have a sort of numb flatness.

Baby blues

About 50 percent of women suffer from 'baby blues'. After the first three or four days, for some women, this feeling of 'the blues' sets in and usually lasts only a day or so. Some women may recognise it as just part of all the heightened emotions in a home with a new baby; but it can be very upsetting. They feel exhausted, disillusioned, even angry. It may mean there are a couple of days of crying, feeling low and anxious and being unable to sleep. It is quite an understandable reaction to all the anticipation and excitement of the birth, the anticlimax after nine months of waiting and the shock of actually having to deal with a baby, who is also having to get used to the world outside the womb.

Post-natal depression

Post-natal depression is different; after a few days of obvious 'blues' it can be a more subtle condition, not always easy to detect, and it goes on for much longer. If you are suffering from it, you may just think of yourself as being tired; giving birth and looking after a small baby is certainly tiring. It can feel as though nothing is right, you are disappointed in yourself and your baby. This can set in after a few weeks of things feeling alright, then you find yourself thinking: 'Is this all there is?' Anxiety that you aren't looking after the baby well enough, or guilt, might keep troubling you and perhaps anger and a feeling that nobody is being of any help to you.

Causes of post-natal depression

Post-natal depression is a sort of emotional loneliness. There are no direct causes, any more than in depression generally, but there are factors that make mothers more vulnerable. The simple fact of having a baby can trigger depression in someone who is vulnerable. Leach describes it well:

> Once the brief drama of delivery is over and the baby declared healthy, most of the care and concern that has surrounded her will melt away, leaving her with her old life and identity in an unravelled tangle in the baby's innocent fists and no clear-cut way of reknitting it to accommodate them both. No wonder a sense of anxious anticlimax is common and depression far from rare.
>
> (2010: 63)

Post-natal depression can interfere with bonding and trying to care for a baby you have not bonded with is also depressing. The relentlessness of your baby's demands can feel too much and guilt about resenting the baby may compound the depression.

Parents' parents

Support from grandparents at this time can make a big difference to a new family. If this is missing and your parents, perhaps especially your mother, is not around, you may find that you go on and on thinking about her, maybe angrily, maybe with sadness. If she has died, you are especially likely to miss her love and care for you and your baby. There does seem to be something special about the confirmation from your own mother, that you are now a mother yourself. It is sad to have to do without this. Brown and Harris (1978) suggest it may be hardest if your mother died before you were aged eleven. This age is significant because it is before or about the time of puberty. It means that you did not have your mother's actual knowledge of your body and yourself becoming a woman, and the pleasure of showing her how you were growing up. Having a loss like this is not an immediate *cause* of post-natal depression but it may mean you are vulnerable to it. It is really important to think about and remember your mother, look at any photographs you have of her, perhaps see a likeness to her in your baby. If you had a happy childhood with her, the memories of this might still nourish you and make you feel that you can pass her mothering on to your baby.

If you had a bad relationship with your mother, whether or not she is alive now, and if you feel you weren't given enough love and care as a baby, it can be really hard to feel you have enough resources inside yourself now to give to your own baby. People who can remember a difficult childhood are more strongly placed to get over it and make a fresh start with their baby than those who have suppressed the memory (see Chapter 4).

Talking it through

If you have a partner you can confide in, you are in a better position to recover. Parents who had unsatisfactory childhoods can be fragile and unsettle each other further. Or, more happily, they find they can 'mother' or 'father' each other very effectively as a part of their relationship. The birth of a baby is one of the times that this is really helpful and can be much appreciated by both parents.

If you weren't well looked after as a child, it may be hard for you to trust people now or to believe that anyone is going to have time for you. However, you might well be surprised at the way people around you seem to want to help. Mistrust might make it tempting to dismiss those people and they may then feel rejected and stop offering. Depression is compounded by the way that those suffering tend to isolate themselves in this way but if you can make use of the help available, you and your baby could make a fresh start together.

Fathers are also vulnerable

Fathers may be equally as churned up as mothers by the change in way of life and status or by the staggering responsibility for a new life, both in keeping a vulnerable little body alive and in the long-term provision for an extra member of the family. Fathers who had unhappy childhoods or inadequate parenting are also likely to struggle to find the emotional resources needed for parenting. They, just as much as mothers, will need the same sorts of support and opportunities to talk about the past and how it is making them feel in the present.

Fathers who are not too depressed are usually the best people to look after mothers. We know that one of the main vulnerability factors to depression is not having a confiding relationship. So the mothers lucky enough to have an understanding partner may well escape from post-natal depression, or recover from it easily.

However, fathers, in providing this support, do not get off lightly. The 'badly-done-to' feeling that can assail a depressed woman means that many perceive their partners as helping much less than is in fact the case. The miseries of this period can even lead to marriage break-up.

The more that fathers become committed and caring, the more vulnerable they are to the pressures of relationships, to being affected by their partner's depression and to being prone to depression themselves. Two key issues for fathers will be how they can best support their partner, but at the same time protect themselves from the depleting effects of having a partner who is depressed.

It seems as though men are more likely to see necessary support as being practical support. However, women who are depressed need emotional support, a chance to talk about their feelings and be listened to properly. They may discount the practical support they are receiving. 'He never helps me, he never sees what I need' may astonish a father who has taken two weeks paternity leave and has been on duty twenty-four hours a day, or perhaps, later, is sharing all the work of the household. A woman who is crying and saying she can't cope, or that no one knows how she feels, may simply need someone to stay with her and listen to her expressing those feelings. She might in addition need someone to watch the baby while she goes off on her own to have a long bath or go out for a walk.

The trouble with depression is that it causes distress in relationships, just as much as relationship trouble causes depression. Having a depressed partner can thus affect a man and cause both to feel further apart. The father can feel useless and unwanted and that he is always getting it wrong. If he allows himself to be sensitive and caring, he may worry that he has become a 'wimp'. If he resists this to feel strong and protective, he may feel out of touch with the emotions going on in the family.

A father's main confidant may well have been his partner, so if she is engrossed with the baby he may feel excluded, not in the simplistic sense of being 'jealous' but that the relationship which gives him emotional strength seems to be unavailable to him, and it is thus harder for him to keep going emotionally. This may be one reason that some men become depressed, or switch off and look for occupation outside the home. Conversely, it can be the father who keeps the importance of the couple relationship in mind, protecting it from being sidelined by the mother–baby couple or from being too damaged by mother's post-natal depression. Emotional openness can help a couple get through the depression, especially when it is partly a result of unexpressed anger. It is important for partners to be honest with each other. A complaining mother may feel patronised if she is not sometimes confronted by the father about her unfairness to him.

Depression and your baby

For a mother afflicted with depression, the last thing she needs is more reasons to feel guilty. However, Murray and Cooper (1999) argue that facing the devastating impact that depression can have on the whole family, and particularly on a young baby, may help mothers and those around her to realise how important it is that she be given the help she needs to recover.

When things go well, mothers and babies spend much time in enraptured looking at each other. As discussed in previous chapters, a 'maternally preoccupied' mother will become very focused on her baby and highly sensitive and responsive to his communications. This facilitates the process of mother and baby getting to know one another and it is also how the baby comes to know who he is and whether he is valued. Mothers and babies seem to enjoy just looking at and mirroring each other. Mothers quite naturally reflect the expression on their baby's face. The baby, seeing this, knows what the feeling inside herself looks like. The baby may then in turn mirror the mother's expression, and perhaps also gets an inkling of what her mother feels. From early on mother, or father, and baby can hold a conversation. The parent speaks; the baby replies with sounds, or simply mouthing, and the rhythm and timing is of a real conversation.

However, when a mother is post-natally depressed something goes wrong with this profoundly basic 'conversation'. A mother who is depressed may look blank-faced or, because she is preoccupied with her own thoughts, may miss her baby's signals or her response may be mistimed. All babies have an expectation that they will be engaged with. A baby who is not responded to will devise some kind of behaviour to deal with the mother's inattention. One reaction may be to give up trying to get her attention and withdraw. Another is for a baby to try to stay close to her mother, matching her mood, and becoming subdued herself. Some babies become watchful, looking after their mother.

Another way that some babies cope is to attempt to stimulate the mother, and a mildly depressed mother can indeed be cheered up by a smiling baby. At worst, however, the mother can feel angry that the baby is out of tune with her mood, and this feeling can increase later on when an active baby perhaps becomes a hyperactive toddler or always seems to be at odds with the mother. This is actually more likely to happen with boys than with girls.

The feeling for a baby of having a depressed mother is of someone who is not responsive to her moods and may not notice what she needs. It can make the baby feel responsible for keeping an eye on her mother. The children of depressed mothers often become sensitive and caring adults, perhaps at a cost to themselves.

However, all depressed mothers do not become unresponsive. Some can remain warm and affectionately in touch with their babies, especially if adverse social factors rather than personal issues have caused their depression. The baby can be the best part of their lives, a ray of hope in adversity. If a mother recognises that she is depressed, she has a better chance of keeping in touch with her baby's moods, rather than requiring the baby to keep track of hers.

From research on the biochemistry of depressed mothers and their babies . . .

At one month after birth, most depressed mother and baby pairs show lower dopamine and higher cortisol levels than non-depressed samples. The extra cortisol inhibits cognitive function and development, which is particularly damaging for the baby's growing brain. Dopamine is part of the reward system so that both mother and baby lose out on the positive mood it gives. Perhaps most worryingly they do not have the link between what they do and how they feel reinforced in a positive way. The babies of depressed mothers are often passive and avoidant, even when given the opportunity to interact with an attuned and responsive partner. Their experience of interacting with a depressed mother forms an expectation about relationships generally that goes something like 'What I do has no impact on others, so it doesn't matter what I do and I don't matter.' Clearly this is a very sad thing to learn about yourself in the world as a young baby and this experience can be hard to move on from because it becomes underwritten in the biochemistry of the brain in the form of low dopamine and high cortisol.

Feeding and sleeping problems

Feeding problems, especially trouble in getting going with breast-feeding, and also sleep problems may well seem to an exhausted mother to be the cause of her feeling depressed. It can in fact be the other way around: depression can make it difficult to get in tune with the baby's rhythms. If someone can look after the mother so that she feels understood and cared for, it may then help her to solve the problems with the baby (see Chapters 9 and 10).

From psychoanalytic theory and clinical practice . . .

Having a difficult birth can make mothers feel that the first encounter between them and their baby has 'gone wrong'. It can leave you feeling full of anxiety, humiliation and misery. One mother hated her own body afterwards. Some mothers feel angry with the baby and that it was the baby's 'fault' that they were cheated out of the birth they were expecting. Unexpected caesareans are a case in point: mothers who knew they were due for a caesarean are not so much affected.

Anyone who has had a previous miscarriage, stillbirth or, of course, cot death will be likely to be carrying grief that gets stirred up again by the birth of a baby. Depression stemming from this can become compounded by anxiety about whether the new baby will be alright. All such fears become limitless if a mother sits and ruminates on her own. If they are put into words, they can become manageable. One mother who had lost a previous baby was understandably very anxious when she had another baby. She was able to talk about her fears and gradually calmed down when her next little son was born. 'He taught us to trust our instincts again.'

The sex of the new baby can be relevant in whether a mother becomes depressed or not. Parents may be delighted with whatever sex their baby turns out to be; or have a fixed idea that it must be a particular sex. If this wish is not realised, the disappointment can lead to depression. Also, the sex of the baby can stir up painful feelings about relationships in the past. A boy may feel alien to his mother, or provoke memories of abusive relationships. A girl may make a mother, who is in conflict with her own mother, despair that this must be the start of another generation of hostility.

What to do about post-natal depression

It might seem to be very gloomy to think so much about depression and its adverse effect on babies in a book for new parents. We would like to think that the opposite is true: that there is a hopeful purpose in it. It has recently been realised that post-natal depression can in many cases be prevented and, just as important, women who do suffer from it can quickly recover. If mother and baby can be helped to get on the right track together, then that relationship can itself be a source of sustaining hope and pleasure. Because the cause lies so often in intimate relationships, the cure also lies in improving relationships, and this may strengthen a new family. Sometimes a mother who has been depressed previously in her life, can understand the causes for the first time.

From parents . . .

> *'I had an idyllic home birth followed by a beautiful hour with my baby before I had a post-partum haemorrhage and was rushed to hospital. It was some time before I regained consciousness and I was weak and traumatised. We had great difficulty establishing breastfeeding and I had no idea how we were going to survive this time. Over the following weeks things got so bad I even thought about ending it all, but the equally crazy consideration that I would then have to kill my baby and husband stopped that line of thinking! Although I did not give it any thought at the time, the one thing I made sure my daughter and I did every day was to have a bath together. I had started to bond with my baby while she was inside me. I would think about her floating around in there. Then we had a water birth and I now think I was trying to reconnect with her through being together in water. Eventually things did get better. We bonded, perhaps because I recovered but then I also think that I recovered because we bonded. This took all the effort I could summon and I don't know what would have happened to my daughter and I if my husband had had to go back to work after two weeks. Luckily he had managed to arrange six weeks and that was long enough to pull us through.'*

The period post-partum has been described as the 'fourth trimester' in an attempt to capture the way in which mother and baby don't

From research on the biochemistry of breastfeeding . . .

Breastfeeding can help a depressed mother. Although she may find it harder to get breastfeeding established because the sense of hope that enables perseverance may be lacking, if she can be supported to connect with her baby in this way, she will have got into a virtuous cycle that is powerfully reinforced biochemically. Depressed people have higher levels of cortisol in the brain and experience difficulties in their relationships. Breastfeeding inactivates a mother's stress response, lowering her cortisol and releasing prolactin and oxytocin, which bolster positive feelings towards others. The sense of calm that this lends her will also help her to manage her baby's stress which will, in turn, bolster her confidence in her capacity to mother him and reward her with the pleasure of a positive interaction with him (Music 2011).

quite separate out emotionally despite the huge physical rupture of birth. As Chapter 3 on bonding discussed, physical intimacy is an essential trigger for all the biochemical reinforcement for bonding our bodies can produce. For the mother quoted above, sharing baths created opportunities for mental and physical connections to be made which, eventually, enabled her and her baby to bond and helped her to overcome her post-natal depression. For others, breastfeeding can work in a similar way. Other forms of physical intimacy can be helpful. Glover (2001) has even found that mothers massaging their very young babies are less likely to suffer from post-natal depression and it improved the quality of interactions with their baby. However, many mothers with post-natal depression will need help from outside the relationship with the baby to recover.

Biochemistry research reinforces this point: that post-natal depression, and indeed the baby herself, can act as a catalyst, the spur to improving relationships with parents or partner. Depression in general, and post-natal depression in particular, can be a time of self-examination. People can come out of such a phase more self-aware and mentally stronger. Post-natal depression can be a time when, in the presence of the new baby, the new generation of parents can think about their own childhoods and perhaps understand their own parents better.

It is such a simple idea that human beings need each other at vital moments in life. Talking to other mothers makes a big difference.

You discover that others feel the same way as you. Mothers who have got through this bad time themselves may be able to help you recover. Professionals, health visitors in particular, can also help parents feel that someone is backing them over the first few weeks. They can only do this if they are allowed to; some depressed mothers feel they must put on a show for the health visitor or they will be criticised for being a bad mother. Resolving to get everything perfect can, in fact, be a symptom of post-natal depression (see Chapter 4). Not being able to relax into the friendly chaos of just being around the baby can be a danger sign. It is now very well known that having a friendly, accepting person around to talk to about all the range of feelings that accompany having a baby can make all the difference in protecting mothers from post-natal depression. Health visitors and others who have a deep interest in the welfare of babies and their parents can often give encouragement to parents to help them support each other. In more severe cases a psychotherapist can be helpful.

Part II

BEING WITH BABY

As the last section focused on becoming a parent, thinking about the changes you might expect to happen in you, the strengths and vulnerabilities you might discover in yourself, then this next section turns to look more closely at you and your baby together. The chapters on conversations, learning through play and your baby's emerging sense of self, really only serve to bring to your attention all that you will do without even noticing, and to help you to see how important this very ordinary everyday stuff between the both of you is for your baby's development. The chapters on feeding, sleeping, crying and weaning do not offer definitive solutions to problems in these areas but we hope to help you reflect on what might be going on for you as individuals with unique experiences.

7

CONVERSATIONS WITH YOUR BABY

Human beings have a deep need to communicate with each other, and your baby is learning how to join in. He wants to engage with you, and as you will have discovered, had started to interact even before birth. In utero he tunes into the rhythm of his mother's movements and can recognise the sound of his parents' voices.

Once he is born, the 'conversations' you and your baby have with each other are one way of getting to know each other. Talking to a baby is part of the process of helping him learn to speak; but it is not just about language, it also gives voice to his emotions and to your own, helping him understand himself and others. When things are going well, whether you talk to him, or sing, your baby loves the sound of your voice. If you express anger or upset, the baby will learn more about real-life complexity but you will also want to protect him from your most difficult and raw emotions.

Watching me, watching you

Parents and babies spend much time gazing at each other. One mother said, 'I could look at her all day.' Of course feeding is the ideal situation for this gazing. A mother sitting, holding her baby close to feed, will often find that as she looks down, the baby's eye will be focused on hers. This mutual looking becomes part of the baby's whole feeding experience.

Feeding is also an opportunity for you to think about your baby, about who he is like, how to understand his character, what he will become, what your grandmother would think of him if she was still alive to see him. This watching and thinking also includes thoughts about yourself, and how much your own hopes and dreams are invested in your baby, or on the negative side, how the baby has got in the way of some of these.

So some of this looking is an internal reflective state, but much of it is a to-and-fro between two people, a two-way exchange right from the beginning.

From parents . . .

> *'My sister told me there would be the pot-plant stage. You know, you feed and water it and it grows but not much else happens.'*

However, if there was really so little going on, why would parents spend so long gazing at and talking to their babies? While some researchers and parents dismiss what is happening right before their eyes, there is a growing body of evidence showing that babies can and do engage 'protoconversationally'. A lovely book that illustrates such 'protoconversations' with photos of parents and babies communicating in this way is *The Social Baby* by Lynne Murray and Liz Andrews (2000). Lynne Murray's *The Psychology of Babies* (2014) has sequences of photos that movingly show how babies flourish in communication with their parents.

Parents and babies begin to mirror each other's expressions, often without even being aware of it. Parents perhaps first show on their own faces the expression on their baby's face, the baby seeing this gets an idea of what the feeling inside him looks like. Your baby may similarly mirror your expression and get an inkling of what you are feeling. It also comes naturally to most parents to put these

> **From research on neonate capacity . . .**
>
> If the birth has not been too stressful, many newborns (some only twenty minutes old) are able to engage with an adult who establishes eye contact then pulls a face. These babies watch, then after a moment and with visible effort, they manage to imitate certain facial expressions such as tongue poking and mouth opening. Not all babies will 'perform' in this way but we can assume that they are all processing what they see, responding internally to the face they gaze at. It is likely that mirror neurons play a part in this (see Chapter 3 on bonding) but they also seem to have an innate understanding that they are involved in a communicative exchange because they do not imitate unintentional acts like sneezes (Meltzoff 2007).

feelings, their own and their baby's, into words so that emotions get formulated into language.

We all do this with our adult family members and friends too. If a friend is feeling depressed, and you have a sympathetic chat with her, you find your face getting serious as you get into tune with her sadness. If you haven't got time for someone else's gloom, you will keep a bright face and suggest something to cheer her up and she will rightly feel that you don't understand. Like your friends, your baby will be able to tolerate this, but not too often.

In addition to face-to-face conversations, parents will use their voice at a small distance – 'Hang on, I'll be there in a minute' bridges the gap to a crying baby.

As the baby gets older, sits up, looks around with a wider focus and longer gaze, so the parent's conversation to the baby takes on a wider perspective. 'Can you see the trees?', 'We're going out shopping soon', 'Here's your teddy', 'Your granny is coming to see you.'

Smiling and laughing together

The most amazing communication between babies and their parents in the first weeks is the smile. Some researchers have suggested that at first what parents see is just a grimace that looks like a smile. Even if this is so, parents delightedly smile back, and babies start to respond to the smiling faces and shining eyes they see. It is thought

Now
Later
Later
Later
Now
Now

> **From psychoanalytic observations of parents and babies . . .**
>
> Holding the baby by the hands, mother blows raspberries, and he appears to be trying to imitate her. She laughs and holds out his arms. He opens his mouth and bobs back and forth. It looks a little like laughing with no sound. Mother uses her hold on him to exaggerate his bobbing movement and makes a laughing noise that is not quite her laugh. She also throws back her head in a caricature of laughing, and it feels as though she were acting as an extension of him and his acts. There is something devastatingly beautiful about this and I feel a tightening at the back of my head.

that real meaning then quickly develops on both sides. It does seem likely that babies learn something about how to communicate because parents treat their unintentional acts as though they had communicative intent. However, the emotional intensity of what seems to be said in a smile – 'I'm glad you're here', 'You're wonderful' – is not produced accidentally. The observation above; of a mother and her three-month-old son, captures the way in which young babies both communicate genuine feelings *and* learn about how to communicate feelings in these early conversations.

The observer's emotional response was not to a dry lesson in when and how to laugh. She was moved by a genuine meeting of minds but also by what Trevarthen (2001) describes as the mother's 'generously shared cognition'. The mother's behaviour was not delusional, but warmly creative, lending him her own communicating strength to express an emotion that was his own. Trevarthen would argue that this mother intuitively recognises her baby's 'innate motives for companionship', and is rewarded by getting to share the joy in his pride at being understood.

Taking turns

So, looking at and mirroring expressions is one of the first ways of knowing about each other's emotions. These exchanges also lay the foundations for language by introducing structure and awareness of expectation.

From parents ...

> *'The first conversation we had was a blinking one, he was only a couple of months old. He would blink, then I would blink and we would both laugh. It was a joke and we both got it.'*

> *'He's five months and we can really get into a rhythm together now. Playing with a large plastic cup yesterday, I put it in front of my face for a few moments and then revealed my face saying 'oh' in a surprised voice. He broke into an excited smile and kicked his legs about. I covered my face again and, although I could not see his face, I could see that his body had gone very still. When I removed the container I noticed his face was quite grave for a moment before he reacted to my reappearance with a laugh. We did this a few times and his laugh got louder and bolder. I began to realise that he was no longer grave when my face was covered. The game was not about surprise any more. It was about him anticipating my cue, which meant it was his turn and he could do his laugh again. We did a few more rallies like that, getting faster and enjoying our competence at it. I then introduced a longer pause. His body became very still. When I uncovered my face his mouth was serious, his nostrils were flared and his eyes were wide open and fixed on me. I wondered if I had left it too long, but then he laughed louder than ever and bounced his body with pleasure.'*

From observing parents and babies ...

Father picks her up and lays her body lengthways along his forearms, her head cradled in his cupped hands. As he gently bounces her, Baby quietens and gazes into her father's face, eyes widening, twinkling and blinking. He begins to talk to her, smiling and cooing. Her mouth flickers in response. In the pauses between her father's vocalisations, her arms give little flicks too. Then Father begins to talk to me about how he likes holding Baby like this. He motions to a picture of them in this position, talking about sending the picture to his family. He has continued to look at her while he talks but she begins to cry and I realise that, because Father is talking to me he has been lost to Baby, the smiling and chatting face opposite her is no longer contingent on her expressions and she feels the loss.

Remarkably, baby and adult do take turns, and the rhythm really is like a conversation. When things are going well, it all seems so effortless and it can be hard to believe that the baby knows he is having a conversation. However, as the previous observation of a father with his five-week-old daughter shows, a disruption in the conversation reveals that the baby has expectations about conversations and is upset when they are confounded.

Repeated experiences of interactions with a partner who is not well enough attuned to provide contingent responses will damage a baby's self-esteem and sense of agency and the feeling that they matter and what they do matters. However, some discord is inevitable, even in good attunement. Indeed, being able to cope with and repair a communication that has got off track is an important skill for life. Stern (2004) beautifully describes these moments as 'mis-steps in the dance'.

While these conversations may seem rather one-sided, with the parent doing all the talking, the baby is engaged in his own wordless way and these chats mean a great deal to him. To begin with, the subjects will be very intimate, just about the emotions in the baby and what is going on between parent and baby. Parents say, 'What are you telling me?', 'That's a good story', 'Was that a nice feed?', 'Why are you looking like that?' A baby can say a lot back without any actual words.

From research on infant expectation of contingency . . .

An innate, or very early expressing, hunger for contingency was observed in the research of Murray and Trevarthen (1985), where disturbances in contingency are contrived. Using a double TV link, the infant watches his mother's face and hears her voice being animated and conversational, and in fact responding to his communications, but with a delay disrupting the contingency of the response. The infants become avoidant and then distressed, experiencing what Trevarthen describes as a sense of shame at the loss of being in a meaning-making exchange with another person.

From parents . . .

> *'At about three months old, he added a delightful new noise to his repertoire. It was a long drawn-out cooing 'Aaaaah'. It was clearly a noise of love, almost exclusively bestowed on me and my husband. One morning, as he was feeding, he stopped and came off the breast. I looked at him enquiringly. He put his little hand on my arm, looked into my eyes and said 'Aaaaah'. It felt as if he was saying to me 'There's no rush. We've got all the time in the world, you and me. We can stop, just to do this, just to gaze into each other's eyes.' The world slowing down, that feeling of completeness – oh, so special, so full of calmness and love.'*

> *'In the evenings, after his bath and final feed but before we put him to bed, we lie him on his front on his mat, which he loves. He makes this sound like a cooing dove. It is the most beautiful sound I have ever heard and he never does it in front of other people, it's a really intimate thing.'*

Babies talking to themselves

The sounds a baby makes become more varied as he grows. At four or five months you can see and hear him enjoying the sounds for their own sake. As well as being part of a conversation with parents and others, babies enjoy talking to themselves. If you let your baby have time out of your sight, you will hear her babble, murmur, gurgle, blow raspberries. Some babies will even wake in the night, and instead of crying, babble to themselves. It is an interesting point that not all talking is part of getting on with other people: conversations with oneself are also important. Babies need to get a feel of who they are in relation to someone else, but with the security of this, they can also enjoy time to themselves, a chance to think their own thoughts.

Towards words

Building on the turn-taking structure established through those early exchanges, word-like utterances begin to make interactions more recognisably conversation-like. From about nine or ten months the baby makes sounds that could be a real word.

From parents . . .

> *'When my son started to say 'da da' I would say 'da, daaa . . . da!' In time I could say 'da, daaa' and he would reply, after the right length of pause, 'da!' and then we would both fall about laughing.'*

The pleasure here seems to be about showing that you know what the other is expecting but this parent is a father, so it is unlikely to be a coincidence that he picked up on 'da da'. These sounds only become firmed up as real words if parents enjoy repeating them and give them meaning. Each new word is a little sign of getting the world under control. Aristotle was the philosopher who first worked out how to classify the natural world. Every baby who learns to name objects, and then has an idea of what goes with what, is re-creating for himself this process of classifying.

Language as loss

Language is a spur to communication. It is also surprisingly a loss. The older baby, into his second year, who is using words to talk to his parents, may feel that he has lost the feeling of being magically understood by his parents.

As an older baby stumbles to get the right words, or finds that parents just can't decipher his meaning, he and his parents will feel the limitations that mere words bring between people. The temper tantrums of these later stages sometimes come from this frustration about not being understood. Even as adults we can easily get into a 'Well if you don't understand what I'm feeling, I'm not going to tell you' with our nearest and dearest.

Twins and language development

> Silent understanding frequently develops in old couples, this usually being preceded by long years of verbal entente. Twins, on the other hand, engage in preverbal and non-verbal forms of mutual comprehension and perception which precede, and sometimes possibly even delay language.
>
> (Piontelli 2004: 118)

Language as a means of knowing and understanding

Babies learn to make sense of the world by their parents putting into words not just emotions but also sequences of activity. Asking a baby 'Do you want some juice?', getting the drink and then saying 'Here's your juice' creates an understandable pattern where words and actions match each other. As Prospero says to Caliban in Shakespeare's *The Tempest*: 'I endowed thy purposes with words that made them known.'

Most parents and babies get special games going to accompany routine actions like nappy changing. Your baby will very likely love the particular words you use and they will be part of his pleasure in being made clean and dry again, and part of what he knows to expect when you change him.

From parents . . .

> *'My baby loves it when I tap his nappy and say: "What's in there?" He thinks it's hilarious.'*

What an older baby may also discover is that one of the best uses of words is for jokes! His playing with sounds and kicking as you struggle to put his nappy back on may make him roar with laughter. If you also enjoy this as a game, it will help him feel really good about himself.

Putting babies' fears into words is also essential. He can feel you making them manageable in your own mind.

Research on the role of language in emotional processing is helpful when thinking about how to handle the unavoidable unpleasant experiences we must all endure. For example, when a baby is immunised, it makes a big difference to how he deals with the injection if parents warn him in words, and afterwards use words

From psychoanalytic observation of babies and parents . . .

I watched a baby girl at three months seeming to enjoy each familiar stage of nappy changing and listening to her mother's accompanying words. Later Mother washed Baby's face, her sounds of pleasure were in the exact rhythm of mother's strokes of the flannel on her face.

From research on language and emotional processing . . .

In Chapter 4 we described research showing that parents who had had difficult childhoods but were able to describe their experiences in a coherent way were likely to go on to have securely attached children themselves. When language is used to describe emotion, it does more than make the feelings communicable. Language imposes structure, which has the effect of marshalling emotions, which could, otherwise, overwhelm. By making the feelings more manageable, it allows them to be held in conscious awareness where rational thought can further mitigate their impact. Music cites research illustrating this effect: 'participants were asked to look at anxiety-provoking pictures that were sufficiently frightening to stimulate subcortical amygdala alarm responses in their brains. When subjects "re-appraised" the pictures, re-interpreting what they saw using language, this lessened their arousal levels and helped regulate their emotions' (Music 2011: 107). The effect over lifetimes is illustrated by the power of a coherent self-narrative to halt the intergenerational transmission of attachment disorder.

to describe his feelings about it. Interestingly, it is not a straightforward matter of simply being sympathetic when talking about a frightening experience – the sympathy often needs to be followed by a brisker 'You're alright now' or even a little joke to help close off the episode. A baby may go on crying when they are really recovering from the injection. At first parents may find themselves instinctively imitating the cry. If you get it right, this can make the baby feel understood, then you might start to imitate the cry playfully and this can make the baby laugh. It is vital, however, never to use a mocking tone of voice.

Crying babies can usually be consoled better when their parents try to put the baby's feeling into words. If they are hungry, only feeding will be the right response, but if not, the parent's words are as much what soothes the baby as any action.

Tone of voice

Parents' tone of voice is as important as their words in letting a baby know that they are in touch with his feelings. It is also through words, used in a particular tone, as well as gestures, that babies learn the 'rules' of life: what must not be touched because it is dangerous, like fires or electric sockets, or what is disapproved of, but not life threatening like throwing food on the floor! While thinking about tone, it is also worth noting how perceptive babies are about the emotional quality of a parent's response. Perhaps because they don't have language and complex cultural rules to distract them, they have a very keen sense of emotional authenticity.

From parents . . .

> *'At the end of a busy morning I realised that I hadn't given my baby daughter much attention for a couple of hours. She had been doing fine with occasional brisk chats and cuddles but I felt bad. Once I had everything else in order, I approached her with a big smile and an extra cheery hello, expecting to have a nice time together to make it up to her. To my shock she recoiled from me. I don't think she knew I was putting it on for her, exactly, but my lack of sincerity certainly jarred her at some level.'*

Talking with your baby helps you both to find out about yourselves and each other: your emotions, sense of humour and temper. Through all this your baby learns the tools of language but he is also building up his knowledge of how people get on with each

From research on parentese . . .

You will notice that you use a particular tone and pattern of speech when talking to your baby. Adults in most cultures around the world use a higher pitch and shorter pauses but, perhaps most importantly, we lend a musicality to the way we speak when we address babies. It's been called 'parentese' but everyone will use it, from children to old ladies in the street. And the baby knows it's meant for him. He will turn his head, look and listen. If you talk in normal long sentences, at a lower pitch, he just won't be listening in the same way and he will find it harder to understand what you say. In experiments, nonsense sentences spoken in parentese were more effective than traditional adult-directed speech as a way of communicating intentions and expectations.

other, and his sense of morality. This does not mean talking all the time – that would be intrusive for your baby and exhausting for you. As in adult conversations, some pauses and companionable silences are also essential.

8

FEEDING

Bowlby (1982) said that the comfort given by the mother, more than the food, was the essential basis for the relationship. It is not, however, always easy or straightforward to get started. This chapter will explore some of the feelings that might make it hard to get going and how fathers can help mothers and babies manage some of the overwhelming feelings.

Your baby's perspective

Being fed is one of the most important experiences of your baby's early life. It not only directly keeps her alive and growing, but also provides the basis for optimism in life. When her hungry cries are reliably answered with a breast or bottle, she can feel loved and cared for, and this helps her build up a feeling of trust. Held close to you, she can study your face, listen to your voice, and get to know the person most central to her world: you, her mother.

Yet, like every other experience she has had since birth, feeding is entirely new to her. After nine months of having had all her food and energy provided for inside the womb, she now has to learn not only how to suck and swallow milk, but also how to digest and excrete it. This may take some time to manage but, instinctively, the baby is ready to get going. She has an instinct to root and to suck and a preconception of something that is there for her to suck on. You could almost say that she expects a breast, or bottle, to be in place for her. Winnicott urges us to:

> Imagine a baby who has never had a feed. Hunger turns up, and the baby is ready to conceive of something; out of need the baby is ready to create a source of satisfaction, but there is no previous experience to show the baby what to

> expect. If at this moment the mother places her breast where the baby is ready to expect something, and if plenty of time is allowed for the infant to feel round, with mouth and hands, and perhaps with a sense of smell, the baby 'creates' just what is there to be found. The baby eventually gets the illusion that this real breast is exactly the thing that was created out of need, greed, and the first impulse of primitive loving. Sight, smell and taste register somewhere, and after a while the baby may be creating something like the very breast that the mother has to offer. A thousand times before weaning the baby may be given just this particular introduction to external reality by one woman, the mother. A thousand times the feeling has existed that what was wanted was created, and found to be there. From this develops a belief the world can contain what is wanted and needed, with the result that the baby has hope that there is a live relationship between inner reality and external reality, between innate primary creativity and the world at large which is shared by all.
>
> (1964: 90)

So, she is establishing a relationship with you but also establishing the kind of relationship she will have with the world and reality.

What you may be concerned about

Feeding a baby can be an enormous pleasure or it can feel completely awful. It's possibly the most responsible job you will ever have to do, literally keeping a baby alive. You may worry whether you are doing it properly, and whether your baby is getting enough – or too much – milk. All the anxieties about being a bad parent can get focused onto feeding the baby. This can connect with what your own infancy was like, an idea explored more fully later. Feeding is as much a learning process for you as it is for your baby and it may take time to feel confident about when, where and how to feed her. Getting a rhythm and pattern going for feeds is one of the main preoccupations of the early weeks.

From parents . . .

> *'I felt so humiliated that I couldn't get the feeding right. I had so much milk that my breasts were engorged, and the*

> *baby hadn't a chance to latch on. The breastfeeding counsellor sat with me until the baby and I sorted it out. I could never have done it by myself.'*
>
> *'I became a breastfeeding counsellor after having struggled to establish breastfeeding myself. The problem is that women are given to believe that because it is "natural" they won't need to work at it. In fact most women have to work pretty hard before they get their "Madonna and child moment".'*
>
> *'The pre-natal breastfeeding classes were informative but the first time I fed her I got a bit too focused on remembering technique – like getting enough of the breast in for her to make a good latch, and then didn't notice how intrusive I was being stuffing her gaping crying mouth. Luckily a nurse appeared from nowhere and told me to slow down and let the baby show me how to do it, then we were fine and I really enjoyed feeding her after that.'*
>
> *'It took us several days to get going and we needed a lot of support at the hospital but once we were at home everything just completely fell into place. Then with my second it was easier from the beginning. As soon as she was born they gave her to me to hold and she latched onto my breast, rooting as if she knew exactly how to do it. I don't know what made the difference: my increased confidence with a second baby, or the babies' own different characters.'*

Breastfeeding is an embodied activity. It reminds us that we are mammals. When it goes well, there is great pleasure in doing a job that your body was designed to do. At other times it can be unnerving to be in touch with your mostly forgotten animal self.

From parents . . .

> *'While my baby was asleep I prepared dinner, listening to a news story about the use of DNA tests to prove maternity and thus reunite mothers with their children that had been stolen for an illegal adoption market. I was only half listening, actually wondering why I wasn't more upset by the story considering I was a new mother. Suddenly I*

> *realised that milk was seeping through my top. I think my body was reacting to emotions I was not even aware of having. I felt like I had been given a glimpse at a more primitive or animal me I don't usually know about.'*

A bit like the lioness who suckles the young of her own prey, women can feel at the mercy of powerful instincts. It might feel frightening or empowering to let the mind relinquish some control and move into a more physical plane of being.

Should I breast- or bottle-feed my baby?

How to feed your baby is one of the first important decisions. Both breast- and bottle-feeding will nourish a baby and support your bond with her. But the question involves much more than just straightforward facts. Your feelings are just as important, so don't let anyone else pressurise you into doing something that just doesn't feel right.

From parents . . .

> *'External pressures can make normal difficulties seem so much worse. My baby cried to be fed almost constantly. My family referred to this as "the famine" because they felt I ought to have given him formula to fill him up. Others told me that I did have enough milk, I just needed to believe that I did. I felt undermined and patronised by everyone but in the end we found our way.'*

Breastfeeding

There are a lot of advantages to breastfeeding. First is the irreplaceable satisfaction of being able to nourish your baby from your own body. There are also the direct bodily pleasures. Some mothers feel an intense physical enjoyment as powerful as sexual feelings in feeding their babies. The sensation of the baby's mouth on your nipples, her hands stroking your breast can be very enjoyable. However, these pleasurable feelings can be a deterrent to some women, it can make them feel shy and embarrassed, or indeed feel that the sexual connotations of breasts make them unsuitable for babies. Such worries usually subside once you get used to breastfeeding.

From research on the biochemistry of breastfeeding . . .

It can be helpful to be reminded that physiologically both sex and breastfeeding are about making and growing babies. Both breastfeeding and sex release oxytocin which makes us feel good physically and well disposed to others. It is a biochemical that supports bonding between couples and between parent and infant. From an evolutionary perspective, the function is to support the survival of our genes. This works on two levels. Because oxytocin makes us feel good, it rewards the two behaviours, breastfeeding and sex, in the moment. In the long term it supports those relationships that the infant's survival often depends upon. The hormones prolactin and vasopressin are also produced during breastfeeding. These further support bonding because they are involved in feelings of protectiveness and love.

The practical facts are that breast milk is easy for your baby to digest and contains important antibodies that will help her fight disease and protect her from allergies. It changes in composition to suit her changing needs as she grows, and reduces the risks of stomach infections. From a mother's point of view, breastfeeding is convenient as it's always available, clean and needs no preparation; easy for night feeds and travelling. It also helps you regain your shape more quickly. However, it can feel frightening at the beginning or burdensome after time. You might even feel that this strange new little creature is going to attack you or drain the nourishment out of your own body.

From parents . . .

> *'I would look at him and feel scared.'*
>
> *'Because she was in with us I wasn't really disturbed by the night feeds. Sometimes it was a nice sleepy little interlude but the four o'clock feed always made me bad tempered. It felt like I had a limpet stuck to me. I'd think "oh just get off!" but by the morning it would be all lovely again.'*
>
> *'Once we got going I found breastfeeding quite pleasurable, but then he started to want to feed for hours and hours of*

> *every day. Pinioned to the sofa I got quite low. I never remembered to make myself tea before we started, so I did end up feeling depleted.'*

This is a tiring time and although producing milk is not tiring in itself, it can feel like it contributes to the exhaustion. Many mothers worry they are not producing enough milk to nourish their babies – particularly as it is impossible to see just how much milk is being drunk. Weighing is useful here. If the baby's weight is following a normal growth curve, you must be producing enough milk.

Despite the naturalness, breastfeeding has in the past gone in and out of fashion. Today it is becoming increasingly popular and more widely accepted, but it was less so amongst the previous generation. If you weren't breastfed yourself, it can be hard to make the decision to breastfeed your own child: it may seem like a criticism of your mother and her parenting.

Of course, the more women who breastfeed, the easier it becomes for others to do so. If as a girl, or more recently, you've seen babies being breastfed, you have an example to follow. It can be a great help during your pregnancy to watch and talk to a breastfeeding mother. What you observe may vary widely, the process can look very peaceful, and as though two people – mother and baby – have got into a very nice rhythm of doing a job together; or it can look turbulent, as if the baby were attacking the mother. In either case, breastfeeding is a very physical and 'earthy' business. The excitement of feeding and the passionate expression of loving and aggressive feelings can be seen more openly when the baby is dealing directly with the mother, without the intermediary of the bottle. Winnicott said 'the survival of the mother is more of a miracle in breastfeeding'. Certainly the sight of a breastfeeding mother and baby can be overwhelming at first. You may feel you shouldn't be looking. Breastfeeding cafes can be a wonderful place to start if you are worried about feeding in public. You can look up your nearest one online: www.thebabycafe.org/your-nearest-baby-cafe.htm.

After the birth: the best time to start

If you are able to hold your baby directly after the birth, you may find yourself quite naturally putting her to your breast. It's a good way not to notice any medical procedures that are still being done to you. This first little nuzzle can break the ice and help you feel you know how to do it. Even so, most mothers and babies have some problems at first. It takes some getting used to. Give yourselves time to calm down and work out what to do. Babies can coast along for a day or two with a bit of a suck, getting the colostrom, and with a bottle if necessary for a few days without you losing your milk. Penelope Leach (2010) talks about newborns needing to learn the sucking = food = comfort equation. While all babies are born with a sucking reflex, in some it will be stronger than others. Some will have discovered that they can suck on their fingers in the womb. They emerge already knowing about sucking something and will not take long to find the breast. None has yet experienced having their hunger sated through sucking. Some babies will need more time and careful attunement in order for them to make these connections. Getting started is a process, not an event.

If you had intended to breastfeed and it doesn't work out for you, don't be overwhelmed by feelings of failure. When it works, breastfeeding is practical and pleasurable but being able to breastfeed, or have a natural birth, is not a virtue. Closeness and being there for your baby are what matter most to her and breastfeeding is only one of the ways to provide this.

The pleasure of breastfeeding

One of the pleasures of breastfeeding is getting to know a baby's particular ways of asking to be fed or conducting a feed. A great deal is going on in this apparently simple scene. A feed is a gratification of an instinctual need; it is also a sensual experience and a learning one. When you sit, holding your baby close to feed, you and she are likely to gaze at each other. She has your nipple in her mouth, the taste of the milk, the feeling of being held by arms and body, the sounds of her own swallowing, of your heart beat, perhaps stomach-rumbles, words or murmurs from you and the sight of your face, especially your eyes and the feel of your breast if she strokes or clutches it. So touch, taste, sound and sight all come together to form the experience in the present, and build up memories for the future. When she digests the feed, she is also digesting the learning she has done about the texture of the world and how she can come to know it by putting together all these cross-sensory experiences. Babies can distinguish the smell of their own mother's milk at the age of forty-eight hours. They come to anticipate your particular milk and the particular experience you have together. The rhythm of these repeated experiences also help to orientate her in time.

We see how in pauses during the feed or in time afterwards the baby is able to do several things: to go on exploring mother's body, away from the urgency of taking in the milk; and to assimilate the experience and deal with the *idea* of mother who is there to feed her, but also exists in addition to this function. An idea that grows in this time is of mother and baby as two separate beings who have been wordlessly together and are now about to move apart. It could well be that how a mother and baby manage this time influences and is significant for how they will manage the separation aspect of the baby falling asleep (see Chapter 9). If, on the one hand, the feed is carried out only as a necessary routine piece of care, with no time allowed for exploratory playing, then there is not a period of transition for the baby to change from the i*dea* of being fed to the *idea* of the end of the feed. If, on the other hand, the mother plays too long after the feed, it may be because she is not able to face with the baby that 'all good things come to an end' and cannot bear the small separations that happen many times daily. So, a great deal, indeed, is going on during and after a feed.

Feeding twins

> Mothers with twin babies often feel frantic and guilty as they are unable to give their full attention to either baby. If one baby sleeps while the other feeds, there is some peace. But this is not an ideal solution as it cannot be relied upon and it may be that the sleeping baby is avoiding overwhelming feelings by cutting off and sleeping. The babies will each have their own individual pattern of feeding. This might play on the mother's guilt about not treating both babies equally.
>
> (Lewin 2004: 64)

Mothers of twins generally want them to be treated equally but right from the beginning the differences between their two babies will be evident in the way they want to feed. Piontelli (2004) describes how one twin might cling to the mother during a feed while the other just sucks from the tip of the nipple, keeping his distance. Another mother she worked with always used one breast for one twin and the other breast for the other: one nipple was smooth and unscathed while the other was nearly torn, evidencing their different feeding styles.

From research on the relationship between feeding and sleeping . . .

Research has shown that having a period of play after a feed is important in establishing sleep rhythms. Babies who spend ten to twenty minutes in their mother's arms after they have finished sucking, sleep better than those who spend either more or less time in such play. It seems that mothers who do this are able to discriminate between their baby's need for playful and loving contact with them, and do not confuse this with a need only for feeding.

From parents . . .

> *'My first would stroke my breast, and I felt very much appreciated. My second baby had a way of going Tap Tap with her little hand on my breast with cheerful assurance that a feed was coming her way!'*
>
> *'Some feeds were hungry purposeful ones, head down, concentrating. At other times it was about sucking herself to sleep. Then there were feeds that were social occasions. She would love lying in my arms, having a suck, pulling away to "talk" to me or look around the room and then settle back to the job in hand. It was touching to see how rosy cheeked and round faced she looked after the feed. She looked full of love and satisfaction.'*

The difficulties of breastfeeding

There can be more difficulties involved in setting up breastfeeding than bottle-feeding. It can take time before mother and baby are at ease with breastfeeding, it can hurt at first and it may not feel worth it to everyone. However, most feeding problems are about getting started and most who do persevere are glad that they did.

Bottle-feeding

Breastfeeding may not feel right to you, especially if you weren't breastfed yourself, and bottle-feeding may come much more easily.

Bottle-feeds involve more preparation but it might feel 'safer' not to have the baby latched on to your breast. Paradoxically, having the bottle between the two of you, creating some distance, might actually help you to feel more relaxed and confident about coming together emotionally. You can still hold the baby close, enjoying the feeling of each other's bodies, and getting a nice rhythm going. Feeding a baby with a bottle separates her physical well-being from your own, and you may feel happier if you can see exactly how much milk your baby is taking. It can also allow fathers to participate. Emotional security does not seem to be affected by whether the feeding is by breast or bottle. What matters is that the baby is held close when fed, looked at and responded to. If such intimacy still feels too frightening, you might need to talk to someone about it.

If you can leave the decision about bottle- or breastfeeding until after the baby is born and you have held her a few times, if you give her the chance to have a little nuzzle at your breast, making her own little sounds, then you leave your options open. Sometimes mothers find that when they have got the whole experience of the birth over with, they feel more able to take on the challenge of breastfeeding than they had anticipated.

It is probably best even with a bottle for you, the mother, to give your baby most of her first feeds. A new baby may find it simpler to learn the style and rhythm of one person only. If you have a maternity nurse or someone else to help in the first week or so, don't let her help you out by taking over the feeds. If you are feeling really exhausted or angry, you might think you must have time to yourself, or even that you want to protect the baby from your feelings. If not, you need the privilege of giving your baby her first feeds more than you need a rest. Maternity nurses may have expertise but they are not you. Each feed is a separate experience, but there is also a continuity between feeds, and in the first dream-like days and nights, the baby should, as much as possible, be fed only by someone closely emotionally involved.

Fathers and feeding

Some mothers may feel, not necessarily correctly, that the father, or indeed other people in the family, will envy their unique relationship with the baby, and they may not be confident enough to claim it for themselves. In fact now that fathers tend to be more involved in the intimate physical care of young babies, they are less likely to feel excluded by the bond between mother and baby or jealous of the intimacy of breastfeeding. With generosity, the father can vicariously enjoy the closeness and enjoy looking after both of them.

From parents . . .

> *'My son has Down's syndrome, which meant he was very docile and apt to fall asleep with the effort of feeding before he had got enough. In the night my husband would tickle his feet to keep him awake.'*
>
> *'In those early weeks I needed both hands to hold my daughter while I fed her. My husband would bring me water with a straw and hold it in position so that I could drink from it hands free. I felt a bit like a feeding baby myself, face tilted up to suck from proffered straw, arms down by my body. We were like a nest of Russian dolls, each feeding a smaller one.'*
>
> *'My husband read a book with all sorts of good positions for feeding. We had such a laugh, lying on the carpet, him showing me these positions with pillows and what have you; it was like we'd taken something. We just couldn't stop giggling. Later feeding came to be more of a bore because my son wanted to feed all day long, but it had been lovely, we had got off to a good start.'*

As a father you can be the most valuable support to mother and baby as they struggle to get to grips with each other and the whole business of nursing. It is a great advantage to a family that one parent is not breastfeeding and can get a wider perspective on the emotions going on.

If your partner is afraid of being trapped by breastfeeding into something too intense, she may be glad to know that you are there, able to help take some of the heat out of the situation. Or she may become too enmeshed in her relationship to the baby and exclude you. This actually means they both need you to help them separate a little, so that they can let you in and so that they can come to appreciate each other as separate people. Don't let your concern be dismissed as 'male insensitivity' but your ideas about solving problems may be more welcome if you are involved practically. Doing some of the care of your baby during the night, changing the baby's nappy, or if she has difficulty in settling, rocking her back to sleep after a feed, will all bring you closer to your baby and help your partner.

Feeding on demand or routine

Many mothers find they naturally choose a pattern of feeding that seems to suit their own personality. If you like everything organised and tidy you might feel your baby should fit into a clear routine. If you are more laid-back you won't mind the lack of order that demand-feeding can bring to the day.

Perhaps there is a middle way to aim at, in which you slowly work out a compromise with your baby. New babies are still establishing a pattern in their lives; they may wake, feed and sleep at irregular intervals, regardless of day or night. They do, however, need attention whenever they cry. It can be difficult at first to work out what they really need, so offering the breast or bottle seems the obvious thing to do. If you are breastfeeding, your baby may well be asking to suck very often at the beginning. Because it is a supply and demand system, it may be important at first to let her suck when she wants to. Leach (2010) says that at this stage if you ration sucking then you ration food. While this is true, it is also true that many breastfed babies seem to get enough milk even when a routine with three- or four-hour gaps is imposed on them from early on. This might be explained by research (Daly and Hartmann 1995) showing that mothers' capacity to store milk varies by up to 300 per cent (this is not correlated with breast size). Mothers with smaller storage capacity will be likely to need to feed their babies little and often. This does not mean there is not enough, just that the pace of feeding is likely to be different to a mother with greater storage capacity, whose babies are likely to have bigger, more spaced-out feeds. As ever it is about getting to know yourself and your baby.

Part of getting into a rhythm of feeding that suits you both will be noticing that your baby's cries have many other meanings too. As the weeks go by you may both come to appreciate the space between feeds – a time to digest the previous feed emotionally as well as physically, and also to look forward to the next feed. At this stage you and she can start to negotiate with each other, finding some sort of pattern that works for you both. She needs to know that you are there for her when she really needs food or comfort, but you both need to establish where the boundaries lie, and learn that she can sometimes wait a bit longer. The negotiating of this, as much as the achieving of it, influences how you and your baby get on together in the future. It can be helpful to keep this in mind. You are establishing a relationship as well as a routine in all that you do around feeding and it is the relationship that will endure. In the context of the rest of your lives together the period of coming together in this particular way is relatively short.

Overcoming common feeding problems

Parents often worry that their babies are getting too much or too little to eat. Such worries are usually unnecessary because, unlike adults, babies tend to take just what they require metabolically. However, if you do find that your baby is gaining insufficient weight or, conversely, feeding constantly, then identifying the cause – which may be practical or emotional – is an important step towards resolving the problem.

Babies who feed too much

Some mothers find they are feeding their babies much of the time, with virtually no space between the feeds, exhausting both mother and child. Only you can know if what is happening feels reasonable. If it does not, it is worth thinking about what your baby's signals mean: she may be crying for you rather than for a feed.

In Chapter 4 the idea of maternal ambivalence was discussed and this is important here too. Parents who can let themselves know of conflicting feelings of love and hate for their babies are in a much stronger position and may not need to act out these feelings so dramatically as those who do not know how to tolerate opposites. It often seems that mothers who let their babies feed constantly are not facing saying 'no' to the baby. It is as though feeding or being with the baby is seen as 'good' and spaces between as bad. You could say that this leaves the baby without having had a feed with a definable beginning, middle and end, followed by a time for digesting the food physically and the experience of the feed emotionally. It deprives the baby of the pleasures both of memory and of anticipation.

Endless feeding becomes a demanding chore which not only exhausts a mother but also saps her imagination so that she can't think what else to do. She may need help from the father or another adult to think about a way out. Some parents have found that they can extend the gap between feeds by gently soothing the baby back to sleep if she still seems drowsy, or by distracting her by talking to or playing with her if she is alert. Similarly, during a feed you might encourage her to keep awake and concentrate on the task in hand, so each feed has a clear beginning and end. So long as you remain receptive to your baby's communications, this sort of thing can be done in the spirit of negotiation rather than domination.

From psychoanalytic theory and clinical practice . . .

Surprisingly often, mothers who feed their babies continuously have experienced a loss, bereavement or another painful separation. They know only too well how it feels when someone they love isn't there, and this can confuse their judgement about what their baby really needs. Mothers who feel compelled to immediately feed their baby when she cries may seriously feel that if they do not their baby will die from lack of nourishment. When in the presence of a mother and baby in the grip of this feeling, the logic seems inescapable, the sense of a hunger that must be met is palpable. Sometimes mothers who endlessly feed seem to be expressing hunger in themselves, perhaps an emotional hunger, and are not able to feel reciprocally fed and satisfied by their baby's satisfaction.

Too little weight gain

It can be very worrying if your baby is not gaining enough weight. You may feel guilty and inadequate – or, even worse, as if the professionals are accusing you of being a bad mother (they're not but they will be worrying about your baby, and about you). Whether by breast or bottle, feeding is a learning process and perhaps you and your baby simply need time to settle down with each other and get accustomed to this rather scary business.

Some feeding problems may have a simple cause – and an easy solution. For instance, your baby may get painful wind swallowing air along with the milk. By holding him upright against your shoulder and gently rubbing his back, you can release the excess air and relieve the discomfort. But even here all may not be as simple as it seems. Swallowing air may come from mother and baby not finding a mutually comfortable position for feeding, perhaps not close enough – it takes courage to hold a baby close. Working out

From research on the biochemistry of breastfeeding . . .

Feeding is of course a physical function, but it can be affected by the emotional state of either you or your baby. Fatigue, lack of confidence, and stress may inhibit the let-down of your breast-milk, while your baby is unlikely to feed adequately if he can sense your anxiety or is stressed or unhappy himself. It is important for both of you, therefore, for you to look after yourself so you can try to be relaxed when you begin a feed. A mother laughing while she feeds will produce milk with higher levels of immunity-enhancing hormones for protecting her baby's health (Kimata 2007). So, just as problems around breastfeeding tend to have physical and emotional elements that compound one another, if breastfeeding can become something you enjoy rather than endure; the rewards will be physical as well as emotional.

how to hold a baby for feeding is an emotional matter as well as a practical one. When the baby is held close to 'wind' him, you may feel the tightness in his tummy – your physical 'getting' of this helps you understand the emotions and he may start to feel that his mother is getting things under control, and he may relax more easily into feeding.

Give yourself time to think about where the problems came from. Anxieties about feeding can be brought on by all sorts of emotions and experiences. Some mothers feel the closeness of their baby as a kind of intrusion on their bodies or an attack, while if you are suffering from post-natal depression you can feel pessimistic about the complexity of it all. If your baby is not easily taking milk from your breast or from the bottle you are offering her, it can feel like a rejection of you.

In rare cases, babies who are under weight may be undemanding and sleep for long periods. For these babies, advice to respond to what they ask for is not helpful. These babies give out weak signals and need to be actively offered feeding.

From psychoanalytic theory and clinical practice . . .

One mother had experienced a bad relationship with her mother. When her daughter was born, she felt as though another generation of trouble was about to start. She said: 'Here we go again.' If you didn't get on with your mother, or worse still were actually neglected in childhood, you may feel you don't have the resources to give your baby the care he needs. Also, many mothers who have had an eating disorder worry about passing their problems on to their baby, and this can in itself lead to feeding difficulties.

Finding someone to help you

If you are having trouble, you really need someone to help you and give you confidence. Most early problems with feeding can be overcome simply with the support and encouragement of your partner or mother, a friend, your health visitor, paediatrician or a counsellor. You need to trust them and let yourself believe they are on your side as well as the baby's. When you feel low, it's easy to feel that people are siding with the baby and blaming you.

If someone can offer you care and attention – sitting with you for a bit, bringing you food and drinks, or letting you cry if you want to, the panic is likely to subside. By listening to you instead of only offering technical problem-solving tips, they will help you calm down so that you begin to notice your baby's signals: how she wants to be held, how to help her get at the nipple or teat, and how not to gulp the milk. You may find that holding her close is less of an ordeal if someone is there to comfort you too. Books about breastfeeding can be supportive and help you feel that someone really knows what it's like and has understood your situation (e.g. *The Breastfeeding Book* by Maire Messenger Davies, 1989). Breastfeeding groups can be especially helpful – the equality of mothers sharing their experiences can be easier to take in than being shown by an expert. As we have said, you can find breastfeeding groups online.

More serious problems

If you have really serious problems about feeding your baby, it might be that you have suffered severe deprivation or neglect in your own childhood and feel you have very little to give your baby. If you felt that the food and sustenance you were given was begrudged, you might not have the chance to develop the altruism that allows people to share. You might feel your baby is just 'greedy' or a 'monster', perhaps that was how you were regarded as a baby – made to feel that having needs was shameful. If so, I think it is optimistic that you are reading this book – you know that there are ideas that can help. It may be a cliché but ideas can feed your mind. We have mentioned before that if you have not been looked after well, it may be hard to believe in the possibility of people who really want to help. Your baby needs you to be able to feed her and this might be the time to make that leap of faith and ask for help.

9

SLEEPING

When your baby sleeps peacefully, it can feel that all is well with the world. When he doesn't, it undermines your confidence, exhausts you and makes you feel unable to cope with everyday life.

New babies need long hours of sleep, perhaps to recover from the experience of birth and to help them grow. At first they cannot distinguish between night and day, and wake to be fed in the night as often as during the day. You will probably take this in your stride, and find that these regular wakings have an enjoyable logic that carries you along with it. A baby's waking and crying need not be as upsetting as you might have expected. The crying is an instinctual signal of need, but not necessarily of distress and you may find that the signal and your response is a pleasurable interaction between you and the baby. It is reasonable to want to move towards less night waking in time, and you probably hope to create an atmosphere in which your baby feels safe enough to fall asleep and to stay asleep, but having a baby sleep for very long periods is not the main aim of parenthood.

Sleep is a physiological function but it is affected by emotional states, and babies' ability to get into regular patterns of sleep is influenced by their parents' care. When things go well, babies do gradually sleep for longer at night, and have more of their waking time during the day.

In this chapter we look at how to understand what might be happening if your baby does not sleep well and how to cope with your and your baby's feelings.

Nobody sleeps deeply right through the night

When you wake up feeling refreshed after a good night's sleep, you might imagine you've slept solidly from the moment your head hit

From research on adult and infant sleep cycles . . .

Sleep can be divided into four distinct stages: Stage 1 is the lightest form of sleep. Adults go first into this stage, giving way after a few minutes to Stage 2, and then to Stage 3. Some time later Stage 4, the deepest stage, takes over. These sleep rhythms go in cycles. After about half an hour in Stage 4, the rhythms move back to a state similar in many ways to Stage 1, though this time with certain vital differences added on: in particular there is now Rapid Eye Movement (REM), the time when we dream. Adults usually have four or five of these cycles a night. We dream more in the later part of the night and have the deepest sleep early in the night. Each kind of sleep has its own particular function. To get the benefit of Stage 4, you need to have a long enough period of sleep in the early part of the night for each cycle to be completed, and to get enough REM, the whole night's sleep must be long enough. Your baby has different sleep patterns. Infants sleep for much longer than adults. Newborn babies sleep for sixteen or seventeen hours each twenty-four hours. They need these long hours for physical growth and for emotional and cognitive development. Each period of sleep is no longer than three and a half hours at a time and of course new babies need to be fed at least three or four hourly. At first, sleep and wakefulness may alternate through day and night, but already by six weeks sleep is more concentrated in the night and wakefulness during the day. This is more pronounced by four months, and at six months they are spending half the time asleep and half awake. By now the longest sleep period usually follows the longest wake period. Some 70 per cent of babies are sleeping 'through the night' by three months, and 90 per cent by nine months, although it must be said that the definition of this is five hours – not a very long night!

As babies get into a day/night rhythm, their sleep cycles also change. Babies have two sleep states: active or REM sleep and quiet or non-REM sleep. Newborn infants go directly into REM sleep, and as they have frequent short sleeps, they have a high proportion of this kind of sleep. As they mature and their sleep becomes longer, the REM sleep moves (like that in adults) to later in the cycle. There is much interest in the function of REM sleep and infants; as with adults it is a processing time, but it has also been suggested that this 'active' sleep could paradoxically have a contrasting function of providing stimulation for the infant's brain to help with the momentum of development.

In REM sleep, the newborn baby twitches, breathes irregularly, with eyes flickering under eyelashes. In quiet non-REM sleep, the baby breathes deeply and lies very still, occasionally making fast sucking motions or a sudden body jerk or startle.

After three months the baby falls, like an adult, straight into non-REM sleep and plunges rapidly through drowsiness and light sleep into Stage 4 within ten minutes. This is an extremely deep sleep in babies and young children and waking them from Stage 4 may be impossible. A child who falls asleep in his parent's arms may wake if put down in his cot in an early light stage of sleep, but not if put down after reaching this later deep stage. (Based on Daws 1993: 65–69)

the pillow. But in fact both adults and children go through many stages and cycles of sleep including several arousals. Usually we will turn over and go back to sleep without becoming aware of the arousal, but at times of stress we may find ourselves fully awake and start worrying. Similarly, as we will see, babies can drift comfortably back to sleep if they are not in need of feeding.

How should parents deal with the arousals?

In the early weeks babies may need to be fed at the times of these arousals. As they get older, waking might still signal a need for food or comfort or it may simply be an arousal in the sleep cycle. What happens then depends on how parents perceive it; whether they let their baby drift back into sleep, or feeling it is a sign of some need, wake the baby more completely.

All this is particularly relevant to the parents of new babies, who are themselves going through tremendous emotional changes. Going through pregnancy and childbirth, having a new baby and the astounding changes this makes in the first weeks has an emotional impact that could be called a form of stress, however enjoyable. Parents have the exhilarating but terrifying task of being responsible for a new life. Ironically, new parents are the people most in need of a good night's sleep. We begin to see how, when disturbances in babies' sleep lead to loss of sleep for parents, their own ability to

From research on why we all need sleep . . .

Sleep is highly restorative, and the different kinds of sleep restore us in different ways. REM, which is also our dreaming sleep, helps us sort out the events and thoughts of each day, and take some of this into long-term memory. The effect of this sorting process means that we then start each new day less cluttered and confused by all our previous experience. We are thus able to focus on one thing at a time. The ability to maintain an optimistic mood, energy and self-confidence also comes from REM sleep, as does the ability to adapt emotionally or to manage days of stress, worry or new learning. Stage 4 sleep is also of vital importance: it helps renew the immune system and is when growth occurs.

deal with the problems is impaired. Focused attention and optimism, which are both affected by REM sleep, are the very qualities needed to help solve such problems.

In addition, we can see how the actual process of waking is difficult, perhaps pulling yourself out of dreams. If you are woken by your baby at that point, then you may have difficulty in dealing with him. In dreaming sleep, you are perhaps caught in the middle of working out your own stress and anxieties. In such a state your baby's needs or anxieties cannot be put into perspective. A parent who is more deeply asleep may awake shaky and confused, not easily in control of their body movements, and not able to work out what their baby needs.

However, the opposite may also be true. Waking in the night, especially in the early weeks, to feed or attend to a baby need not be a sleep problem for either parent or baby. Newborn babies have to be fed regularly to survive and most mothers are more attuned to the baby's rhythms in the early weeks than to their own biological sleep–wake rhythm. In fact mothers of new babies rarely sleep deeply. They don't proceed into Stage 4 sleep because they need to be able to hear their baby cry. This is not to do with mothers being self-sacrificing. These are mutually satisfying exchanges of biological cues and signals between mother and baby. We can see here the connection between physiological and emotional processes. Parent–infant attachment can override the parent's personal sleep rhythms. This also explains why fathers may be less easily awakened in the night than mothers; their bodies have not had the biochemical sensitisation that giving birth and breastfeeding strongly give to a mother. However, as discussed earlier, fathers who have very close contact with their babies will also have their biochemistry altered and may find themselves similarly listening out for the baby even in their sleep, and waking as the baby stirs.

Settling your baby to sleep

Although sleep states are a physiological process, the way in which parents handle their baby affects how he learns to settle into regular sleep patterns. We have seen how, in the first weeks, the sleep–wake cycle goes on, irrespective of the time of day. It may take until twelve to sixteen weeks for the day–night rhythm to get established. This achievement is not just physical. It is partly due to the to-and-fro between parent and baby that takes place through feeding, holding and playing. These affect the baby's level of tension, and hence his ability to get into a stable sleep pattern.

Babies, as we know from common sense, are different from each other. Some need more stimulation or more calming from their parents; others are able to soothe themselves, or even prefer not to be handled too much. You may get the feel of how much your baby likes to be cuddled, from very early on.

From parents . . .

> *'When my baby was very young I discovered a talent for being "the magical sleep fairy", as another mum called me. I could see when he was getting sleepy, in need of one of his daytime naps. I knew that babies like the sound of their mum's heartbeat, so I'd hold him so that he was very securely held in my arms and his head was next to my heart. Then I'd breathe deeply and slowly into my diaphragm, so he could feel it, and say 'Sssh, ssshh, time to go to sleep now' a few times, very soothingly. And he would! That was a highly potent feeling of satisfaction: I could do something no one else could do – it made me feel very pleased and clever, and pleased with him too!'*

The way that parents perceive their baby can make a difference to how the baby develops.

If you find you are giving your baby 'a bad name', thinking of him as naughty if he doesn't sleep, perhaps you hadn't known how

From research on the impact of parental expectations on infant behaviour . . .

Research has shown that teachers' appreciation of their pupils affects how well they do in class. This applies to parents too. If you see your baby as being either easier, or more difficult, than an objective outsider might, this will influence how you interact with him, and thus influence his behaviour. It is a bit like 'Give a dog a bad name . . . ' This is a sobering thought but it can be a chance to rescue things before they get too bad.

little babies usually behave. Perhaps you are finding it especially difficult to have to put someone else first, night and day, without ever being able to rely on a good night's sleep yourself. Talking about these feelings with someone who is sympathetic to both you and the baby could help you sort things out.

Babies, of course, cannot feed themselves or put themselves to sleep, so they need someone else there to help with physical needs such as hunger or getting to sleep. Being put to sleep is in itself an important part of a baby's experience, and how it is done will affect how the baby feels about himself. A baby who is cuddled and played with before being put to bed will feel differently about himself to one who has just been put there in a perfunctory way. He will also feel different about the parent or other person who has put him there, and these feelings will stay with him as he goes to sleep and affect the quality of his sleep.

Feeling close to you will help him to reach the first stages of separation. Physical closeness is essential for intimacy to develop. You could say that this is the underpinning of human happiness – to experience intimate relationships. If your baby has this, he will more easily be able to have a sense of his own worth and to grow into his own identity as a separate person.

So, helping your baby manage his sleep rhythms involves getting close and into a rhythm of feeding him, holding him and playing with him. As well as you responding to him, you will also be encouraging him to respond to you. So sometimes you might be judging that he can wait a bit longer before another feed. You are giving him the idea that there can be spaces between feeds, a time after the last feed digesting it, a time anticipating the next feed.

Similarly you will be encouraging him to see different patterns in night and day. You will, if you are feeling well, probably be able to respond instinctively to his day and night need for feeding in the first few days or weeks. After this, as we have seen, his physiology starts to settle down. He responds to the external cues of light and darkness and to your cues.

Babies respond to mothers as well as mothers responding to babies. So your sleepiness in the night may gradually become a signal to the baby after the first few weeks that you no longer feel as enthusiastic about more than one night feed. This is a dialogue between you. Also, as he grows, your baby's needs change over time.

Sleep and separation

Sleep can be thought of as a kind of separation, and how both you and your baby view this can affect the way your baby sleeps. Something in parents' own lives can make it difficult to put a baby down to sleep. This is not to do with blaming parents. If you can spot how a problem has arisen, you are likely to feel more confident in dealing with it.

From psychoanalytic theory and clinical practice . . .

Surprisingly often when a baby is not sleeping we find that there has been a bereavement or another serious loss or a separation in the parents' lives. This might be the death of the parents' own parents or events like miscarriages, abortions, still-births and, especially, cot-deaths. It can then mean that an ordinary small separation, like putting the baby down to sleep, can feel as though it is unbearable. Sometimes, if you are going through a stressful time yourself, you can find yourself holding on to your baby for comfort rather than the other way round. It can make you feel that your baby can't manage the transition to sleep 'on her own' even though you are actually closely on hand.

From parents . . .

> *'I had a miscarriage at five months and even though we now have a healthy baby girl, I disturb us at night checking to see she's alright.'*

This is a very understandable reaction, and it can take a long time for the fears about the healthy live baby to get more into proportion. It does seem to help to remember such events and to think about how they might be affecting you and your baby now. Talking about previous losses does not make the effect of them go away entirely, but it can lessen the impact it has on your behaviour with your baby. Sometimes anxiety about separation might be triggered by the upheaval of moving house or a worry that has been planted in your mind by a friend or family member. It is worth thinking through what your worries are and where they come from.

Sleep problems

There are two main kinds of sleep problems for babies. Either waking up several times in the night; or having trouble getting to sleep in the first place.

If a newborn baby is continuously crying and sleepless, this may be an 'irritable' baby who needs especially smooth handling. One cause for this is a difficult birth. Difficult births are stressful for all the family, and one of the direct results can be sleep disturbances. Your exhaustion, or a feeling of having started off in the wrong way, can make it much harder for you and your baby to get into easy rhythms together. In any case, it can take time neurologically for some babies' brains to settle down after a birth. Most irritable babies calm down by six weeks but it's a long time to wait. Very often, however, it is when parents themselves have had some very stressful experience that the whole tension level in the family somehow gets over to the baby. You all need to look after yourselves as much as possible, and find someone supportive to listen to you and back you up.

As babies get a bit older, parents feel less panicky about how to deal with problems. It may still be helpful to think in terms of relationship factors but the more practical problem-solving approach becomes easier.

Babies often drift off to sleep while on the breast – if they are then put down asleep in a cot they may wonder when they wake later how they got there. It gradually becomes a good idea to catch the moment before your baby is quite asleep, to put him in his cot, so that he gets used to a few moments of drowsiness there, or perhaps the sort of dreamy going-to-sleep thoughts that you or I might have, even if he hasn't got the words yet for these thoughts.

Then, if he wakes in the night, he will recognise where he is and be more likely to be able to turn over and soothe himself back into sleep, rather than have to call for a parent.

From parents . . .

> *'Because I always picked her up within a millisecond of her starting to make a crying noise, I created such an intense bond that it makes it hard for her to sleep. She needed me but I needed her, to the exclusion of everything else. She is four now and I still stay with her until she falls asleep.'*

'To the exclusion of everything else', even sleep. This mother eloquently describes how her own needs created a relationship that could get in the way of her daughter's need for sleep.

Parents can support each other in helping a baby to sleep. Fathers may often help mothers in trying something new and particularly in setting limits. There can be a useful balance of one parent, often but not always the mother, being in touch with the baby's needs as they are, and the other parent having new ways of doing things in mind. However, if either parent felt neglected in their own childhood, they may 'veto' the other one in setting any limits, perhaps wanting to make sure their baby gets what they missed out on themselves. There will be more on this in Chapter 10 on crying. Fathers can sometimes usefully point out that a mother's willingness to respond to her baby can lead to letting herself become exploited by the baby. If a mother has got into a habit of responding, rather than thinking about what the baby really needs, the father may be able to bring a new perspective to the situation.

Working parents and their babies may need time together at night to make up for long hours away from each other during the day. In this case the baby doesn't usually have a sleep problem as such, but all the family may be feeling deprived of enough time with each other.

From parents . . .

> *'I went back to work when my first baby was eight weeks. I know I wasn't ready. I missed her so much in the day, my body missed her. That's why I kept her in with us at night for so long.'*

> *'I could not breastfeed my son because of his cleft palate and I think we kept him in our bed until he was two as a way of making up for the lost opportunities for physical intimacy.'*

Older babies wake for different reasons – as they grow more independent, crawl and walk away from their parents, they may also worry whether their parents will be there for them to come back to. This new independence brings with it a quite normal period of insecurity and many babies wake in the night at this time. All the excitement of new achievements may keep a baby of this age awake: after a triumphant day of learning to stand up, it can be quite difficult to calm down enough to go to sleep. Teething can wake babies, perhaps not just the simplistic explanation of feeling pain – but perhaps the teeth also represent newly found aggressive feelings, the pleasures of biting which also bring worries about hurting others. The teething baby is a developing little person who is starting to take on the complexities of worrying about other people. As well as 'teething gel', babies at this stage often need cheerful reassurance.

When older babies wake frequently but seem otherwise to be well, they may need to be helped to 'learn' to sleep for longer.

From parents . . .

> *'When, after several months, things were getting worse and my baby was waking every forty-five minutes demanding to be fed, my husband stepped in. He held him in his arms while he screamed. Eventually he would calm in his father's arms and allow himself to be put down. A little later we tried letting him cry in his cot for a while and within a couple of nights he was sleeping through. I know that cruel things are done under the name of "controlled crying" but we had got stuck in a rut and this got us out. We were all so much happier afterwards.'*

Although a baby should never be left alone to cry for long, quite often parents interpret any murmur, or sound of protest, as 'crying'. If parents always intervene, you could think they were censoring protest. Some of the sounds that babies make might be part of a self-soothing process. Letting a baby vocalise is not necessarily leaving them to cry.

If you are changing your approach to the baby, tell him about it in words. Even though he can't talk yet, or understand language in detail, he can understand that you have got something new in mind. It also helps you to sort out your intentions, by communicating them to him. Mothers or fathers firmly saying, 'When it's bedtime tonight I want you to go to sleep' may sound simplistic, but the air of resolve in the parents can help the baby settle into different ways of behaving at bedtime.

Parents may be dutifully attending to a baby many times during the night, but actually feeling really angry about it. Your baby senses this suppressed hostility. He may manage to be comforted momentarily, and go back to sleep, but does not feel secure enough to settle into deep sleep and wakes again wanting more attention. The interaction between parent and baby then perpetuates the problem.

Other parents may feel so exploited by the baby that they attend to him in an automatic way, without responding emotionally; the baby is left unsatisfied and tries again. Of course this conflicts with common-sense advice that you should not be too friendly with your baby in the night and give him to believe it is 'playtime' – hopefully you will know which is relevant for you but many parents do find themselves in a conundrum. A baby demanding endless attention may indeed be ready for less attention, but has got used to a certain kind of parenting. It can even seem like an addiction. Sometimes, however, the opposite is true, and a satisfying moment of togetherness is eluding the pair but might be what is needed for them to separate well.

A demanding baby can be so irritating to a parent that the temptation is to switch off whenever they aren't asking for anything. This of course perpetuates the baby's need to be the one to initiate because otherwise he is likely to be ignored. Depressed mothers can find themselves caught in this trap with their baby. The solution can be to take the initiative for a few days and offer attention to the baby before he asks for it. Sometimes mothers and babies who have become irritated with each other aren't playing or having much fun together during the day, and need to get back to finding out how to enjoy themselves.

Bedtime routines

Babies are helped to get to sleep by having routines that they learn to recognise. This means ending the baby's day with a sequence of events, such as a bath, followed by a feed, with a song just before putting the baby down to sleep: a routine that is enjoyable in its

From research on the Basic Rest–Activity Cycle . . .

Another interesting discovery is the Basic Rest–Activity Cycle (BRAC). We all have these, adults as well as children. In adults they last about ninety minutes, compared with forty-five minutes in newborns. This means that as well as the night-time cycle, we have cycles during the day of being more alert and efficient, followed by times when we feel less focused. This is not just being tired from working but a cycle in the working of the brain. (One practical application of knowing about the BRAC is that if you ever have bouts of insomnia, you should expect to be awake for about ninety minutes. Most people can reliably expect to fall asleep again after this length of time and worrying about getting back to sleep sooner is wasted energy.) The rest periods do not need to be as long as the active periods but respecting them can improve our efficiency and safety. Sometimes a few minutes will suffice. It is useful to think of these less alert periods, while awake, as times for losing focused attention, being reflective or daydreaming. This time will thus be restorative in a similar way to REM sleep. Because this cycle is a natural one, mothers who get in tune with their new babies' sleep patterns may find it easier than they expect to have little naps during the day while their babies are asleep. (Based on Daws 1993: 65–69)

own right – pleasurable things that you and the baby do together. The repetition of each activity leading from one to another helps him get into a frame of mind for sleep and helps him to wind down. He will get to recognise the words you use, and their rhythm. Playing with and being cared for by you makes him feel good about himself and secure enough to sleep. Bedtime routines can be with either parent. Your baby won't necessarily be confused if each of you does it somewhat differently from the other, he knows you are two separate people, as long as you are both genuinely finding the way that works for the baby and haven't got an ulterior motive of putting the other parent in the wrong.

From parents . . .

> *'I pat the baby and say, "It's sleepy time" as I leave him.'*
>
> *'I rock him, singing a lullaby my wife taught me. She stands with us, rocking in time. We both kiss him before putting*

him down, and then we both kiss him again once he's in the cot. It's a ritual, we all know what's going to happen next, which is soothing.'

Where should your baby sleep?

These days most babies sleep with, or close to, their parents in the early weeks. This fits with mothers' feeling of anxiety and of being somehow incomplete when separated at all from their infants. When hospitals remove newborn babies to give mothers a rest, mothers may feel confused and lost without their baby. Despite the hard work of childbirth, they may find they are less in need of rest than a chance to get to know him or even just to get confirmation, through his presence, that he really exists. From the baby's point of view, he needs human company. However, co-sleeping divides opinion. Confusingly, co-sleeping is associated with negative and

From research on the benefits of co-sleeping in the early weeks . . .

Researchers now say that sleeping apart is a sensory deprivation, and that parents and infants respond to each other's breathing and movements. Physical contact may have a mutual calming effect on baby and parent. Mothers' and babies' physiology can connect very closely. One study of co-sleeping showed that infants born to mothers with low heart rates slept for longer and fell asleep faster and generally cried less often than did infants born to mothers with higher heart rates (McKenna et al. 1989).

From research on the risks of co-sleeping in the early weeks . . .

In contrast to the McKenna study, the National Institute for Health and Care Excellence (NICE) advice says co-sleeping increases the risk of sudden infant death syndrome (SIDS), especially when a baby is less than eleven weeks, if either parent smokes, is very tired, has drunk alcohol recently or is on medication or drugs that make them sleep heavily.

positive outcomes. It has been co-related with both cot-death and with good cortisol processing. No causal relationship has been established between either and you will need to make your own decisions based on your own assessment of what the available research suggests, some of which is described above.

From parents . . .

> *'It had never occurred to me and my husband to have the baby in with us at night but after weeks of none of us getting more than an hour at a time I found myself thinking: I'll just lie down with her for a minute before I put her back. The next thing I knew we had all been asleep for six hours!'*

What happens after the first few weeks?

Some parents keep their baby close after this time. They may then find their baby has difficulty getting to sleep; many do not. It seems that some parents and babies can enjoy being very close, but let go of each other emotionally, enough for each to be free to go to sleep. Others seem to find each other's presence intrusive and no one is able to sleep long and deeply. At its simplest, if a baby or young child in his parents' bed is kicking, and thus keeping his parents awake, then he is not being comforted by being with them. Sometimes one parent gives up and goes to sleep elsewhere for a few days or weeks.

From parents . . .

> *'At the moment it is best for all of us if my husband sleeps in the sitting room. I then don't have to worry about disturbing him, I can put the light and radio on and potter about getting the bottle and getting comfortable for the feed. When he's had a good night's sleep, my husband is a morning person so he takes the baby then and gives me a lie-in, usually putting the sleeping baby back in the cot in our room before he goes to work without waking either of us. At the weekend I spend a night next door and he does the night shift. It works for us for now.'*

Making sure that at least one person gets a good night's sleep can do much to support a marriage but there are times when a father leaves the marital bed in response to the disruption in the marital relationship – you could say that the baby is literally kicking the parent out of bed and it might be hard for the couple to come back together.

From parents . . .

> *'My two- and four-year-olds still get me up regularly at night because I let them get in with me. A part of me thinks that in some cultures that would be normal so why not? But I often don't sleep next to my husband.'*

Breastfed babies who sleep with their mothers are likely to wake more often and have brief feeds throughout the night. This may be very satisfying at first for both you and your baby, and breastfeeding mothers may not even completely wake up. Later on your closeness, the smell of you and your milk, may perpetuate your baby's waking and feeding, when he might have been ready for longer periods between feeds with longer time asleep. Going into his own cot at this point may help him to stay asleep for longer and may also allow you and your partner to reclaim your relationship together.

From parents . . .

> *'I enjoyed having my first baby in bed with me. I could sleep well on my side, curled around her, without moving an inch all night. Neither of us really woke when she latched on in the night and it was all rather lovely. In time I started to want to move around more and felt that she could manage a bit of distance. Because we had her cot right up against our bed with the near side down, I could push her away after a feed without fear of her falling out. At six months she was spending most of the night in her cot and we were coming together where the cot and bed met for feeds every couple of hours. We thought that she might go longer if we put her cot into her room. She didn't but it was worth getting up in the night to have our bedroom back to ourselves. Our second baby went into her own room at four months, which meant an even longer period of getting up several times a night. They both started to sleep through at around a year.'*

When a couple doesn't spontaneously come to feel that it is time to move baby out, it might be that the 'sleep problems' are in fact disguised marital problems.

You and your dreams

You will probably find that you dream about the baby during your pregnancy, and just before and after the birth. Dreams are an important part of mental functioning. These dreams can be romantic and enjoyable, or disturbing and shocking. This is probably nothing to worry about. They are usually part of the mental processing of all the changes your body and mind are having to deal with. Dreams that are not remembered may help the dreamer assimilate all the activities of the day into settled long-term memory; all the day's conflicts seem to get connected with experiences from the past (Palombo 1978). Remembered dreams can be a useful source of information about what is going on below your conscious thoughts. Even shocking and violent images in dreams are a way of illustrating the fantasies that most women have about what is happening to their bodies and their feelings about the 'alien' creature inside or the devouring creature outside.

From parents . . .

> *'I find breastfeeding very enjoyable but there were nights when I would be haunted by an awful image from a nature programme I'd seen. It was a close-up of a munching caterpillar – its whole face taken up with a circular machine of tiny devouring teeth. When this image flashed into my mind I would nearly jerk with the urge to pull her mouth off my breast.'*

However, if you have the same dream repeatedly, and you feel upset by it during the day, perhaps anxieties about having a baby aren't running their normal course and you might find it useful to talk to a therapist or counsellor about them.

After the birth many women will find their dreaming time cut by the lack of continuous sleep. If the baby is waking frequently, the very fact of losing sleep and particularly dream-time makes this waking seem all the more insoluble. However, if you can in the early weeks relax into the same sleep–wake rhythms as your baby, you may find that some of the time awake with your baby, especially feeding at night, becomes a dreamy reflective time that is almost as restoring as being properly asleep.

Fathers and mothers may find that the change in their own identity and the many new responsibilities, welcome or not, will be shown in their dreams. As the baby grows, parents may find themselves dreaming about themselves and their baby and find that the dreams include half-forgotten memories of their own childhood – this can be a fruitful way of the past connecting with the present.

From psychoanalytic theory and clinical practice . . .

When working with parents of sleepless babies, a parent's dream often anticipates progress before it has openly been achieved, not as a 'prophecy' but as an acknowledgement of mental work. One father dreamt that his pre-verbal son asked: 'Daddy, why don't you show me how to get to sleep'. This dream released into consciousness memories that helped Father connect what was happening now with similar problems from the generation before – he felt his failure to help his son now was connected to his experience that his father had generally failed to help him when he was a child. I felt that it also heralded the progress that this sort of thinking and linking-up of ideas allows a family to make. He was beginning to imagine himself as being able to help his son.

10

CRYING BABIES

Listening and comforting

All babies cry. They cannot yet talk, so crying is a way to communicate their feelings. Some babies do cry more than others, but when a new baby cries, there is always a reason: they are not trying to manipulate you, they do need you for something.

A newborn's cry is almost irresistible. It pulls adults towards the baby, often without them consciously noticing they have responded.

From parents . . .

> *'When a friend visited with her three-week-old baby, I found myself halfway up the stairs as the baby gave her first cry, before remembering she wasn't mine – even though my own children were long grown up by then!'*

Why babies cry

Crying is instinctive: its purpose is to bring an adult close in order to keep the baby alive, by feeding and keeping her safe. There are several main causes of crying: such as hunger, pain, discomfort, loneliness, or overstimulation. Your baby will probably develop a number of different cries and in time you will be able to differentiate these, although you may not be aware that you are doing it.

Babies are not always in distress when they cry. At these times the cry will not be upsetting to listen to nor will it be an ordeal to sort out what they want. In fact hearing the sounds your baby makes can be part of the amazing discovery of this new, little person. The cry of a baby a few weeks old can have a musical lilt that is very pleasant to hear. By crying, your baby not only lets you know that she's hungry or tired, or that she just needs some attention, she also wants to sense your nearness and feel safe. Your response to her cries shows her that you are available and helps to strengthen the feeling that she can depend on you. Babies do not always know themselves why they are crying – they may have a general feeling of misery or of just needing 'something' and need you to understand this. Giving them attention may then be sufficient in itself to satisfy them.

Many babies have a 'crying period' at a certain time daily that doesn't appear to be related to hunger or any of the usual causes. This 'unexplained crying' often happens in the evening when you are also at your most tired. Fortunately it is often followed by your baby's longest sleep period, so you all have a chance to recover. It is also helpful to think that babies who cry a lot are being assertive, and that this is a very positive character trait. They are able to let their parents know about discomfort or dissatisfaction. Some 'good' babies, who rarely cry, may not be able to assert their own wishes so effectively. Ill babies must of course never be left to cry – your doctor or health visitor can help you to differentiate the sound of a sick baby's cry if you are not confident that you will know this yourself.

Comforting your baby

Babies are usually very ready to be soothed. They will stop crying as soon as an adult picks them up, either because they enjoy being held or because they can anticipate that their need is about to be met. A baby of only a few days will stop crying at the sound of her mother's voice, apparently knowing that she is there and is coming for her. This is also one of a baby's first experiences of cause and effect. Soon a baby will start to pause between bouts of crying to listen to whether someone is coming.

From parents . . .

> *'Getting ready to go out with a newborn was hard. Having put him in the buggy I would be hurriedly going to the loo, getting my coat on and so on, all the while chatting to my baby boy because he would cry at our physical separation. At about three weeks old, I noticed that he would, for a little while, stop his crying to listen, clearly paying attention to (and comforted by) the sound of my voice. I, in turn, found this decidedly reassuring.'*

> **From research on the biochemistry of cuddling . . .**
>
> Schore (2001) describes research showing that when a distressed infant is held ventral to ventral (chest to chest), heart-rate matching occurs which resets the baby's autonomic nervous system. The mother's autonomic nervous system thus acts directly on that of the baby, bringing it back to normal. This not only calms the baby in that moment but the mother's body is 'training' the baby's body to adjust the balance of adrenalin and noradrenalin in his system in order to bring it back to normal. (See more about the biochemistry of 'holding' in Chapter 3 on bonding.)

Learning to recognise the meaning of your baby's cries is one of the main ways that you get to know each other. In fact, most babies will react to whatever their parents try. At first, babies will need to feed, or at any rate suck, many of the times that they cry. But they may also simply enjoy bodily contact with their mother or father. Holding your baby close to you, chest to chest, is one of the most successful positions to soothe a baby: it lets her know that you are emotionally open to her. The physical proximity enables you to feel her distress, while she in turn can feel, through your body, your wish to know about her feelings and to comfort her. Some babies like to be held higher, against your shoulder.

Talking to your baby, rather than just holding her silently, is also important. Provided you are not feeling too upset yourself, your voice can echo some of the lilt of her cry as you ask her how she is with something like 'Poor Baby. What's the matter?' Having got in tune with her emotions like that, you may find yourself calmly telling her 'It's alright, Mummy's here.'

The fussy or inconsolable baby

Each baby requires a unique approach from her parents. Some babies seem to be born more fussy or irritable than others. They cry more than their siblings or peers and it may demand sensitive thinking about how to help them. If she goes on crying after you have been through all the usual checks of whether she is in pain, hungry or wet, it could be that it is simply taking her a while to settle down after her birth. The world is a very different place from the womb! If the birth was difficult, she may have had a jangled start and you may have to work harder than usual to find ways of soothing her. All babies have their own preferences for sounds, rhythms and ways of being held. You may even have detected some of these personal preferences while she was still inside you – such as her reaction to music or a particular noise.

From parents . . .

> *'My firstborn cried a lot and really loud. I only started to realise that not all babies were like her when I went to a breastfeeding meeting. She had slept through it but woke as people got up to leave. Everybody stopped and stared in stunned silence at her blood-curdling scream. I was taken aback by their response. That was just the sound of her waking up. My son was completely different. His cry was a quiet mewing, at first I thought he was just talking to himself and didn't realise he was asking me for something.'*

> *'When she would cry inconsolably and heartbreakingly and I couldn't calm her I felt so bad, so worried and then at times angry. I wish I could have known then that she would always have this thing where she would get on to an emotional trajectory and not be able to divert from it. Once she is mad, she stays mad, until she's done and then she's fine. I wish I'd understood that my job was to bear it with her, be there while she did her thing. Not necessarily to make it stop.'*

A baby who is crying may be communicating intense and passionate feelings of all kinds, but especially of misery or anger. These are normal kinds of emotions but when a mother or father, perhaps because of their own experiences, is frightened of what their baby is expressing, they will not be able to reassure her. She will be left unsettled, perhaps still crying, unable to sleep. If a parent can understand these feelings and help the baby to deal with them, repeated instances lead her to remember this, and learn how to manage them herself. By trying to soothe your child, you demonstrate to her that you are doing your best to understand why she is crying and that you do have the resources to help her feel better.

Coping with prolonged crying

Soothing a crying baby is partly trial and error. The trouble is you are not a dispassionate scientist doing an experiment in a quiet laboratory. The crying can get to you, get into you, while you are trying to figure out how to respond.

From psychoanalytic theory and clinical practice . . .

In Chapter 4 we explored the idea of maternal ambivalence. It is often only during a bout of prolonged crying that a mother is confronted by her own ambivalence, just at the moment when your baby most needs you to be available to her. One mother told me that her baby's crying made her so angry that she had to keep silent, or 'The things I would say to him would be too awful.' In fact, it wasn't until she was able to talk to me about these 'awful' thoughts of hostility towards her baby, and have them understood, that she was able to convincingly calm him when he cried.

From parents . . .

> *'When she gets like that it feels quite crazy. I struggle to be the calm one because as much as she gets lost in that feeling, so can I. It's like she pulls me in with her.'*
>
> *'Sometimes I had to speak of love when I was feeling hate and in time we both started to believe in, or remember, the fact that I do love her and we would both calm down. Other times I had to ask someone else to take her for a short while.'*

Your baby has got herself into a state, and doesn't know how to get out of it unaided. If you can just bear her feelings with her, you may be able to lessen their force and prevent either her or you from becoming too distraught. If your body or voice are shaking with suppressed hostility, you will make her feel frightened; so if you are feeling very angry, you need the help of somebody else. This could be the other parent, a friend or professional. They are not trying to take her from you, but to help you both sort it out. It can be helpful to think about it in terms of your deserving support because what you are doing is important and difficult, not because you are no good at it.

From parents . . .

> *'When I've been up for hours with her crying and arching away and I'm physically and mentally exhausted by the work of feeling those desperate feelings with her and the effort of trying to keep a lid on my building anger, I do resent the lack of status this work has. If I were doing some other job that demanded such self-sacrifice and exposure to raw emotions, it would be well paid and I'd have back up – not a lonely sense of doubt and failure.'*

'Ghosts in the nursery'

So, we know that all parents could experience feelings of hostility towards their baby but some will struggle with this more than others, and especially when their baby is crying.

If your mother was rejecting, you may find turning away or becoming angry are the only responses you know to the sound of a crying baby. The feelings that you had, that you were no good, when your mother seemed to be pushing you away, get stirred up again. You feel rejected by your baby and reject her in return. However, it can be the very fact of being rejected that makes babies 'go on and on' crying. Babies can actually make do with and be satisfied with quite a small amount of comfort but it can be hard to discover this if you don't feel you have what they need. You can feel that your crying baby is telling you that you are no good, and that in turn makes you just want to shut her up. Parents who batter their babies often feel the baby is criticising them when she cries. (An amazing 80 per cent of parents with new babies said they could sympathise with people who batter their babies. This shows vividly how testing a crying baby can be.)

However, you need not have experienced neglect or abuse to find yourself grappling with 'ghosts in the nursery'. Many aspects of the way you parent will be influenced by the way you were parented in ways that it can be hard to bring into conscious awareness.

From psychoanalytic theory and clinical practice . . .

Sometimes parents are unable to soothe their babies because of something in their own history. Fraiberg et al. (1980) used the phrase 'ghosts in the nursery' to describe the way that problems between a parent and baby can often be traced back to the parent's experiences in infancy. Often, if people were neglected when they were themselves babies and their cries went unheard, their baby's crying stirs up their own unmet infantile needs, and actually makes them feel unable to muster sufficient adult resources for their baby. It usually takes someone to listen to their memories of childhood, to help them get in control of these unmet needs. If parents are listened to, they will then most likely be able to listen to their baby's cries and console them.

In the terrible (and thankfully rare) cases when babies are battered, it is usually when they cry and parents have not been able to stop the crying. These are usually parents who feel they have no good experience of parenting inside them to draw on.

From parents . . .

> *'Sometimes his crying is so intense that it sets going a vibration in me. My pain gets stirred up by his and I worry that my pain will then amplify his. That's what happened when I was little. When I was feeling pain my mother would feel pain, but it was not an empathic response, it was an automatic reaction. Sometimes she would get angry if I was upset or she would shut off from me, wash-up with her back to me, but mostly she would try to 'gee-me-up' with an anger-driven hysterical happiness. She would hold on to me and to happiness like her life depended on it. I had to comply. She doesn't do calm happiness. The hardest thing for me is to resist the urge to rush in and quiet the awfulness for my baby. I know that he needs me to hear it and bear it rather than chase it away.'*

Parents also may feel that they can't comfort their baby if they are on their own, lonely and feeling someone else should be there to help them. The resentment towards the missing person for not being there can get in the way of dealing with the baby. Single parents can feel like this; so can parents who have not got the support of their own parents. If you feel like this, it is important for you and your baby that you find a friend or professional to help you through this bad patch. You won't be criticised, everyone needs support at times. In fact, people are relieved to get a chance to be involved. It is worrying for outsiders to see a mother and baby suffering but feel that they would be interfering if they tried to help when they're not invited to do so. Most mothers have a worry that people will want to take the baby away. Like feeling guilty when you see a policeman, it is not rational yet it is quite powerful. If you can let people in, you will be reassured that they don't want to take the baby from you but to help you and your baby settle down with each other.

Colic

When a baby's crying seems completely inconsolable, it is often called 'colic'. The crying inexplicably develops into violent and rhythmical screaming attacks. Colic generally begins in very young babies, when they are about two weeks old, and may go in a cycle peaking at two months and usually disappearing by three months, or four months at the latest. When a baby has these screaming attacks, she may scream frantically and relentlessly for two or three hours daily, often at about the same time each day (usually late afternoon or evening). The crying is different from crying at other times of day, with a higher, more intense pitch, and with spaces between the cries. The baby may not respond to the usual comforts or only temporarily; she stiffens her whole body, arches her back, thrashes her limbs, clenches her fists, draws her knees up to her abdomen, and makes facial grimaces, all of which make her look as though she is in pain.

These screaming attacks can make parents feel panicky. You may feel upset, helpless, and can easily become angry. This particular kind of intensive crying really gets into anyone who hears it. You are likely to feel demoralised because you can't calm the baby and criticised or rejected by the baby, for not getting it right. The irritated feeling in the baby's body is illustrated by an irritating cry, which makes the parents also feel full of an irritating pain. So as well as having to deal with the baby's state, you have to deal with your own feelings stirred up by the crying, in order that your response does not exacerbate the problem.

What causes colic?

The baby's body movements often look as though she has wind and one theory is that it is painful wind caused by an immature digestive

There's no such thing as colic – it's just a problem affecting nervous new mothers
Dr. BRISK
Two years later:
Dr Brisk at home.

system. Another theory is that the baby's pain is the *result* of taking in air during the crying, not the cause of it. The suggestion is that colic is ordinary crying that has got out of hand and then escalated into this desperate kind of crying.

Does it help if a parent thinks of a colicky baby as one having a difficult temperament? It might help move on from feelings of personal failure to the problem-solving of dealing with difficult behaviour. However, there is a danger in thinking of the baby herself as 'difficult' or 'naughty'. An important principle in thinking about human beings is how innate characteristics are affected by our relationships. To some extent we *all* have difficult temperaments and rely on our family and friends to neutralise some of the more extreme signs of this, and babies need their parents' help in this way. However, babies are not just a reflection of their parents' care, they are also separate individuals with their own strengths and vulnerabilities.

Colic and feeding

It seems that colic is rarely caused by a gastro-enteric problem. So, changing the method of feeding is not usually the answer. Breastfeeding mothers do not need to worry that their milk is causing the problem, and bottle-feeding mothers do not need to keep changing the formula.

The upset of the baby crying can make mothers lose confidence in themselves and keep trying something different. Sometimes, if mother and baby have not got into a comfortable feeding relationship with each other, this can lead to tentative positions for feeding, where the baby does not latch on effectively. Such feeds could be experienced as 'indigestible'. Taking in wind while feeding at breast or bottle might be a consequence of this uneasiness or awkwardness in the way that the baby is sucking. Perhaps an anxious baby gulps too quickly or strains away from the mother's body as she sucks. However, perhaps it has nothing to do with how you and baby come together for a feed. If you are able to keep an open mind to the fact that it might be partly about that, without being hard on yourself or your baby, you might find you can work your way out of these difficulties.

Mother and baby often need a sympathetic person to help them get together in a comfortable way. Certainly, a mother with a colicky baby needs the father, or someone else, to take turns in holding the baby. Often, a father can calm a baby when a mother can't. This need not mean that he is a better parent, but that he can give the baby a fresh start, away from the tension built up in the previous few hours between baby and mother. If both parents get the same reaction from their baby, there is no escape from the fraughtness; but if one parent can succeed in calming the baby, that can also be upsetting for the other who has 'failed'. It is helpful to think that one parent has to go through the intensity of feeling what the baby has been unable to deal with, and the other parent is able to give the baby a respite from this. Being the one to receive and bear the baby's communication of pain is just as heroic, if not more so, than being the one who breaks the cycle.

It may save your sanity to know that colic doesn't go on for ever so that you don't let it completely overshadow your relationship. Try to have pleasant interactions with her when she is not crying. It can be tempting to enjoy respite from one another but you also need to be building up a bank of good experiences together to see you through the tough times.

Should you leave a baby to cry it out?

Some parents worry about responding immediately to their child's crying for fear of 'spoiling' her. Little babies need to be responded to; they don't become spoilt by being picked up and comforted. Confirming your love and reliability is part of the whole relationship that will grow between you and your baby.

It is not that a baby should never be allowed to cry. If a baby cries and is properly attended to, she needn't be picked up again if she cries for a few moments after being put down. As she gets older, she may need some firmness and a chance to soothe herself. Encouraging her to use other comforts such as a thumb or teddy

From research on infant crying . . .

Research suggests that responding promptly and appropriately to the crying of very young babies actually reduces the amount they cry later on; it makes them feel more secure, and able later to explore and confidently enter into other relationships etc. What's more, leaving a baby to cry will make her more and more fretful, and less likely to respond to your eventual attempts to calm her (Bell and Ainsworth 1972).

bear can enable her to take charge of her own emotions. This is not a question of leaving her to cry but of allowing her the chance to be separate and to feel and express her mood.

How to calm your baby

Holding

As we have said, holding a baby upright, tightly against your body, often works. Even a baby can sometimes feel psychologically as though she is 'falling apart', and crying can be an expression of this. Holding a baby physically can help them to feel emotionally 'held'. They may also feel that what they are going through in their body can be felt in the body of the parent holding them. A baby who is kicking and thrashing about all over the place may be relieved by firm holding. There is evidence that a desperately crying baby may be overbreathing. If held face to face, by the parent, they can breathe in carbon-dioxide from their exhaled breath and this may have a physiologically soothing effect. Alternatively, some parents find themselves holding the baby outwards, to get a view of things outside. Looking out of the window may help both parent and baby to get out of a claustrophobic, stressed, shared state of mind. Other babies may not be able to bear too much handling and you might have guessed that your baby is one of these. Maybe you and your baby need some relief from each other. Putting a baby down in a safe place, his cot or pram, and walking a short distance away, can give you both a chance to recover.

Dummies

They can work miracles, but not always.

From parents . . .

> *'I can't think why now but I had not liked the idea of giving him a dummy. At two months I tried one out of desperation. It completely resolved our sleeplessness problem. There is no more to say than that.'*

> *'Someone suggested a dummy might help her to get to sleep off the breast but every time I tried putting one in her mouth she would make a funny face and spit it out.'*

> *'I can still remember feeling desperate when one of my babies wouldn't stop crying, deciding to try a dummy, and, I must confess, even practically ramming it into his mouth. He calmed down immediately, the fury between us disappeared, I could see how the sucking focused him.'*

The baby who feels emotionally all over the place is calmed by the neurological process that sucking sets in motion. She gathers herself together through the focus of her sucking mouth. It relaxes the movement of the guts and major muscles while the regular, rhythmic stimulation from the mouth reduces the random thrashing about. Some babies are able to find their thumb or fist, others need a dummy. There doesn't seem to be any good reason for not using a dummy with a baby who needs extra sucking. Sucking has emotional significance as the way the baby is in contact with the mother when at the breast. Sucking on a dummy can represent a memory of sucking at the breast, when separate from the mother between feeds.

From parents . . .

> *'At home I don't mind her asking for a feed when she isn't really hungry, it's just like a special cuddle, but in public places it can be quite a hassle getting her latched on in a discreet way. When she then hears something interesting going on and pulls off sharply – leaving me hanging, literally! – I feel really annoyed.'*

> *'Sometimes I know he's not really hungry, then I think I'm being used as a dummy.'*

So, babies who cry a lot, or who have colic, can often be calmed by sucking on a dummy. The effect can be instantaneous, as the baby starts to suck the thrashing about of limbs stops; it seems as though the sucking focuses the baby physiologically and calms him emotionally. Thumb-sucking can be equally successful.

Parents may, however, worry about giving their baby a dummy to suck. Does it looks as though they haven't been able to satisfy the baby? They may feel 'shame' about dependency feelings and may worry that it will become a habit which will be difficult to break.

From parents . . .

> *'I felt mortified. I was afraid of being made redundant.'*

> *'Thumb-sucking is fine, it's natural.'*

> *'I'd rather he had a dummy, at least then I can take it away when the time comes.'*

A dummy is not a good idea when it is used to shut a baby up – that is, to stop sounds of protest that are a communication to parents. Older babies can be delayed in talking if their parents' reaction to noise is to shove a dummy in their mouth. It stops the exploratory sounds that a baby makes as part of the process of learning to talk. Dummies constantly used can delay the development of the mouth muscles that are needed for talking.

Teddies and blankets

Teddies are a different kind of comforting object. They come into their own when the baby is older and starting to deal with the idea of separation from their parents.

From psychoanalytic theory and clinical practice . . .

Teddies are sometimes thought of as a 'transitional object' (Winnicott 1958a). Transitional objects are one way in which a baby gets through this stage of becoming more separate. A teddy, some other toy, or perhaps a blanket, may become special to the baby, particularly at bedtime. It always needs to be there before the baby can settle to sleep. Tiny babies do not have these security objects – they need to have their mother with them for much of the time. These objects come into their own when the baby is in a period of change, they help the baby to start to feel separate while still in close contact with their parents: it does not replace the parents but is a bridge between them.

From parents . . .

> *'I found that giving him my own T-shirt, still smelling of me, seemed to soothe him.'*

Parents cannot, however, choose which toy or other object is going to be important to their baby; the baby finds its own meaning in something, and this in fact becomes its first 'possession'. As the baby

From psychoanalytic theory and clinical practice . . .

I have noticed that when parents and a baby are having particular trouble in separating, especially at night, parents may have been feeling that only *they* can comfort their baby. Although parents can't choose their baby's special possession for them, suggesting that a teddy could be a comforting person-substitute in helping an older baby get to sleep, can sometimes release the parents into seeing the possibilities. One mother joked with her baby, 'Here's teddy. Give him a cuddle to help him get to sleep.' Her baby seemed to be relieved to be allowed to get on with it and was able to settle.

gets older, this possession may need to be carried around, and the whole family recognises its importance.

As with dummies, babies will usually give up their teddy or blanket when they are ready to; they can help a baby eventually to become more independent, not less. Toddlers may use them as an anchor as they go out into the world. If a child really goes on being rigidly addicted to any of these, she may still be having trouble with separation issues and perhaps the family need to think about the meaning of this. However, many adults still enjoy special objects that anchor us.

Massage

This can be very comforting, a physical way of organising your response to your baby's distress but should not feel intrusive. You need your baby's 'consent' to touch him as much as if he was an adult. Done respectfully, massage is known to improve interactions between carer and baby and to be a protective factor against post-natal depression (Glover 2001). Perhaps the mutual creating of a rhythm together by mother and baby has a neurological effect that is healing to the mother as well as the baby. The learning about and responding to each other physically enhances each one's emotional state.

Rocking

Rocking is an effective way of stopping rhythmic crying. Gentle, rhythmic motion, about the speed of a very slow walk, helps to calm a baby's heart rate. Perhaps the rhythm first attunes to the rhythm of the baby's crying and then is able to take the baby out of its agitated state of mind and body. Some parents find that an agitated baby can be similarly calmed by being pushed in a buggy, or driven in a car. However, they can then find themselves driving around at night to get their baby to sleep and to keep him asleep. This can be very useful short-term but if it continues, it may be a desperate measure and a false solution; it perhaps represents something about getting out of the house away from the emotions built up inside, or of one parent feeling that they need the other one to take the baby away, out of the house. Less extremely, going into another room or out of the house can change your baby's mood and yours. If you tell the baby what you are going to do, 'Come on we're going for a walk,' you can help her feel you have some ideas for a fresh start.

Swaddling

Swaddling is an old-fashioned practice which has been rediscovered. It affects the physiological state of the baby, and through this her emotional state. When babies are wrapped in a tightly folded blanket, it seems that they sleep more, have fewer startles and a lower heart-rate variability than non-swaddled babies.

From parents . . .

> *'My first baby was, at the suggestion of the midwife, wrapped in his shawl. A peaceful look came over his face each time he was wrapped up; he would close his eyes and fall asleep instantly. After a few weeks he struggled to have his arms out, though still liking his body to be closely wrapped. As he got older and his movements increased, the shawl soon worked loose and the calming effect lessened but was no longer needed. This did not work at all for his younger brother, who preferred from the beginning to have freer movement of his limbs. This was a very simple example, for me, of how babies' temperaments differ and of how they have their own distinct preferences, right from birth.'*

Singing

Sounds are important to babies, especially parents' voices. Babies in the womb can hear their mother's voice and can recognise it soon after birth. Tapes can also be useful to soothe a baby and ones with a heartbeat sound are now available. But parents singing to their baby is the real thing. They can moderate the rhythm and pitch to what they perceive the baby is responding to. The sound is so personal, and the particular melodies and words can have a private meaning between them and the baby. When you sing to a baby they often, at the same time, fix you with their gaze, as though they are also 'listening' with their eyes. Sometimes parents find that loud music of their own choice will absorb some of their own anger with the baby for his noise, and even though it's not the conventional idea of soothing music, it might help everyone calm down.

Bouncing a baby

Sometimes the heightened feelings between parent and baby mean that your 'rocking' gets taken over into a fast strong rhythm so that you are bouncing, or jigging her up and down. If this starts off as a getting into tune with the rhythm of her crying, she will feel you are with her. You will then be able to steady the rhythm and this may calm her. However, if you find you are always 'jiggling' her, this may demonstrate the tension inside you and, in turn, make her feel more tense.

If you are ever tempted to shake your baby, put her down safely, and walk away. Shaking your baby can cause serious injury.

Carrying

Babies given extra carrying in the early months, cry and fuss less later on.

Mothers and babies who are close to each other for long periods have a chance to learn about each other and respond. However, mothers who carry their babies also have to work out when the time is right for letting the baby be more separate and starting to manage their own feelings.

From research on attachments . . .

One study also found that when babies were carried close to their mother's bodies in the first two months, they were more likely to be securely attached emotionally. This made more difference than whether they were breast- or bottle-fed.

From psychoanalytic theory and clinical practice . . .

In her book *Saying No*, child psychotherapist Asha Phillips (1999) describes a mother and baby who have had difficulty in letting go of each other. Mother and baby have a good relationship despite a difficult birth but he hates being put down and 'whimpers as soon as he is out of contact with her'. She ends up carrying him in a sling all day while she does her chores. 'What began as pleasurable contact . . . turns into an inability to part . . . He seems stuck on to her, even occasionally like a parasite, living off her rather than relating to her. She feels this has nothing to do with who she is, as an individual, and finds him most irritating at times' (1999: 11). By always responding to his whimpering by picking him up, the mother is reinforcing the idea that he can't manage without her. Once a baby has a good bank of experiences of being comforted to draw on, 'saying no' to him can liberate him to discover that they can manage a little independence. They will need this space between them in order to get to know each other as separate people.

Crying is not criticism of you

Try to remember the following points:

- Your baby is complaining to you, not at you, and her cries are not a criticism of your parenting.
- She believes in you and thinks you can make her feel better.
- She first needs you to know how she feels. This will start to make her feel a bit happier. It gives you time to sort out what she needs.
- It will help her to know that you are getting in tune with her feelings if you can tell her in words what you think she is feeling and what you are trying out to help her. Your tone of voice tells her more than the words.
- Putting it into words helps you to feel there is some limit to what is going on between you. It is no longer endless misery.
- It might help you to help her if, as you hold her, you try to remember a time when someone listened to you and made you feel better.

There will be many times that you never discover what the matter was but your job was to bear it with her all the same.

11

WEANING AND TEETHING

Weaning is a long, complex process that means different things to different families. The word itself is used in diverse ways: as a giving up of the breast for a bottle; as the introducing of solid foods to a baby who is feeding from either breast or bottle; and as moving to a cup.

Weaning from the breast can feel like a terrific achievement. It signals moving on and the first stage of your baby's independence. Conversely, it can feel like a very sad time of loss of special intimacy. Both mother and baby may wish that all these new experiences didn't have to be attempted. It is certainly a period of change and a baby at this stage can seem very different from one moment to the next; snuggled close one minute, sitting up on your lap or in a baby-chair the next. The time of weaning can bring a sense of exciting newness to your baby's life.

Most babies try some solid food by twenty weeks or so. However, if your baby seems hungry and needs more frequent feeds, your health visitor may advise it sooner. At this time the mouth is a real focus of interest and sensitivity. A baby ready for solid foods will already be spontaneously putting toys and anything he can get hold of into his mouth, it's the way babies explore the world. He is initiating actions and it means he is ready for the idea of taking in new tastes and textures.

New perspectives, new skills

It takes a few days for a baby to learn how to feed from a spoon. A baby who is skilled at sucking from the nipple or bottle teat has become used to a flow of milk that may be continuous when he sucks. He can feel in control of the supply even though he does have to take into account the mother whose nipple and breast this is, or the person holding the bottle.

Feeding from the spoon is quite different. He has to learn to get into a rhythm with the person holding the spoon, and he has to tolerate gaps between spoonfuls. The flow is not continuous like the milk. These gaps are not just failures in the supply, they are time for the more complex munching and swallowing of this differently textured food.

The introduction of feeding from a spoon depends upon another important stage of development: that of sitting up even though still needing support. From this new position for eating, a baby can get into a rhythm with the person feeding him and understand the role of 'turn-taking' as he waits, responds and practises his co-ordination. It gives him a whole new perspective on the world: rather than lying in his mother's lap to feed, watching her face, he can now face out, looking at the people and objects surrounding her.

Baby-led weaning

Baby-led weaning can start when your baby is sitting up unsupported and free to make his own choice of what and when to pick up with his fingers from what is offered. Examining the feel and texture of food is part of a baby's learning process. He needs to connect up the information from his different senses, so that he knows what the food in his dish feels, smells and looks like, as well as how it tastes.

Weaning also encourages the development of language. Whereas your baby's mouth used to be focused mainly on the nipple or teat, from four months he is well into using his lips and tongue in different ways. Experimenting with blowing bubbles and making different sounds and expressions can be seen as the beginning of language. Now your baby can communicate with you from a distance; you can 'talk' to each other from across the room.

From parents . . .

> *'We were weaning and I tried her on some apple puree. She spat it right out and I laughed, so she did it again, and again in a more exaggerated way. It was a joke with no words that we could share. It felt really special.'*

From psychoanalytic theory and clinical practice . . .

One mother realised that her seven-month-old wouldn't eat anything with 'lumps' in. She thought he was protesting about all this newness. She realised she felt a bit panicky herself about whether she and her baby would ever find their old intimacy with each other again when the closeness of feeding was diluted with this more grown-up way of eating. She had felt fine when he was born, but she did feel rather depressed now. She reflected that she often found starting new things rather an ordeal. As mother got this into perspective, baby in turn started to take the lumps in his stride. He had perhaps been sensitive to his mother's worries and with these out of the way he was freer to experiment.

Letting go

Sometimes the significance of weaning in terms of development and change can be difficult for mother as well as baby.

Parents can anticipate problems with their baby letting go, only to discover that when the time comes they are quite ready.

From parents . . .

> *'I had decided to wean from the breast to the bottle at six months but as that point neared I could not see how I was going to deprive him of this thing that he loved so much, I began to feel bad about what I was going to do. In fact he rather liked the bottle, the way it could supply so much so quickly. You can over-think these things and forget the baby will have opinions too.'*

Fathers and feeding

Fathers may have been glad to stand by if the mother was breastfeeding. They can come into their own when the baby is being weaned, enjoying introducing their baby to new foods, or feeling they have less excuse now for not sharing the work! Fathers can be invaluable in helping mothers and babies out of an entrenched position when things are difficult. Babies who won't eat for their mothers may do so willingly for their fathers or, indeed, grandparents. If the weaning process has become emotionally charged between mother and baby, with the baby perhaps upset or angry about losing the breast, eating with father can be an escape from the tension. Fathers are sometimes less conservative than mothers, and may more easily help the baby master new experiences with less regret for the old.

From parents . . .

> *'Our baby has two mums as we are a gay couple. Yet, partly because of our different characters and partly because I carried him, gave birth, stayed at home and breastfed him, my partner was the one who was more spontaneous and willing to let him have a try of things he looked interested in. I was more reticent, wanted to follow a plan of gradual weaning.'*

Self-feeding

At about nine months, your baby will be used to holding finger-food in his hands and probably taking food from a spoon. He is now likely to also want to start using the spoon himself. This is an important moment of independence. Feeding himself, from either fingers or a spoon, is a baby's first experience of 'work' – the feeling of achievement from managing to do this may give him confidence to stretch his capabilities in the future. Of course babies still need you there, sitting with them and helping things on. Rather than feeling you are now redundant, you can be pleased that he is identifying with you. Preventing him from practising the skill often leads to tantrums and this is an important sign that a real need is being thwarted. More seriously, it can lead to a feeling that things aren't worth trying. If parents can tolerate mess, and also sit sociably with their baby, eating a meal or at least having a cup of coffee or a snack, then he will eat better and enjoy his mealtimes. Praising his skill when appropriate works better than scolding your baby over stray food and mess. The social anthropologist Mary Douglas (1966 [2002]) said that: 'dirt is matter out of place'. If you were brought up to believe that mess was always disturbingly 'out of place' and therefore dirty and shameful, it can take courage to ignore the critical voices inside you and prevent such ideas getting into your baby.

Giving yourself a second spoon so that some food reaches its target is often a good compromise. It reduces your anxiety over him gaining enough weight or over wasting food as long as you use it tactfully and don't get in your baby's way. Working as a team, you and your baby can enjoy mealtimes. Some mothers feel more comfortable with this new distance, and enjoy using new food as a way to include exciting new things from the world beyond mother and baby. Others may find this stage more difficult.

From parents . . .

> *'I have been reluctant to wean my second child. I think it is partly because breastfeeding is so easy. You don't have to plan, shop and cook for it, all to have it rejected. I find mealtimes a bit of a trial, boring and stressful. So unlike the peace of breastfeeding.'*

If the atmosphere has become bad-tempered between you and your baby at mealtimes, make sure to have some fun at other times of the day. Do you play games with each other that are started by your baby? Do you let him take the lead when you play with him? Allowing him to use his toys in the way he chooses can increase his confidence and skills. The feeling of enjoyment at doing things together in the games will help him feel co-operative at mealtimes.

Weaning from the breast

Some babies go on wanting to breastfeed for a long time after they can happily chew solid foods: sucking from the breast provides its own unique pleasure and feeling of comfort. Some mothers also mourn the loss of this special relationship and worry that they will never be close to their baby again. They cannot imagine themselves into a new kind of way of being with their baby. Others may be feeling impatient, waiting for the baby to decide it's time to give up. They may worry about depriving the baby but mothers shouldn't feel obliged to continue longer than *they* want to. Breastfeeding is part of a relationship, a two-way process, and negotiating the ending of it is an important stage. A breastfed baby needs to be able to perceive his mother as someone in her own right, with her own needs, not just as an adjunct to himself. He needs to know her as someone who can set the limits – and it forms a basis for considerate negotiation with other people in future relationships.

From psychoanalytic theory and clinical practice . . .

The phrase the 'good enough mother' (see Chapter 4) describes a mother who tries to adapt to her baby at first and make everything just right for him. This gradually lessens when the infant becomes more able to tolerate the results of frustration. If the mother continued to adapt perfectly, the growing baby would have the illusion of being in magical control. The mother has the task of 'disillusioning' the baby, and weaning is one of the fields of action where this happens. The experience of one family I worked with helps to illustrate the importance of this process of disillusionment.

Mother was reluctant to wean her eighteen-month-old son, as they both enjoyed the closeness of breastfeeding. She became uneasily aware, however, that he was beginning to consider that her breast belonged to him, not to her. He would importunately pull up her jumper to get to her breast and tended to look triumphantly around the room at the rest of the family as he fed. His father was a gentle person who thought babies should indeed come first. It took a bit of courage for the couple to realise that their baby had started to rule the roost and that he might actually feel relieved if they could co-operate as his parents to help him be less domineering. When his parents became stronger, the baby lost his rather bossy air. He had found it difficult to play and explore, but when he gave up his need to stay in charge of his mother, he became more creative with his toys.

A mother who has weaned her baby will indeed start to have a different self-image, body and mind, feeling she can walk unencumbered – perhaps becoming more interested in sex again. Some will have enjoyed sex from early on, others need a bridging time of having their bodies to themselves.

One mother was starting to wean her baby, the youngest of four. I said sympathetically to her, 'You want your body back.' She replied, 'I want my mind back.' This mother's comment about wanting her mind back is very important. It reminds us that the mother of a young baby has given over much of her mind to sustain the communion with her baby that has been described variously in terms of 'maternal preoccupation', 'generously shared cognition', 'reverie' and 'careful attunement' (see Chapters 3 and 4). As much as a young baby needs this, he then needs to begin to do without it while a mother gets her mind back.

For other nursing couples, the cue for weaning comes from the baby. Although weaning is a long process, some mothers feel that there is a particular moment when several different facets of development coincide. Seeing their baby sit up unaided, acquire the beginnings of speech, and achieve a sense of individuality and strength, can be such a turning point. Weaning from the breast then seems like an acknowledgement of a stage already reached and not the actual cause of it. Sometimes it is not until you start that you realise how ready you both are.

From parents . . .

> *'My mother saw me begin to refuse my son breastfeeds. She was taken aback by his capacity to protest. "I didn't know he had it in him," she said. It was then that I realised that I had been worried that it would be cruel to deny such a meek and gentle soul. In fact, he needed me to challenge him in order for us to discover his strength. Once I knew he was a lot tougher than I'd thought, it was then easier to hold firm myself.'*

Teething

Connected with all of this is the coming of teeth. Babies often delight in their teeth: in their hardness and in the new ability to bite. As emotions develop, biting can be used to express new feelings of aggressiveness but at the same time a burgeoning awareness of the feelings of others means that a baby will also have to learn how to be careful with his teeth and not bite his mother's breast. (One of my sons tactfully bit my arm instead.) Being able to bite into hard biscuits takes the worry out of getting his teeth into something, and weaning can be a relief. Some more subdued babies, however, may not get the same pleasure out of biting, and this could be one reason why they might have a poor appetite at this stage.

Teething can be a painful business for babies, but these pains are not a sign that anything's wrong: the coming through of teeth is of course both universal and necessary. Parents naturally feel that any pain borne by their baby is their own pain, but carried too far this can prevent your baby from learning to deal with his own sensations. We've all experienced occasions when we can sleep through pain, and other times when we are too frightened of the pain to sleep. The way in which you comfort your baby can affect his ability to deal with the discomfort himself. Letting your baby know that you realise how he feels, giving him cuddles, and making him as comfortable as possible, will give him the confidence to allow himself to fall back to sleep. Becoming agitated about his pain can make things worse and make it more difficult for him to calm down.

A new experience for you all

Teething can also be a difficult stage for parents, particularly mothers. The presence of teeth can feel like the first sign that your soft, cuddly baby is turning into a strong, fierce little creature; in fact, it is quite common for mothers to dream about wild animals at this time.

If you talk to your baby about his teething, even if he can't understand the words, he will realise that you know what he is feeling, and realise which part of his body has the pain. Rubbing teething gel onto his gums is helpful for two reasons: first, it does ease the pain, and second, having you gently touch the sore area informs him that you do know just what the trouble is.

12

LEARNING THROUGH PLAY

Babies play on their own, discovering their own bodies and using things close around to explore sensations and the characteristics of objects. They also love playing with their parents. As well as having fun together, the games that parents naturally play with their babies of touching, stroking, kissing, taking turns, songs and rhymes, all help the baby develop in different areas. Through these games your baby learns how to enjoy co-operating and improves her co-ordination. Language, counting and the developing of abstract concepts also start as a form of playing. After all, many scientific or philosophical discoveries have their origins in 'playing with ideas'.

What is important about games between parents and babies is that everyone should enjoy them. This sometimes means letting the baby take the lead, with parents not being too quick to initiate what form a game takes.

From parents . . .

> *'When I want to play with my baby, I do try to see what she's doing and join in with her play, at her level, but soon I find myself trying to "extend the lesson". I think I do it to keep myself interested. I watch my husband with her and he can stay with what she's doing, giving it his sustained attention in a quiet and steady way that she seems to love. I don't know if he doesn't get bored like I do or if he's better at tolerating a bit of boredom. There are times when she surprises me with a new twist on what we've been doing, and that is such a delight.'*

Perhaps this mother is a bit hard on herself. Her baby surprises her with a new twist and maybe her previous boredom is a sign that they were both ready for some newness. As babies mature physically and mentally the games naturally change. The first play is usually at the breast, or with the bottle. As well as sucking to feed, you may early on see your baby doing some extra 'non-nutrient' sucking, seemingly just for the fun of it, savouring the sensations of the nipple in her mouth. After her hunger is satisfied, a baby often enjoys a bit of playing about with the breast, using her mouth and also her hands, stroking her mother's breast or neck. Sometimes this feels to a mother like a loving caress, at other times annoying, especially if sharp little nails dig into her. The baby may be exploring the shapes or sensations of skin or clothes, or attracted to colours or sparkle and pull at necklaces or earrings. In this play she is showing her interest in you, and also perhaps working out what is *not* you, the difference between people and objects.

Learning by herself

Your young baby can spend long periods just looking at objects, especially anything in motion – mobiles, trees in the wind, the washing going round in the machine. She will also lie kicking her legs and discovering her own body and its capabilities. She puts her two hands together and looks at them. In her mind perhaps she is putting ideas together, perhaps even ideas about parents being together. She reaches towards things, and later manages to grasp them. Once she has learned to control her movements, she is more able to understand and manipulate her environment. She starts learning how things fit in with other things. The baby who spends enjoyable hours putting small objects inside her plastic containers is not only practising her co-ordination but is also getting to grips with the concept of 'in' and 'out'. She may also be having a sort of 'What goes on inside?' speculation.

Learning about herself with others

The games your baby plays with you will teach her about herself and about others. By touching noses for instance, she will experience what her own nose, and what somebody else's nose, feels like. She learns where her body ends and someone else's begins. Later these games include the learning of words like the names of parts of the body. 'This little piggy went to market' involves touching toes, and parent and baby enjoying getting into a rhythm with each other. Clapping hands involves the delight of imitation and the achievement of physical co-ordination. Waving signals, saying hello and especially goodbye help in anticipating and managing feelings about separation.

From parents . . .

> *'The first game I remember playing with my daughter was before she had any words or could clap or high-five, she didn't even smile much but she loved this game. She would get your attention then put her head to one side and then straighten it again. If you copied her she beamed and did it again. She would do it to any new person and often I would have to prompt them to copy her. I think she liked it because it was a way of being with people but I think she also quite liked the power of being able to make other people do something.'*

In Chapter 7 on 'conversations', it was seen that while adults induct babies into ever more complex ways of communicating feelings and ideas, babies are born with feelings in relation to others and a capacity to express them. Trevarthen (2001) has termed this 'readiness to relate'. He argues that a baby can feel pride at being understood when her existence and her feelings are acknowledged and validated by an adult. It is through play that an adult is able to demonstrate that she is attending to her baby and her experience by imitating her and playing with her expectations.

From psychoanalytic observation of parents and babies . . .

Mother draws the helium balloon towards him on the string, speaking in a slightly teasing, anticipation-building sing-song. When the balloon is very close to his face, he wriggles and kicks out his limbs with great excitement. Mother then pauses for a moment and he holds a little more still, staring at the shiny foil balloon until she releases it accompanying its ascent with a drawn-out ascending phrase. At this, his body flips into jiggly action and he makes explosive little noises. Sensing his pleasure at seeing it right up at the ceiling, she leaves it there for a while. She then repeats the whole process several times using very similar timings. His pleasure in this is infectious and we both laugh with him. I have the feeling that our pleasure in his adds something to the quality of his pleasure. He seems to be taking something in that keeps him topped up and in this state of excitement. Mother then tries leaving a longer pause between the drawing down and the letting go. He notices and bounces himself wildly with a big gummy smile until mother 'gives in' and lets it go.

In all these games, a level of excitement builds up between two people that one person on their own can't have. Here it is specifically the mother playing with her baby's expectations. By doing this she demonstrates that she knows what is in his mind, what he expects to happen, and she intensifies his experience by building up his anticipation, exquisitely, almost painfully drawing it out. The name given to this sort of interaction, where it is the experience of being experienced by the other that gives it its special quality, is 'inter-subjectivity'.

While emphasising the crucial role of experience within relationships, we should also note what your baby brings to these interactions. Even newborns have been shown to have a preference for interactions with an 'element of surprise'.

From research on neonate playfulness . . .

'A burst-pause pattern harbours within it surprise, while a static pattern presents no such opportunity. And Nagy and Molnar (2004) have demonstrated that neonates less than 3 days old will go as far as to "provoke" adults to engage with them, if they have already experienced "irregular" response patterns (i.e. ones that contain an element of surprise) with those adults' (Nagy and Molnar 2004, cited in Zeedyk 2006: 329).

It would seem that a hunger for playfulness is in-built and sustains the kinds of interactions needed to build a mature human brain by wiring-up the pre-frontal cortex as discussed in the bonding chapter.

There are also the special games that go with ordinary care-giving activities like nappy changing. The games that parents and babies develop together at feeding or at bedtimes, affect deeply how a baby feels about herself. These games show her that her parents enjoy being with her and are not just performing a duty.

Learning about being with other people

Babies have an urge to share emotions with other people, and they do this through play. Returning to Stern's phrase 'affect attunement', mentioned in Chapter 3 on bonding, we can see how play helps you and your baby to be on the same wavelength. As you perceive your baby's emotional state and synchronise with it, you are able to communicate that you have understood what she is feeling. When your baby imitates, she is letting you know that she is aware of you and what you do. When you imitate her, she discovers that you are attending to her, her states and her actions. You let her know how interesting she is to you.

Then, at around nine months or so, more complex games get going. When your baby claps, instead of clapping back, you might find that you tap on the table in the same rhythm. If she bangs two toy bricks together, you might find yourself singing a little song to the beat. These are spontaneous games, and they show that you and your baby have got beyond just imitating each other and that you each know enough about what the other feels and thinks to create a new game together. At this stage babies become able to share jokes and to tease, a real sign that they have a mind of their own and are starting to know what is in other people's minds.

From parents . . .

> *'At ten months my daughter learnt how to tease me. For a while we'd been playing a sort of peek-a-boo game. When my husband was holding her on his shoulder, I would come up behind them and reveal myself on one side then move to the other until she could predict which side I would appear next, then I would change my routine to surprise her. One day it was my turn to be surprised. She was not there when I would have expected her to be. I looked around the other side to see if she had lost concentration but she was, in fact, waiting there wearing a huge grin! She had not got confused but had learnt that she could be the one to confound my expectations. As she saw the penny drop for me she started to laugh.'*

This kind of teasing is such fun, and so significant developmentally, because it involves a 'you-know-that-I-know-that-you-thought-I-was-thinking-something-else' moment. In our complex social world,

From research on how babies know minds . . .

Research suggests that we can know *when* babies have developed an awareness of the intentions of others through their capacity to play with those intentions. In longitudinal studies they found that provocative or disruptive actions, like the one described opposite, with a playful or watchful look to the adult's face was *clear* in less than a quarter of eight-month-olds, but was evident in three quarters of eleven-month-olds. Babies also tease by offering and withdrawing objects, or themselves for a hug or a kiss (Reddy 2008).

inferring intention and expectation is of paramount importance. The early mastery of these skills in such play is therefore crucial to becoming a competent member of our social group. As the example above shows, it also helps to cement each relationship in which it occurs because of our innate pleasure in being understood. Confounded expectations are also the basis of much humour and this shared laughter is a great bonding experience.

Learning about how the world works

The peek-a-boo game in the last anecdote describes the culmination of a lot of learning through play. A little baby who drops a toy does not look for it; as far as she is concerned it has 'gone'. When she is a bit older, she starts to have the idea that the toy could still exist when she can't see it and so looks down to see where it has gone. She has now reached the stage of appreciating 'object constancy'. When babies grasp a new idea, they have to practise it and it becomes a 'game'. So, a six-month baby, sitting in her high-chair, will drop a toy on the floor, look down, laugh and expect you to pick it up for her. A delightful game for you and her to play but you might often have to be the one to say, 'enough'. Sometimes this kind of play can seem to parents like just being awkward. It is easy to get annoyed when your baby repeatedly throws things on the floor. It can take all your sense of humour to remember that this 'game' represents a major conceptual leap for her. One grandmother enjoyed a slightly more sophisticated version of this game with her twelve-month-old granddaughter.

From grandparents . . .

> *'She had pulled a loose bit off a cardboard box and then dropped it in the box, She pushed it on its side and looked at me. Neither of us could see the torn piece any more but we both knew it was in there. She started to reach in and feel about for it. She was delighted to pull it out and show it to me and then put it back. I then fished it out for her. She seemed to like the fact that we both knew about its whereabouts, even though we could not see it, a sort of shared invisible thing.'*

In fact, being able to play such games has important consequences. If your baby can think about where a dropped toy has gone, she can also think about the fact that people, as well as things, still exist when they have gone out of the room, or even out of the house.

This theme is continued in many of the games played between parents and baby which are to do with disappearing and re-finding. These games of peek-a-boo and hide-and-seek are universal in all cultures. The games are ways of mastering separateness. They are also to do with identity: 'There you are, here I am.'

Pointing

At first, your baby points to indicate that she needs something out of reach. In time pointing will be used to bring another's attention to something she is attending to. Later on you see mother and father pointing out something to the baby, and the baby pointing out something to a parent. This simple act is a sign of one of the most important aspects of our human condition: that as individuals we need to share our interests and our emotions with others. Babies need someone else to take an interest in what they are discovering about the world. Without that, it would be a lonely business.

Playing alone

Having said that, when babies feel secure, knowing their parents are near, and interested, they can enjoy playing alone.

From parents . . .

> *'Even before he could sit up, he loved playing with his toys in his bouncer as I cooked. He would give a little cry, but*

> *was quite satisfied if I looked over to him or just spoke to him. He would look at me, smile and go back to his toys. When he had had enough of this, he would call out in a different tone, and I knew he needed me to go to him.'*

Toys

Parents often feel as attached to their baby's toys as the baby herself is. It is partly love for the baby spreading over into love for their possessions. It is also the attunement to the baby's stage of development that makes the parent feel involved with the 'tools' that the baby is using. Parents who are following their baby closely can often spot just what toys they are ready for next. Your baby is also likely to incorporate everyday objects into her play. After all, much of her play is about trying out what being an adult in their world will involve.

From parents . . .

> *'Babies watch you using everyday objects and start to imitate. Mine loved looking in cupboards, taking everything out and sorting it, putting things in piles.'*
>
> *'My baby has started to use the remote control as a telephone.'*
>
> *'I thought it was so sweet when I realised he was pretending to feed the teddy bear with his spoon.'*
>
> *'At one year she would balance a long piece of Lego on a squat piece and sing "see-saw" while making it tip one way and then the other.'*

These examples of using one thing to stand in for another are charming but this is also an important conceptual leap. They are beginning to use symbols, a capacity that enables us to use language and have abstract thought.

When a baby starts to play with things, it affects the way you play with the baby. Some parents will find it easier than before, other parents will discover new challenges. Some mothers may feel rejected, that they and perhaps their breasts are no longer all the world to their baby.

From parents . . .

> *'I was excited to see her start to explore the world, and she usually wants to share her discoveries with me but I have to admit that I quite liked it when I was her world.'*

> *'Once he started to crawl he could show me what he was interested in. I found it so exciting, it was like I suddenly had access to his thoughts through his actions.'*

In the second year, as games become more ordered – as children, for instance, line up rows of bricks or toy cars – they may be getting into the frame of mind where they are ready for the self-control and organisation needed to manage toilet-training.

Exploring further

Many of an older baby's games seem to involve making a mess, or a noise, or both. Babies need to be helped to explore their environment safely, and to find out what happens if they try certain actions. Real learning comes from this. Imagine the pleasure of discovering that if you bang a spoon on a saucepan it makes a big noise. Of course a lively-minded baby is going to relish both the sound and the power of being able to make it. Parents can either enjoy their baby's innovations or feel regretful that they no longer have a static little baby under their own control. At low moments it is easy to think your active baby is 'getting at you' when she is into everything. If you can take pleasure in her initiative, her exploring is likely to be calmer and she will check back with you to see if what she is doing is safe. Children who have been played with by their parents as babies and allowed to explore are most likely to do well at school. They have learnt both how to work things out for themselves, and how to co-operate with other people.

13

YOUR BABY'S EMERGING SENSE OF SELF

Being a parent is a role that is always changing. From the beginning babies need to be closely and reliably looked after. This gives them the security to become independent. Then they need the space to develop that independence. This will not be a neat linear process and there are no general timescales to follow. It is about being in touch with a baby's changing needs. As your baby's capabilities grow, his sense of self also changes. Parents and babies interact differently as the baby becomes mobile and gets a 'mind of his own'. This process, of course, continues through childhood, with adolescence being the real testing ground of whether secure attachments have enabled successful independence.

Temperament and a readiness to relate

'Selfhood' is something that emerges out of interactions with others. However, your baby does not come as a blank slate. Babies are born with their own temperament, which will effect their behaviour, right from the beginning, which in turn will influence the care they receive.

We have seen that babies quickly come to expect you to engage with them conversationally. Newborns imitate tongue poking and a nine-month-old will enjoy teasing you. They are born ready to relate; their interactions quickly become quite sophisticated. Many parents have an intuitive understanding of their baby's capacities and get on with getting to know their baby without giving all of this any conscious thought. If you are feeling a bit flat, it might not come so easily but it can be motivating, a spur to get involved with your baby if you can persuade yourself to notice and believe in his active desire to get to know you.

From research on temperament . . .

Temperament is thought to be a collection of 'biologically rooted individual differences in behaviour tendencies that are present early in life and are relatively stable across various kinds of situation and over the course of time' (Bates 1989: 4). Temperament is not related to differences in cognitive ability, it is the genetically inherited first building blocks of personality. Personality is the outcome of a complex interaction between temperament and experience. Experience can modify or exaggerate behavioural tendencies but then behavioural tendencies will impact on the kinds of experiences a baby will have.

Piontelli (2004) did long-term observations of several sets of twins in utero, using ultrasound scans, and continued to observe them into their third year. She discovered that twins showed distinct temperaments and patterns of relating to one another that were still observable into their third year.

Pregnancy, before separation

In pregnancy the mother's body is performing certain vital functions for the foetus. There are two bodies but they are not yet divisible. Even at the physical level things are not clear-cut and emotionally things are even less clear. It is normal to feel a bit confused about whether the foetus inside you is a part of your body, or something separate. However, a mother who has particular difficulty about this may be more afraid and unwilling to face the next stage of separation, which is birth itself. The birth is a 'letting-go' by the mother of the baby, into his own individual existence.

Birth as a separation and a coming together

The birth establishes two conflicting truths. The baby is now demonstrably physically separate, but the mother is now much more aware of his dependency on her because she must act to meet his needs, whereas before her body had just got on with it. Some women feel they have lost themselves, the demands of the baby eclipsing all that formed their previous identity. Others feel they have lost the baby; others that they are getting to meet the baby. You will probably experience all these feelings at different moments.

Mother and baby as one unit

Babies are born with their own temperament and their own experiences of the womb and of birth but, in many ways, they are not yet their own person.

From psychoanalytic theory and clinical practice . . .

Winnicott (1964), who was so good at memorable phrases, said 'There is no such thing as a baby,' adding, 'only a baby and someone'. We have looked in previous chapters at the implications of a baby's absolute dependency on adults for survival in terms of how they experience inattention as a threat to life. Winnicott was interested in how this dependence was experienced in terms of a developing sense of self. He went on to clarify that when he had said that there was no such thing as a baby, he meant that at the beginning the 'unit is not the individual, the unit is an environment–individual set-up' and the self emerges from the total set-up, not the individual.

We all have an approximate understanding of this idea that baby and mother are two parts of one unit, as a lone baby just doesn't look right. If in the street or park you see a baby sitting in a pram, apparently alone, your eye will most likely check until you have mentally connected the baby with a watchful adult. For a moment you will have been on guard on behalf of that baby, even if the baby was not doing anything to attract your attention.

You and your baby's emerging sense of self

So, a newborn is a part of a unit in that he is not yet viable in isolation. He is also not yet capable of experiencing himself as a 'self' because his brain is not mature enough, his pre-frontal cortex has not been wired together to allow such higher cognitive function. What of the other half of the unit? You existed before this new person started to grow inside you. How and why, then, do you become a part of this new whole? The state of 'maternal pre-occupation' described earlier, a state of powerful identification and obsessive concern with the needs of the baby, can lead to an experience of merger with the baby. Such a moment of merger seems to be captured in the box below. The mother found herself bringing her hungry baby to the breast, despite herself and her wish to follow a routine.

From psychoanalytic observations of babies and parents . . .

Baby cries and mother picks him up. It seems to me that she instinctively holds him in a feeding position. He starts to mouth. She says that he may be hungry, but she is reticent. While stating that it is not really time for his next feed, she brings him to the breast and all three of us relax. He becomes still and drops off, waking and feeding and going back to sleep in a blissful cycle.

The observer went on to explain that when the three 'relaxed', it was as though a communal hunger had been sated. The baby's wish was felt by the adults, almost as though it had been their own, and the mother's body acted independently of her conscious thoughts and even defying the words she spoke. Perhaps in this moment the baby did not experience his mother as a separate individual to whom he needed to communicate a need, any more than she experienced a conscious decision to meet it. It seems that the mother had lost some autonomy in the service of his needs, almost as though he could bypass her self-will and take up control of her arms to get the feed he needed. An idea mentioned earlier was that the selflessness of parenting is made possible by this identification with the baby. The well of altruistic love is replenished because a part of you feels as though it were your own needs being met. An unconscious fantasy that baby and self are one seems to serve both baby and mother.

From your baby's perspective

We know that a newborn cannot have a mature self-identity but we can only guess at how he does experience himself and others. There are two different views on whether a newborn feels separate from his mother or not: one view is that he feels 'fused' with her, as though she is an extension of himself and as though her breast that appears when he is hungry really belongs to him. However, the recent

From psychoanalytic observations of babies and parents . . .

This ten-day-old baby looked like he came to feel merged with his mother during a feed. As his mother got him into position to suck, his eyes were wide open and he looked up into her face. While he fed, mother and baby gazed at each other. Gradually, as he became fuller, his limbs relaxed, his eyes lost focus, and by the time the feed finished he was snuggled into her body with his eyes closed.

research showing that infants recognise their mother by sight, sound and touch straight away suggests awareness, from the beginning, of her as a separate person in her own right. There must be some appreciation of the 'otherness' of the mother, in order to want to bridge the gap by 'talking' together.

The infant's body can 'melt' into the mother's body at times of falling asleep, while in a more alert state he will be clearer about his mother and himself being separate persons.

From parents . . .

> *'The second time I left my five-month-old with my mother for a couple of hours he blanked me when I returned. After much singing, coaxing and kissing he finally stopped avoiding my eye and allowed himself to smile. This may seem quite unremarkable except for the fact that the very first thing we had done on my return was to have a breastfeed. I had known he would be hungry and barely noticed myself putting him to the breast before really trying to say hello.'*

It does seem odd that a baby would be happy to feed from someone he won't look at. Perhaps he did perceive his mother as someone separate, who could disappear and therefore needed to be punished, and yet the breast had a slightly different status, more like something of his that his mother had wandered off with. Perhaps this reflects the fact that the reality is rather paradoxical. The baby is able to recognise separateness at times, and at other times lapses into a sensation of merging with mother. Your baby will need you to be open to merge with him at times but also be capable of noticing his attempts to understand your separateness from one another.

Being in touch with your baby's feelings and his self-regulation

To your baby, you will seem to be the whole world at the beginning. Through your attempts to understand what he needs, he comes to feel that the world is a place that can know and accept him and his feelings. A parent who is in touch can take in feelings of loving and hating, understand them, and help her baby manage them. So, your baby puts into you intense and passionate feelings of all kinds. To many mothers it is all in the day's work to receive them and give back to the baby a sense of understanding, and an idea that these feelings can be got into perspective. Repeated instances lead him to remember it and learn how to manage to deal with his feelings on his own. This is the baseline for all relationships in the future and determines whether he will grow up able to temper his emotions or be at the mercy of them.

Being in touch with your baby's feelings and his self-awareness

In previous chapters we discussed the significance of imitation, turn-taking and joking for bonding, language development and play. These experiences are also crucial to a baby's emerging sense of self. It has been argued that in order to come to know that we exist, we need to experience existing for others.

To recap then, being in touch with your baby's feelings enables you to help him manage them now and in the future. It lets him know that he exists for you, which is how he comes to know that he exists in the world. This is part of the higher cognitive function that is made possible by the pre-frontal cortex getting wired together. This happens after birth and then only really effectively within good enough relationships.

Some distance between you can be a good thing

Once your baby has come to trust in the world as a place that is reliably responsive to him, he will be developing a sense of self as reflected back by that world. To develop his sense of self and a sense of agency, he will also need a little space. One kind of thinking about

From research on 'readiness to relate' . . .

Trevarthen (2001) has shown that newborns have 'intrinsic motives for companionship'. They appear to want to engage with others for the sake of it:

> Even a prematurely born infant can, if approached with sufficient gentleness, interact within rhythmic 'protoconversational' patterns in time with the adult's vocalisations, touches, and expressions of face or hands, turn-taking with the evenly spaced and emotionally enhanced movements that are characteristically displayed by an attentive and affectionate adult . . . They are not only selecting support of internal physiological regulations, nor are they only responsive to caregiving that aims to directly regulate emotional displays.
>
> (Trevarthen 2001: 100)

If this getting-into-a-rhythm-together happens even when the baby has no need of external support with how he is feeling, then it would seem that the purpose is simply to show the other that you are aware of them and what they are doing. But what bearing does this have on the emergence of self?

Studies of so-called 'feral' children, those found living wild with animals, have shown them to lack certain self-reflexive functions. They don't seem to have an objective sense of their own existence, only their experience of existing, so that they don't even recognise themselves in mirrors. It is argued that it is through protoconversations, which can only be had with other people, that such self-awareness develops. Initially through expression-matching and then mutual imitation, the infant is given the experience of being the object of his carer's attention. 'This experience leads to anticipation, for a contingent and therefore directed-at-me act, and this anticipation is so psychologically and physiologically stimulating as to awaken a new level of consciousness' (Zeedyk 2006: 329). Reddy (2008) describes how we can see evidence of that new level of consciousness, as it emerges from such interactions, when we see a baby take pleasure in teasing. When an expectation is confounded, in that moment of I-know-that-you-know-that-I-know – something that is not manifest – we know the joke relies on the presupposition that there is a mind that contains a thought about the content of another mind. Hobson describes this as the 'primordial sharing situation between infant and carer', from which the infant comes to 'distil out self and other as persons-with-minds' (Hobson 2002: 258).

very young babies suggests that they divide everything into 'good' and 'bad' (Klein 1946). When the mother is there, offering a feed, she is 'good'; if a hungry baby has to wait a while for a feed to come, he may feel she is 'bad' and leaving him to starve. Gradually, as he has repeated memories that she does always turn up to satisfy him, he will be able to look forward in her absence to the next feed. By 'absent' we are talking about a mother who is actually within reach, perhaps bustling about in the kitchen, stopping the potatoes from burning before dashing to her baby's side! The point is that through these experiences he comes to know that he can have helpful thoughts, that he can be satisfied, for a time, by the *idea* of a mother who will come.

From psychoanalytic theory and clinical practice . . .

It has been pointed out that there is a logical connection between absence and thought itself. Bion (1962) proposed that tolerable frustration, initially in the form of the absent breast, gives birth to the first thought, in the shape of a wish for the breast. If his hunger is always immediately met, there is no opportunity to have a thought about what is missing, only the experience of hunger followed by feeling sated. However, if the absence is intolerable, then the baby will be too preoccupied with his frustration to have the thought. A parent needs to allow just the right sort of gap at the right time. Luckily most will do this without any conscious awareness of how carefully attuned they are to their baby's stage of development and mood in a particular moment.

Language can bridge gaps. One person not knowing what the other is thinking is a spur to use language. A little benign neglect can create the space needed for certain kinds of development. Giving this space is important.

From parents . . .

> *'I use loads of language with my daughter, always describing what we are doing, putting words into context, the physical world, our feelings – everything. As a result her comprehension has always been amazing but she is still not*

> *talking. I think it's because she knows that I know what she's thinking. She knows she can point and grunt and I'll know just what she means.'*

While many mothers find themselves slowly but surely trusting that their baby can manage a little more frustration with time, others struggle to make a judgement. A father can often be the one to suggest the time might be right. Sometimes the demands of a growing family release a mother from too attentive a servitude to the baby.

From parents . . .

> *'Looking back it is quite funny to think about how the holy grail of the routine dominated life with the first child, then it becomes completely irrelevant with the second because of all the other demands – toddler's classes etc.'*

> *'Having never left my first child to cry or settle herself to sleep, when my son was born and needed feeding at her bedtime, she would scream blue murder. I would be in the next room feeding our son and crying my eyes out while my husband tried to comfort her. I thought this was evidence that her heart was breaking when I failed to go to her. I was really worried about how I was going to parent two children. I was then really shocked when, within a week, she was calling for her dad at night, not me.'*

In fact absence is a necessary part of any relationship (see Chapter 4). We talk about getting a look at something from a bit of distance, of 'getting things in perspective', and babies also need time away from a close relationship to get an emotional perspective on it. Appreciation too is sharpened in absence.

Twins and emerging selfhood

This is all so much more complicated when negotiating your relationship with two emerging persons. The mother of twins must balance her desire to treat each child the same; with her wish to allow individuality. This requires not only acknowledging differences in them but also allowing her attention to them to be responsive to their individual needs. It can feel an impossible task to provide an equitable experience whilst fostering individuality. All families with more than one child will face this dilemma, and the difficulty of intense rivalry between siblings for parental attention can lead to a split in the family. The children might take one parent each, as it were, and become possessively identified with that parent. For some parents a similar defensive split can happen, in their own minds. This allows the parent to experience all their loving feelings, undiluted by their mixed feelings, in relation to one child. Parents may then begin to feel that their negative feelings have been provoked by the more challenging child, rather than being an ordinary part of all relationships.

Developing a sense of others

In the early months, your baby is still pretty much egocentric. He sees his mother as being there for him. The phrase 'at home alone with the baby' is often used and contains an interesting paradox. A mother with her baby is not alone and yet the baby does not perceive the complexity and richness of who she is in the way an adult partner in an intimate and demanding relationship might, and his personality is still unfolding. In time he does start to perceive her more and more as her own person with feelings of her own, which he might take account of. He starts to see the effects of his actions on her and to have some concern for her. A simple example of this is the one we have described of the baby at the breast who has cut his first teeth. His pleasure in his ability to bite means that he is likely to have a nip at his mother's breast, by accident or not. At this stage, he is able to see that he has hurt her, that other people feel pain, and to be sorry about it, or upset if she is angry with him.

Another instance of having other people's needs in mind is the delightful game where a baby of nine months or so 'feeds' his mother or father from the spoon he has just learnt to hold. It is rewarding when your baby does this; it seems like his grateful wish to give something back for having been fed.

From psychoanalytic theory and clinical practice . . .

Creativity may be sparked off in the company of others, but often needs solitude to flourish. Winnicott has also written about the ability of a baby to be alone in the presence of the parent – that is to be able to play, or follow a train of thought, in the security of the parent's presence, but without having to check back at every moment on the parent's knowledge or approval of what he is doing.

How to be alone

One of the main tasks in becoming separate is how to be alone without being lonely. If a parent is always there, the baby may never have the opportunity to be in a room on her own, thinking her own thoughts. Many families don't have the luxury of space, but where possible, sometimes to be on one's own is an important experience.

The connection between physical and emotional development

As your baby begins to sit up unaided, he is literally in a different position in respect to the rest of his family. As a tiny baby he had to be helped to sit up, with his head specially supported. It is an entirely different way to view the world and your family if your own backbone is supporting you and if your head doesn't wobble. Previously, a bouncer chair may have allowed him to sit separately, looking on, but this is not the same as the achievement of sitting up independently. Similarly, when he is placed on the floor, he will be practising turning over, perhaps flexing his knees, and intentionally reaching out for objects.

When a baby is able to crawl, to stand up and then to walk, life has really changed. Babies need to practise these accomplishments over and over again. It can look obsessive to anyone watching but this is personal triumph and needs to be done in the context of a relationship. Your delight in seeing your baby start to crawl is part of the joy of the achievement.

As well as attaining motor development, babies at the latter part of the first year are feeding themselves, starting to talk and moving with intention to get what they want. The ways in which they can express themselves are increasing in every direction. All of this changes your baby's feeling about himself, and about his relation to others in the family.

Growing independence – leads to doubts

Soon the pleasure of crawling and walking includes moving away from the parent. Independence is at hand. However, a baby who crawls away from his parent needs to know they are there to come back to.

Babies who are practising moving away from their parents need their continued presence to return to. We see this again in

From psychoanalytic observation of parents and babies . . .

One nine-month-old crawled out of the kitchen into the living room. She turned back and her mother, who had only moved to the other side of the kitchen, was out of her sight. The baby wailed dismally, until mother called out to her and quickly came back into view.

adolescence when young people, in the first stages of leaving home, are affronted if their parents are out when they unexpectedly pop back for a visit. In fact teenagers when first staying out late probably rely on the idea of a parent at home worrying as their protection while they tackle the dangers of the outside world.

Independence and adventure bring a backlash of feelings of insecurity and babies who have always slept well may be more wakeful at this period, sometimes crying out in their sleep as though having bad dreams. They may refuse to let parents out of their sight, and we might guess that their own urge to move has made them worry that their parents are also anxious to escape. Of course, they may be partly right. Once the baby can manage to do more on his own, the tie between him and his mother and father lessens. As they feel he needs them less, they may have thoughts of taking on extra commitments in their own outside lives. Mothers can be surprised to find that although the baby can happily move away from her, he may panic if she moves away from him.

At this point you will be feeling a bit more separate from your baby, because he is able to start thinking about being separate from you. Paradoxically, he may make more fuss when you go out because he has a better idea that you as this person separate from him have left him. However, he is also better able to manage the time apart and to anticipate your return.

At about eight months, your baby may be upset just at the sight of a stranger coming near or even, embarrassingly, a close friend of yours whom he hasn't seen for a bit. This new anxiety does not mean that he has only just started to recognise you and tell the difference between you and other people – he has known you for a long time. It does mean that he has started to realise that you and he aren't stuck permanently together and he might worry about others getting between you and him. As his mind develops, he has more curiosity and is fascinated by what is new. Through this he has more anxiety as to who and what other people are about. You will often notice that he looks to you to check whether or not to approach the stranger, and will be guided by your reaction. He is learning to take clues from you about who is friendly and what is safe.

Giving your child the space to explore

Security and the ability to explore confidently come in the first place from being in the presence of attachment figures, the people he is closest to. Your baby needs to know that you are interested in what he is doing, and that you approve of it. Babies pick up their parents' anxieties very closely. As your baby starts to move about, to crawl and walk, he will frequently check with you for feedback on what he is doing. If you give him clear messages about what is safe and what is not, he will learn from this, and feel that you are able to protect him from danger. He will then start to get a feeling inside of how to keep himself safe and his own judgement about this will develop. It is important not to confuse him with too many messages that the world is a dangerous place. He needs to learn how to explore safely, not to be stopped from discovering. He will understand from your tone of voice and expression that it is dangerous to touch certain objects, such as electric sockets; if you use these vetoes sparingly, he will usually respect them. However, as a baby becomes mobile, it is necessary for parents to simplify their home and make it as safe as is feasible. He needs to be shown how to climb safely on furniture, not to be stopped from doing it. Always saying 'no' to a baby can crush their spirit of exploration.

It can feel as though your baby is no longer under your control – always on the move, making a noise or a mess, starting to be defiant, closing their lips if they don't like the food offered, waking up at night when previously they've been good sleepers, getting into everything or getting at them. A docile, grateful little baby has become their own person. This stage may be a delight but it can be a big shock for parents. Parents who have felt themselves to be beautifully in tune with their baby can feel very 'out of sync' now. Increasing independence sometimes coincides with the end of the weaning phase, mothers and babies losing their special relationship with each other. A mother may feel the baby is now part of the wider world, not just belonging to her, and both parents may have to grapple with the realisation that their baby now has a mind of his own. Exploring together with a parent is also important. Going out from home and coming back differentiates 'home' from 'outside world' and reinforces an idea of self in relation to the place and people he belongs to.

From parents . . .

> *'When we come back from our walk he looks up at the window of our flat. He knows it's his home.'*

Conscience

Babies at the end of the first year start to have a moral sense, a feeling of what is right and wrong, in relation to their parents. This moral sense goes along with the development of the baby's capacity for self-reflection. He gets to recognise his own states of mind through his parents' interest in them. He then progresses to realising that 'there are other minds out there' and he, in turn, can perceive his parents' states of mind. He starts to realise the effect you and he have on each other. It matters to him that you approve of him, and he will regulate his behaviour accordingly. Babies do have to experiment, both with what it feels like to do something, and also what your reaction will be. If your baby throws some food on the floor at the end of his meal, he is working out cause and effect on different levels, the laws of gravity and the rules of parents! You have the difficult task of working out the balance of encouraging self-expression and deciding when enough is enough.

This negotiation is the basis for many future workings-out of the balance between freedom and compliance. One major arena in the following year will be the beginnings of toilet-training. Success in this is a toddler's achievement of self-regulation, and wanting to please his parents. It need not be a matter of 'discipline'. It is a mistake to try to toilet-train a baby in their first year; they are too young to understand and give consent to the process. The time to toilet train is when a toddler can recognise their own bodily signs and has his own words or signals for needing to do a 'wee' or 'poo' because the control of bodily functions is matched by control over language.

Gender and identity

We have spoken about the importance of the fluidity of roles and functions in a family; the idea that it needn't be the father or even a man who complements the mother's role is familiar. Yet there is

a biological necessity for an actual male, or at least his sperm, at conception. The idea of a parent of each gender seems to persist in the minds of children, even when all their needs are being met by a single-sex family. Perhaps this has something to do with needing to know oneself in relation to each gender, in an intimate way, in order to know who one is, to have a fully rounded sense of self.

From lesbian parents . . .

> *'We are a lesbian couple and we adopted my partner's niece when she was taken into care due to her parents' drug and alcohol problems. She knows she has a tummy mummy and a daddy who we don't see because they're not well, then us – her two forever-mummies. My partner and I both noticed her watching a little girl playing with her daddy in the park and we felt it was important to acknowledge her interest in them. She has asked if she will see her own daddy when she's big. She is very curious about her uncle and has a really special bond with her grandfather.'*

Another lesbian couple had a baby through sperm donation and the process of choosing a donor raised interesting questions about the formation of identity. They had agreed that given the limited information offered on sperm donors, his age was probably most important because of improved chances of healthy sperm. Yet, they were both drawn towards an older donor who had said a few words about his motivation for donating sperm. They came to realise that they had not only his sperm in mind but an actual person who their unborn child might seek to make contact with at eighteen. They were confident that between them they could provide what their baby needed but they could still keep a space in mind for a child's wish to know their biological father. The business of genetic inheritance and how it impacts on emerging identity is also an issue when choosing a donor.

From lesbian parents . . .

> *'My partner had never wanted to carry or give birth but I guess I was conscious of her not getting to pass on her genes because I found myself wanting a donor with her colouring. She seemed totally uninterested in this at the time but I do think it is hard for her now when we see that our baby is starting to look like my mum, for example.'*

When family members note shared genetic characteristics, it is a sort of claiming which might underpin a baby's emerging sense of himself as belonging. However, these things are rarely straightforward. The mum quoted above was reassured to remember that another lesbian couple they know found that their baby looked like her biological mum but grew up to have her other mum's character. After all, identification is an ongoing process, much more complex and fluid than a simple looking-like the other and often has more to do with the roles taken up in the family.

From lesbian parents . . .

> *'My partner feels a much stronger impulse to thank our donor and more curiosity about his features and about whether our son has siblings through him. It is hard to know whether that is because he represents her contribution – the other half of the genes that aren't mine – or whether it is because I'm the stay-at-home, breastfeeding mum that she then identifies with him as "the father", the one in the other role.'*

Part III

THE WIDER WORLD

We started with the adage about it taking a village to raise a child. What constitutes a village in a modern global world and what a baby needs from that village is an infinitely complex subject. There is a conflict between, on the one hand, wanting to share your baby with the wider family and the outside world, and indeed your own need for some separation and childcare and, on the other hand, the opposing desire to protect your special intimacy with your baby.

14

WIDER FAMILY AND OTHER SUPPORT

Your baby belongs to a wider family than just her two parents. Your parents, siblings, aunts, uncles and cousins share her genes and are likely to claim her as one of theirs. She is affected by the relationship you have with your parents and the rest of the family. Her order of birth in the family will also be influential. A first-born baby will have a different view on family life than one with older siblings.

Your own parents

Much of the influence your parents will have on your baby flows through you. They pass their genes through you and you are likely to pass on certain traits and values that are recognisably of your family through generations. A recurring theme of this book is the profound effect your own experience of being parented has on how you bring up your children. This takes the shape of complex reactions to experiences rather than a straightforward inheritance. Your parents will also have a direct relationship with your baby. How you got on with them in the past will probably affect how you feel about them in this role. When things have gone well between you, having your parents seeing your new baby can be the best confirmation of your achievement. Their approval can feel like they are giving you and the baby their 'blessing'.

From parents . . .

> *'Being abroad, it was just the three of us after he was born. We were in a blissed-out bubble, but it saddened me not to be able to show my parents our perfect baby boy.'*

> *'My parents separated when I was four and my father and I have not been close. Yet when my children were born*

> *I had to take them half way round the world to him. I can't quite explain why but I needed him to see them and acknowledge them.'*

Different generations, different attitudes

New parents need to work out a new relationship with their own parents. The real test of being adult is if you can be separate and free-thinking when you are actually in the company of your parents. You are likely to have different ideas about parenting because styles change. With luck, your parents may also enjoy new ways of doing things, but you could find yourself as much in disagreement as you were over your teenage choice of music. You need to have the confidence that you are following what your baby tells you she needs. If you can trust yourself in this, and enjoy your baby's satisfaction when you get it right for her, you will be less interested in pursuing old battles with your parents. They may be able to acknowledge your newly developed expertise as parents. The more confident you feel, the more you may be able to think about and make constructive use of their advice.

Even when you are clear that you don't want to repeat certain things, you might find it hard to know exactly what you should be doing. Much of what you do in the throes of everyday interactions with your baby is informed by unconscious memories of your own experiences. Or, to put it another way, you cannot draw on experiences you did not have.

From parents . . .

> *'My mother was strict. "Because I say so", was all the explanation she offered. I want my daughter to feel she can negotiate boundaries and understand the decisions I have to take for her, but in the moment, when she's doing something she shouldn't, I can hear in my mind what I don't want to say but nothing else. It can leave me a bit wordless. I guess I do have some difficulty knowing what I think is OK.'*

> *'My family are not short on love but there is a fear that emotions could overwhelm, so a certain amount of emotional distance is kept, as a sort of precaution. I am determined to be more emotionally available to my children but I sometimes notice that I'm so busy thinking through*

how I want to respond to something that I am not present in the moment, inadvertently repeating the pattern.'

If you or your partner had an unhappy childhood, there will be concerns about letting your parents, as grandparents, do to your baby what they did to you. Any of the serious shortcomings in parenting that we have talked about can make you feel reluctant to let your parents have too much contact with your baby. Talking to a professional might help you sort out some of your feelings about this.

Sometimes parents have actually changed since their days of rearing babies and small children. They may have matured, or been able to get into better circumstances and have more to offer a baby now. You might feel quite bitter about this, or alternatively perhaps be able to enjoy watching your baby get more from them than you did.

Even if you got on pretty well with your parents, you may find they are different with your children from how they were with you. Because they don't have the responsibility of bringing them up, of exercising discipline, they may be much more indulgent now. It can seem that they have the freedom to give all the treats and you have to do all the limit-setting. It can be annoying to have to behave more sensibly than your parents!

Managing unexpected feelings in relation to your parents and your baby

Letting your parents and your children have a relationship with each other can be surprisingly difficult. All sorts of complicated feelings come in. One that you might not be expecting is that of being jealous of your own baby. 'What about me?' Many new mothers and fathers think when the grandparents make a bee-line for this precious addition to the family, 'Am I only there to answer the door?'

As a young adult you may have spent the last few years trying to escape your parents' attentions, but having a baby and being exposed to her dependency on you can stir up your own infantile longings to be looked after. So, just at the moment when you could do with some parenting yourself, you are ignored in favour of this little usurper. It can take you back to some of the jealousy and pain you had when your little brother or sister was born twenty-five years ago.

If your parents were very competent at looking after you as a child, and seem to be just as good now with your baby, you might end up feeling de-skilled or redundant. It can seem as though there is only room for one generation of parents, and if they are so good at it, you can't be; and of course the older generation can also be jealous of the new parent's generation – we are all vulnerable to such feelings. If you can trust your own skill, you may be able to use your parents' experience without feeling it detracts from your own.

From parents . . .

> *'At the beginning, before I'd found my groove, I could not take any advice from my mother. I remember taking the buggy down the steps in the most alarming lurching fashion because I would not tip it back on two wheels as she'd suggested (and everyone else does). The thing is that we agree on all the important emotional aspects of parenting so I guess I was just trying establish this as my territory now. I must have looked ridiculous though!'*

> *'I felt a mind-numbing rush of jealousy when I saw my mother-in-law with my newborn baby girl, I wanted to snatch her back and claim her as mine. I did not have a good relationship with my own mother, which is likely to have something to do with it but then it is complicated with my mother-in-law too. Our pregnancy was unplanned and we'd only been together a couple of months but we decided to make a go of it. She had had to give up her baby when she got pregnant out of wedlock as a young woman. Perhaps I was scared she would try to replace her lost baby with mine.'*

The temptation for either of you, mother or father, to become your own parents' 'child' again, preoccupied with old concerns and dynamics, can undermine the bond between you and your partner.

From parents . . .

> *'I was very glad of my mother's help when I had my baby but my husband got annoyed with her bossiness. I realised that we had been ganging-up together in a pleasurable female child-bearing bond, but that the effect was to freeze him out.'*

What grandparents offer

These are the difficulties; there are also the pleasures. Grandparents can feel like the most natural back-up to new parents; the ones who will drop everything to help you when you really need it, because you and your baby matter to them more than anything else. It is also necessary to get the balance right so that you don't impose on them; you may rather envy their freedom and feel they should be there whenever you need them. Aside from that, make the most of the help offered and enjoy it. Grandparents can help you get problems into perspective and take the heat out of the moment. Many new mothers have a fantasy when everything is too much, of walking out and leaving their baby. You are lucky if you have the reality of asking your own mother or mother-in-law to stand in for you for a few hours, to rescue you from feeling too trapped. Grandparents have probably come to the end of their own child-bearing years and can often offer an unselfish parenting to the new generation and take pleasure in doing it. Even at a distance grandparents are invaluable.

From parents . . .

> *'I rang my dad from Australia to tell him about our one-year-old son who was pulling all the books off the shelves. "What did you do when I was at that stage?" "I shouted at you," my dad joked. It's funny because he was such an indulgent father. It felt good to remember my childhood with him, and acknowledge that we are both fathers now.'*

The relation between grandparents and grandchildren is also important as the link between generations. Grandparents represent the past, grandchildren the future and the continuation of the family. You might enjoy seeing likeness between your baby and other relatives, feeling he belongs to a wider group. Your baby's intimacy with her grandparents now may develop into a very precious relationship later on where each can feel really valued by the other without the conflicts of the parent–child relationship. As the old joke goes: 'Grandparents and grandchildren are united by a common enemy.'

Grandparents and adoption

The love that you feel for a grandchild is almost tribal, because of the feeling that the grandchild is one of the family. Whilst many grandparents might feel similarly, these feelings can be a little more complicated when grandparents have adopted their child, and that child goes on to conceive a child. The feeling that the baby represents the continuation of a family line is rather altered, as the baby will not physically resemble the grandparents. Therefore, there may not be such a strong sense that grandparents have 'handed down' something to the future generation, even though the baby will have benefited from the parenting that the grandparents have 'handed down' to the parents. If the grandparents adopted their children because of fertility difficulties or pregnancy losses, the feelings of loss may then resurface as they witness their child growing a baby. The second and third generation will share a biological link and an experience of gestation and birth which excludes the first generation and reminds them of what they couldn't have. This can lead to worries about being excluded from their child and grandchild.

Some of these grandparents may struggle with feeling envious about their children's ability to grow a baby and give birth, and potentially to breastfeed the baby. For parents it can be hard to turn to the grandparent for support about these issues, both because they are not areas that their own parents have direct experience of, but perhaps also for fear of reminding the grandparent about their lack of experience. Parents may feel guilty that they have been able to conceive and carry a pregnancy to term, and this may generate anxiety about things going wrong, such as the child becoming ill. Additionally a parent who has been adopted may also now think about their own birth parent's decision to place him/her for adoption, or the circumstances that led to him/her being adopted. This may be very painful, as parents directly experience the love that they have for their own infant, and get in touch with the infant's helplessness. This may provoke parents into contacting their birth parents, or can lead to renewed feelings of anger and rejection in relation to the adoption. This can be complicated when the parent is trying to negotiate a new relationship with his/her partner and child and can result in the rejection being acted out within the new family unit. Therefore, it might be helpful to seek help about these issues at this time from a therapist if these feelings are bothering you.

Grandparents and disability

In *Loving Andrew*, Romy Wyllie writes about extended family coming to terms with a disabled baby being born to the family: 'Grandparents, especially have a harder time changing their thinking and adjusting their dreams than the parents themselves who have the daily activities and close intimacy to further the baby bonding' (2012: 40).

Adoption, disability and identity

From parents . . .

> *'I was adopted and did not know my birth parents. One of the things that really excited me about having a baby was the chance to have a member of the family with whom I would share a family resemblance. When she was born with Down's syndrome, this was one of the hopes that I had to mourn.'*

Your older children

If your baby is not your first, her experience of family life will be different. She will be born into a noisier and more eventful household than first babies usually are. How do you introduce her to her older brothers or sisters? Their lives have been changed as much as yours. They may easily see the benefits of having this new member of the family but it is likely that their reactions will be mixed. You may worry if your children are jealous – but in fact you could think of jealousy as being quite a positive emotion – they are letting you know that they have something to lose, that they value your attention and realise they will now have to share it. Some mothers feel that they would be being disloyal to their toddler if they allowed themselves to become preoccupied with their new baby. The dynamics become very complicated.

From parents . . .

> *'Our three-year-old had a radical suggestion: "Let's all eat the baby up and keep me."'*
>
> *'My two-year-old son became very accident-prone and he would almost always fall over just as I was picking up the baby.'*

> *'I have seen the best and the worst of my two-year-old daughter in relation to her baby sister. She can be so kind and thoughtful but sometimes the jealousy is so raw it distresses me. Despite the occasional attacks, the baby lives to be noticed by her sister.'*

If your children seem very jealous it's worth thinking about whether they are raking up some feelings from you about the difficulties of sharing. You might think about whether there's any connection with your childhood. Where do you come in the family? Did you feel you were replaced by a younger sibling? Or did you have to cope with an older one who resented you turning up? Talking about these memories with your partner or a friend can help get them into perspective. You might even be able to discuss them with your sister or brother.

Jealousy is normal and should be acknowledged and accepted but that does not mean children should be allowed to act aggressively towards the baby. They may be very relieved to be able to tell you how angry they are with you for having the baby, as with the baby for turning up, but talking about anger is one thing, acting on it is another. It is important for you to show that you are serious about protecting the baby and probably necessary to make sure that the baby is never left alone with a toddler until you see how everyone is settling down.

From parents . . .

> *'My toddler was watching TV, apparently quite happily, one afternoon. The baby was in his Moses basket at the other end of the room and I thought nothing of leaving the room to answer the phone. Suddenly I heard the baby scream in pain. I rushed into the room and my toddler was sitting calmly in front of the TV as before on the opposite side of the room to the screaming. When I went to the baby, however, there was the unmistakable mark of teeth around his little nose. Only then did I realise that the embers of hatred had been quietly burning, ready to ignite at the first opportunity. I felt sorry for both of them.'*

> *'I am told that as a toddler I took my infant brother from his cot onto the landing and held him over the banister. Thankfully I did not drop him but instead called out to my*

father. My father was not very involved in our care but probably was a figure of authority.'

Perhaps this toddler was asking for help with getting her jealousy and aggression under control.

From psychoanalytic theory and clinical practice . . .

Feeding a new baby may provoke jealousy or worry in older children, who often show signs of wanting to be babies themselves, keen to breastfeed or suck on a bottle. They can become angry and disruptive. One couple came to see me because their two-year-old son, John, was like this since his sister Marie had been born. They told me he was especially awful when Marie was being breastfed. Luckily it was time for a feed so I could see what they meant. John became noisy and upset, and touched the baby's head as if he were trying to pull her away from the breast. He asked, 'Why is the baby eating Mummy?' It struck me that he was not just worried about this idea but also about the intimacy of breastfeeding. I suggested that when they got home his mother should show him some photos of himself being breastfed as a baby and ask him to talk about his feelings. I also thought that exciting toys to play with, during the baby's feeds, could help to take his mind off feeding. When they came back two weeks later, his parents reported that John had calmed down considerably, relieved that his upset had been understood.

Toddlers may be quite pleased and excited with the new acquisition at first but then be dismayed to find it is there permanently. 'Can you send him back?' is a very frequent request. Toddlers may be happy to identify with parents, be a 'big boy or girl' and help care for the baby. They are likely, even so, to need to act like a baby themselves at times. It is frustrating for parents to find there are now two little babies in the house who need to be carried everywhere. It is quite usual for toddlers to regress, to behave as though they are younger, and perhaps to lose ground on toilet-training and need to go back to nappies for a bit. Seeing the attention that goes to the baby can make them feel left out, and think that parents really only care about little babies. Giving them some special 'babying' for a while usually works. They may even be able to joke about pretending to be a baby. This beginning time of having a second baby often seems as though there is too much to cope with. Gradually it is actually likely to become easier than just having one. Each child with their own character brings out different responses in their parents. The emotions in the family can have more variety and be less intensely channelled. Children also can be supportive of each other and band together as recipients of their parents' attentions! A baby's development can be stimulated by wanting to join in with his older siblings. It has also been shown that older children benefit from adapting to the demands of communicating with a younger sibling, often using that sing-song 'parentese' way of speaking. It is thought that the most cognitively and socially stimulating part is having to think themselves into the shoes of the younger sibling, to imagine what they must be making of a given situation according to their limited knowledge of the world. Getting good at this sort of perspective-taking confers all sorts of benefits on the older children which they make use of in their lives beyond the realm of the family too.

Stepfamilies

These days many mothers or fathers are having their first baby with a partner who has already had children by a previous marriage. How do you cope with the feelings about this? It is really important that the 'experienced' parent remembers their own anxieties and does not get impatient with their partner for their uncertainties now. To have one experienced parent around can be a great confidence booster, but it can also be difficult – the new parent feeling that the other one already knows better than he or she can. There are bound to be moments of jealousy, of knowing that the partner has already shared this precious time with their previous partner, so the mutual discovery of becoming parents cannot take place together.

If one partner already has children, this is the time to include them as much as possible. This is easier said than done. Parents of a new baby can find it difficult to include their own older children in their attention and help them manage their jealousy of their younger sibling. It is even harder to do this with your stepchildren, especially when they may already be jealous of you with their father or mother.

However, this is the big chance to help reconstituted families move along in growing closer. The new baby, who is the half-sibling of the other children, may be a great force in 'bonding' the new family constellation. He or she is related by blood to all of you. Whether he or she is resented or loved by the older children will partly be influenced by how generously you are able to share the baby with them. One of the difficulties at this point can be mothers feeling that life would be simpler if the father made a 'fresh start' and concentrated on you and your baby, and less on his older children. It is important to get this in perspective. If he opted for the simplicity of this, you would have bought his attention at a very high price – the impoverishment of him as a father who sticks by his children.

From parents . . .

> *'My husband's daughters are heading into their teens and they're lovely with our new twins. It does feel like we can pull even closer together over these little shared blood relatives. I'm also grateful, particularly with twins, that I don't have to wait for him to be broken in. He is already an experienced father and has no existential crisis to get over. He knows just what needs to be done and he gets on with it.'*

Friends

Your friendships are likely to undergo changes. You may find that you get closer to old friends who have children and you are likely to make new friends through meeting other parents in your area but you are also likely to find some friendships receding. Most mothers feel that it is impossible to commit the time and energy they once had for friendships with their childless friends. Some friendships can survive this and evolve into something new. Some friendships may suffer because you just don't have the same interests any more. Kate Figes writes with great honesty and humour about the impact of having a baby on friendships and social life in her baby book *Life after Birth*. She notes that:

> Even girlie chats over a cup of tea become difficult because only the most saintly childless girlfriend doesn't get insulted when you have to break off mid sentence in order to tend to the needs of your child. When you return to talk to her, the topic has moved on, and rarely do you get to discuss one subject in depth without interruption until it is resolved.
> (2008: 214)

From parents . . .

> *'I was determined not to become a baby-bore with my childless friends. With a young baby it was fine because they were interested in cooing and admiring for a while and then we could get on to more adult topics. As baby got older and then baby number two came along it got harder and harder to give everyone the attention and consideration I wanted to. I felt envious and left behind as childless friends started to invest in other friendships more, although I knew that it was me who had withdrawn first.'*

> *'Being at home with children, I've got to know my neighbours, all the other families in the street and even the postman and the park keeper and the shop keepers. Although at the beginning I felt isolated, I now feel much more plugged in to my community than I had before.'*

> *'When I need to let off steam about how awful it can be at times only another mum friend will do. Friends who don't have kids don't get it and my mum wants to fix it for me. I know she really means well but I don't want to be told that I need to try some other strategy. I just want someone to listen and know what I mean.'*

For some families a community of friends is vitally important. One lesbian couple spoke of their appreciation of having other gay families around who were dealing with similar issues but they were also thinking about the importance of this community to their children in the future.

From parents . . .

> *'I know that there will be a time, when the kids are older, that they will be really resentful and angry about having gay parents but it reassures me to know that they will all be able to get together and bitch about it together in a supportive environment.'*

Back-up for parents

Parenting is probably the most rewarding and the most difficult role you will ever take on. You will need, and deserve, support. Parents need to feel someone is behind them. If you can get that support from each other and from your own parents, or from friends and professionals, you are fortunate.

Handling criticism

At this vulnerable moment in your lives, interventions from outside your own new family can feel to be intrusive. You suddenly find yourself exposed to all sorts of 'advice' and 'expertise'. Some people take the offering of advice as a sign that they are not succeeding as parents. Parents often feel criticised, and they can be easy targets.

One stimulus for criticism may be envy; the older generation criticising the younger one who are going through the passions of family life. The more immersed in it they are, the more left out the older generation may feel. This can include professionals just as much as family members.

From parents . . .

> *'I found that the "advice" I was given most frequently seemed pretty innocuous at first: "Oh, they grow so fast, you must make the most of it" or "she won't be a baby long, enjoy it while you can". But soon these comments began to grate. While I could see how fast she was changing and understood in some abstract way that time was going fast, it could also drag. I began to feel guilty. Why wasn't every moment with her unadulterated bliss?'*

Perhaps the wistful comments of the experienced spoke of their own regret that it had not been possible for them to enjoy every moment of parenthood.

From parents . . .

> *'I remember feeling attacked when people offered advice but it wasn't only me being defensive. Things can get quite charged because the person offering advice might need you to affirm the decisions they made and can't go back and change. Others invest your choices with the power to allay their doubts. Sometimes it is the advice giver who feels accused if you do not do as they have done.'*

You may feel criticised for going out to work or for staying at home, for choosing to bottle-feed or to breastfeed, for having your baby sleep with you or alone in a cot, for being a teenage parent or an older one. You need, however, to think about what the criticism means to you. Too much can indeed 'get to you' and lead to low self-esteem and sway your confidence. But have you let yourself get into a one-sided view about any of the important issues, so that any statement of the other side of things feels intrusive?

It is a subtle matter to examine whether you actually see any advice as judgemental. When you are a new parent struggling to get it right, any suggestion can feel like the last straw; there you are trying to sort something out between you and your baby, and the health visitor or your mother confuse you with yet another idea! If you are in this frame of mind already, they can make you doubt your own judgement. There is an art in finding a balance, of trusting your own instincts with your baby but letting yourself entertain other people's views. Although the stakes are high and anxiety builds quickly in new parents, it is helpful if you can hold on to the pleasure of arguing round a problem. If you can bear with the anxiety of not knowing, of not yet being sure what is best, you will not get entrenched. Being entrenched hampers your critical faculty as much as letting yourself be told what to do.

From psychoanalytic theory and clinical practice . . .

When I see families about problems such as sleep, they often tell me that they have 'tried everything'. They and their baby have become more and more confused, and can't remember what works and what doesn't. Some parents feel so unsure of themselves that they will take up any new idea from a helpful outsider.

The most serious aspect of feeling criticised is that if you let someone else do all the criticising, you can end up not having the capacity to reflect on yourself at all. This can happen if, say, a baby is failing to gain weight. Parents can become so worried that, paradoxically, they can't deal with the worry and feel they are being unfairly 'got at' by the health professionals. Instead of getting together about the problem, all concerned might start arguing about whether or not the measurements are correct.

New parents do need concern from someone outside, and a validation as to whether they are doing a good job as parents.

If you feel responded to in this way, it is easier to face any real worries about the baby. If you just feel criticised, you may shrug off the worries or even blame the baby for them.

One effect of being short of confidence yourself is feeling that your baby is also blaming you. If she won't stop crying, it is easy to feel like that. It's important to remember she is complaining to you, not about you. The more you let yourself get close to the baby and let her show you that she recognises you or perhaps smiles at you, the better you may feel about yourself as a parent. You may then find a way of being mutually co-operative with your baby so that you can each appreciate the other.

Sources of advice and help

Baby clinics

In the UK there is the superb system of family health clinics, popularly called 'baby clinics', often now taking place in a general practice. These clinics are usually run weekly, with health visitors and doctors available to see babies and their parents on a drop-in basis. There are developmental checks at fixed ages, but the aim of this service is for health visitors to see families informally to discuss the baby's progress, and any worries that parents have. There can be specific problems such as feeding or sleeping, or more nebulous ones like a worry about making a relationship; bonding with your baby. There is now much evidence that talking to your health visitor or other professional about your worries can help you get going with your baby. It is especially important if you are suffering from post-natal depression to have this opportunity. If you had a difficult birth, talking about what it was like and what you felt about it can help you recover. You may in fact find that you have to tell this story more than once, especially if it has affected how you feel about your baby.

Your health visitor will do a 'new-birth' visit at your home at ten days, when the midwife stops being responsible for you. You may already have met her ante-natally but this first meeting after the birth is often a memorable one. It is really important for fathers to be present so that you all get to know each other.

In most baby clinics the weighing scales have pride of place. They are a useful focus for thinking about how your baby is doing, although you can probably tell that from your own common sense anyway. However, if your baby is growing well, it can be nice to have it confirmed, and if she is putting on too much or too little weight, the measurements give you a baseline for talking about the problems with your health visitor. It is important to remember they are not going to blame you. They are there for you and your baby.

If you are not feeling confident, you can feel very exposed in the baby clinic. You can feel judged by the professionals and all the other mothers can seem to be so much more competent. Babies often tremble as they are undressed to be weighed or examined, not so much from the cold, as from a feeling that they have lost the protection of the clothes that 'hold them together'. I think mothers can feel almost as exposed as their babies. Baby clinics can also be an opportunity for reassuring parents that everything is fine.

From parents . . .

> *'I remember being all thumbs as I clumsily put my baby's nappy back on and thinking that everyone would see what a bad mother I was.'*

> *'After a year or so the health visitor told me that, although I was very welcome to carry on bringing her in once a fortnight, I didn't have to. I was rather embarrassed when I realised that although we didn't need them for anything in particular, I had come to enjoy the routine of bringing her in and having her progress discussed.'*

Perhaps both mother and health visitor underestimated the value of these routine visits. They may have had an important role in the mother's capacity to look after her baby.

Immunisations

Your health visitor and GP share in the responsibility for protecting the population as a whole from serious infectious diseases. In order to control diseases and prevent epidemics, the majority of babies need to be immunised. Professionals will, of course, also respect your family's particular medical history or particular beliefs or anxieties. This may be the first arena in which you have to consider your baby's welfare in a wider context.

It can be very difficult to take your baby to be immunised. Any fears of your own about needles are intensified at the thought of this happening to your little baby. Holding her as steadily as you are able, do try to tell her, just in a couple of words, what is going to happen. Although she cannot understand your words, it is part of the pattern that will build up in her mind – that you are there to prepare her and help her deal with unpleasant experiences. She will probably cry at the prick and may go on crying for a little time afterwards. This crying is akin to telling you what it was like. You can actually think of this positively, that she is crying *to you* because you are there to hold her and listen to her. It is one of the first 'grown-up' decisions you have had to make on her behalf, that something painful and with a (very small) risk factor protects her from worse harm.

After immunisation, a few babies may have a reaction that might include a high temperature. Very occasionally, there are serious reactions to an immunisation. Although these are rare, the waiting time after the immunisation until all is clear can be quite an ordeal.

It is vital that a baby is never given an injection while asleep. This is a real betrayal, the awakening is traumatic, and it takes away from her the ability to start to prepare herself and understand the situation, including that you were consenting on her behalf.

Baby books

Reading books can be helpful and supportive (as we hope this one is!). They can be a source of essential factual information, and can put into words what you are observing about your baby, what your worries are, and how to find solutions. You can read them quietly, and take things in, in your own time.

The limitation is that you can't have a conversation with the writer. You can argue with them in your mind but you can't ask them what they mean, and they can't ask you what lies behind your questions, in the way that your doctor or other health professional might. So the problem with reading books that give advice is whether you take in and use only the sort of advice that fits in with whatever you are already doing, or whether you are released to try something different.

Books that give very specific advice, for instance on how to get children to sleep better, may rescue some parents from a feeling of not knowing what to do and make both parents and baby feel safer, with someone in charge. The danger could be if someone unaware of the communication in their baby's crying uses this as an excuse to concentrate on stopping the crying without ever having understood its meaning.

Advice from professionals

Advice on bringing up children has always swung from one extreme to another: no one is obliged to take it. Getting your doctor or health visitor to give you advice can be a way of getting them to take the responsibility for ideas you have but don't want to own. For instance, getting a professional to recommend leaving a baby to cry can be a way of not owning to a cruel part of oneself, or to the worries that this could be a cruel way of dealing with the baby. Sometimes parents who can't set limits themselves do need help in being firmer, but need first of all to put into words the feelings evoked by their baby crying, and then to talk about their fears of, perhaps, being violent towards their children. Talking about firmness is only helpful in the context of the professional knowing about these very real fears.

This is the sort of moment when parents may be able to tell someone about their own childhood. Children may have difficulty knowing whether their parents have behaved cruelly to them or not. They have neither the experience nor the objectivity to evaluate it. It can take much effort in later life to sort this out and, when you have a baby yourself, this may be the time when you can manage it.

Advice works best in the context of a relationship – when you have the feeling that you and the professional know each other. You need a GP and health visitor whom you can get to know and trust. It works much better to have your own named health visitor – not just one of a 'pool'. She is then able to keep you in mind between your visits to the clinic, and you will feel better looked after if you have a known person to ring up when you are worried. If your clinic doesn't run in that way, you could ask why not. How you feel towards them will of course depend on their own personalities and competence. It may also depend on relationships you had in the past, and whether you have had people you could rely on at important moments. How they treat you will, in turn, be affected by your attitude to them; if you are dismissive of them or distrustful, it can make it harder for them to be helpful – health visitors are human too.

15

TO WORK OR NOT TO WORK

Financial worries or fears of job loss conspire to drive many women to an early return to work. Some women find their self-esteem needs validating through work, and fear losing their identity. However, the early weeks of babyhood are precious, and you may find it difficult to enjoy them fully if you are anticipating the imminent separation of returning to work.

Timing is all-important

It does make a difference at what point during the first year you go back. This is to do with the stages of separation – biological and emotional – between mother and baby, not to do with any moral point. Going back early can be a real wrench for both mother and baby but it's not just a case of gritting your teeth and being brave. You risk losing out on irreplaceable time and an effective way of creating a strong attachment that makes for healthy separation later on.

At three months, mother and baby are still in the exciting stages of exchanging smiles, looks and sounds. As his mother gazes enraptured at him, the baby sees himself mirrored in her expression. He learns about emotions, he feels his communications are valued. Of course, he does not need this interaction all the time, nor does the mother, but if she has to go out to work at this stage, they cannot *choose* when to be involved, and when to have a rest from each other.

Six months is a time when babies are able to feel more separate from their mothers – sitting up, they can watch her across the room. They have more of an idea of coming and going; they will be eating some of their food from a spoon or holding finger-food so that feeding is a less intimate process than for the three-month-old baby needing to be cuddled as he sucks.

At a year a child has some language, words in which to say goodbye and greet his mother on her return. These words are also a sign that he is mastering the idea of her coming and going. Older babies of this age make more fuss when mothers go out than do tiny babies. Some parents feel this means that the younger a baby gets used to his mother's absence, the easier it is for him. In fact it seems that having been able to take his mother's presence for granted in the early months helps a baby have a more secure relationship to her and thus helps him manage her absence better later. The protest he makes when his mother goes out is his right, and a sign that he notices whether she is there or not, even if he can do without her.

There are many practical aspects to deciding whether or not to return to work, but the emotional ones are key. Timing is a crucial factor. Try not to feel pressurised by your employers to make the decision before you've had your baby. You may well feel different once you are away from work and particularly after the birth. You may find that if you could, you would choose to stay with the baby but find that you have already locked yourself into returning. Plans made beforehand are unfairly weighted towards work as even a pregnant woman cannot know what she will feel when she has had her baby.

From parents . . .

> *'I just had no idea, until after the baby was born, how strongly I would feel about just being with her.'*

> *'I managed to negotiate having my job kept open for a year but I only did it because I thought it was the right thing for my baby. It wasn't until he was born that I realised how much I would want to be with him.'*

> *'Before having the baby I was a career woman, running my own department. That's all gone now. I don't know if I could be that person now. I would only have had to go back to work for three months at full time to be in a position to negotiate my old job on a part-time basis. But I couldn't do it. When I did go back later, taking a more junior part-time post for a short time, I had to work under the boy who had got himself my job as maternity cover and was still in post despite being incompetent. That was hard to swallow. I don't regret it though; it was worth it to be with our son.*

Also, my husband and I are now writing a play together, which we would not have been able to do if I had gone back to my old job.'

Make the most of your maternity leave

From research on the impact on maternity leave of early return to work . . .

One of the most important discoveries by America's best-known paediatrician, Dr Brazelton, is that when pregnant mothers commit themselves to return to work before three months, this seriously affects their thinking about the future baby as a person or themselves as parents. They talk instead about the concrete problems of timetables and finding substitute care for the baby. He suggests that they are already defending themselves against too intense an attachment, because of the pain of separating prematurely from the new baby. He implies that the impending return to work robs parents and baby of some intimacy ahead of the actual separation.

From psychoanalytic theory and clinical practice . . .

Several mothers have told me that the prospect of going back to work has broken into their experience of the early weeks, even when they were actually able to be full-time with their babies at the beginning. They have told me that it has interfered with getting breastfeeding going. The separation to come has confused the rhythms between them and the baby. Similarly when a mother does go back to work, one of the greatest stresses is losing the freedom to tune in to the baby's sleep rhythms rather than having to also be subject to the alarm clock. Mother and baby have the problem of working out a sleep–wake rhythm with limited time available for them to do it.

The need to return to work

When a separation for external reasons looms, mothers often seem unable to understand the normal phases of needing to be close, and then to move apart that they and the baby might otherwise naturally have. It feels as though only the job takes them away and not the normal process of separation, and preparation for being apart seems too difficult. However, it is important to add that some mothers cannot happily settle into this time at home with their baby. Feeling trapped with the intense dependency needs of a baby can be very uncomfortable. You might decide that you can be a better mother by letting someone else attend to these daily needs, and that you come back to your baby more fulfilled yourself, and with more to offer the baby. But don't assume that it will be this way for you: give yourself the chance to find out.

From parents . . .

> *'After I went back to work he got quite clingy and I felt annoyed. It had been just him and me for a whole year and now I felt: "Look, you, I've done my time, now I want to get some of my life back." Of course I thought about it from his perspective too, and I knew that he was missing me but for a couple of months it was like I had to swing the other way. In retrospect I can see that I sort of had to in order to make the separation but I can also see that there was something a bit savage about the cutting of those ties.'*

It seems likely that maternal ambivalence plays a large but silent role in decisions around returning to work and use of childcare. Perhaps part of the motivation to return to work is to side-step an important part of the process of 'gentle disillusionment', the getting bored, disengaging and re-engaging, and dealing with the feelings of glee and guilt as one disentangles oneself. If you are able to build respect for yourself as an ordinarily flawed parent, you might find the role more rewarding and feel less inclined to hand over to the 'experts'. When you do come to hand your baby or child over to someone else to care for, accepting that those looking after children all day will have good and bad feelings about it also helps to keep expectations of carers realistic and relationships between the adults open and honest.

Choosing a carer

Decisions about what work and how many hours are often made according to what childcare is available and affordable.

From parents . . .

> *'Now that my youngest is one I would love to do some freelance work, and it is out there but I can't arrange childcare on an ad-hoc basis so I have to let it pass me by.'*

If parents can share the care themselves, or if grandparents are available, this may well be best for some families. Some fathers are exhilarated by working out how to have some time at home with this special responsibility for their babies.

From parents . . .

> *'My wife has gone back part time which means I can now work four days a week and have the children myself one day.'*
>
> *'I am lucky. I can leave him with my parents. Their eyes light up when they greet him. He knows they look forward to him coming.'*

If it means someone outside the family, how do you choose? Little babies are probably better off in a quiet place with one carer – but that person needs to have as much support, other adults to talk to, and interesting places to go to, as a mother at home would need. A childminder or nanny stuck at home with someone else's baby may find herself counting the hours till the mother comes home, and be equally prone to the depression that the mother may be escaping. Some parents also find it hard to let their children make real bonds with carers outside the family.

From parents . . .

> *'I know that individual care is thought better than group care but at the time I had to make the decision I was haunted by an irrational fear I could not get out of my head. I thought that if I left her with an individual, she might run off with my baby.'*

This mother was asked if perhaps her fantasy was an extreme manifestation of the more rational fear that her daughter might make an attachment, which would in some way 'take her away' emotionally. She agreed that it probably was and went on to explain that in the end they moved to a cheaper area so that she could give up work and take her daughter out of nursery. She added: 'I thought I had to work, but in reality we did have a choice.'

A day nursery can be a confusing place for a tiny baby – he doesn't need too much sociability yet. However, a nursery with good morale can be a supportive place for a carer to work in, with colleagues to chat to, as well as the baby. How do you know a good nursery? One that will let you observe for several hours before you make your decision is one that recognises the significance of your feelings about your child's care. Little babies should have one main carer who can make a real relationship with him or her. You need to see whether the carers are really able to get close to the babies and children, or whether they feed or change nappies without making enough contact. You need to see whether the person in charge treats the staff with respect. You need to assess the emotional atmosphere. In fact, do you feel mothered when you sit and watch?

It is easy to be critical of whoever cares for your child in your place. This can often be a displaced self-criticism for not being there looking after the child yourself – many childminders are found fault with unjustly. Or you can feel that she is an expert, critical of you for abandoning your baby, especially if you are feeling that your work is more important or more skilled than looking after a baby. You may have had to hype yourself up to leave the baby and also

> **From research on childcare decisions . . .**
>
> Most parents surveyed claim high satisfaction with the childcare they have. However, a study comparing what parents said would be their ideal childcare choice at three months with the childcare they actually had at nine months showed that most had not got the childcare they thought they wanted. Penelope Leach suggests that: 'expressed childcare ideals are largely rationalisations of personal situations and childcare "choice" could be for some families a misnomer as they have not as much control over what kind of childcare they use as they would like' (2009: 21).

had to dress smartly for work. These clothes can in themselves make you look rather unapproachable, and out of tune with casually dressed nursery nurses or childminders.

The ongoing process of individuation, of becoming a separate self, is complex. It involves exciting gains in development and painful losses too, for both baby and parents. As parents re-enter the world of work, the highly emotionally charged task of moving towards independence must now be played out between child, parent and carer. This three-way relationship is bound to be messy and intimate, also fraught at times. Yet, the relationship must also be professional if it is paid work. In short, decisions about childcare are tremendously important and complex, requiring difficult and honest reflection on your own feelings about it. Sadly, it seems that thinking about these decisions is often incongruent.

Successful separations

Parents leaving their baby for the day need to think about how they manage the separation in the morning, and the coming-together later on. You need to think about how you say goodbye. Most babies appreciate the honesty of letting them know you are going, reassuring them that you will be back and then leaving. (Anxious hovering upsets everyone.) Your baby will probably cry – this means that she cares about you and minds you going. She may, however, settle down happily with her minder when you have left. It would be far worse if it did not matter to her whether you go out or not. Having said that, some babies do seem to be provoked into being very upset by big goodbyes. Slipping away quietly may even sometimes be best. One child asked her mother on the fourth day of nursery if she would mind very much if she didn't cry this morning! You can find the way that works for you and your baby.

Working parents with babies who are sleeping badly do sometimes realise that trying to slip away without saying anything, 'so as not to upset her', may be exacerbating the problem. If you do 'just slip out', she may not be sure when to expect you to be there or when not. This may leave her feeling insecure and at night make it harder for her to relax into sleep. One common reason for babies of working parents having less sleep is that both parents and babies do need a substantial amount of time together after the working day apart.

As well as partings being important, the coming together in the evening is also important.

From parents . . .

> *'When I collect her from the childminder's she beams at me before she remembers how furious she was with me for leaving, and then she cries. Her tears are as bitter as her smile was joyful.'*

Other babies may be more guarded in their response:

From a nanny . . .

> *'Most of my charges have had a similar response to their returning parents at the end of the day. One eight-month-old knew the sound of the car on the drive and would look up and about the room excitedly, taking short breaths and blinking fast. However, by the time her mother entered the room she had composed herself, taken up a rattle or something and would be studiously exploring its features. Her mother would be welcomed with a cursory glance before she returned her attention to the toy. She did not appear indignant or rejecting and responded to her mother's embrace when it came but she had affected a relaxed indifference, which was persuasive and painful to her mother. Yet, it also perpetuated a family myth: if the reunion is a non-event, then the separation cannot have caused any pain.'*

This is not to say that the mother should not have worked or that the childcare was not adequate. Indeed, the carer was very sensitive and thoughtful and probably did much to contain the feelings of both mother and baby. What we hope to highlight is the importance of acknowledging and dealing with the difficulties of separation.

However your baby deals with reunion, you need time for a kind of reconciliation. A day apart is a long time for a baby. You need to save enough energy for this time of getting together, perhaps sharing a bit of relaxation time before tackling the evening's chores. If a mother has used all her energy at work, it can feel to a baby as though all her interest and excitement is in her world out there and that there is nothing left for him.

Does working lead to less incidence of post-natal depression in mothers? Researchers seem to have conflicting results. Some women find their self-esteem needs the validation of work outside the home, others that the opportunity to discover the world through their baby's development, and the relationship between them, is an enhancement of their own mental state. However, a warning note comes from health professionals who have noticed an unusual amount of illness in mothers who go back to work early. It does seem that premature separation has physical as well as emotional repercussions. It is likely that the need to get into a more highly focused state of thinking, and pressured interactions with people, necessary in many jobs, is in conflict with the biologically adaptive state of attunement to a baby's signals. The stress of this mismatch can affect the immune system. The shortage of sleep that some mothers have, because of their need to stay awake with their baby, to make up for the separation of the day, can also cause problems with the immune system.

Part-time work

Qualities that many mothers at home with their babies develop are flexibility and the ability to do several things at once – both very useful in any job. Negotiating working part time is one of the most successful ways in which mothers can have both the outside stimulation of work, and the pleasures of being with their children.

From parents . . .

> *'Initially I thought I would be a stay-at-home mum for the first few years, both our mothers did and I know there are*

> *lots of benefits but I just got bored. I was much more able to enjoy him on the other four days once I was back at work part time. I just felt such relief – ahh, I'm back. You are not so frustrated and tired, you are you again, which has got to be good for them too.'*

The issues around working and babies will be different for each family. As with all the issues discussed in this book, honest reflection and acknowledgement of the feelings being aroused will help you to make the right decision for your family, assuming you have choice. If you don't have much choice, then being thoughtful about the impact on you and your baby will help to protect you both from any potential ill effects.

End of our journey: baby's first birthday

Getting through the first year of a baby's life is a wonderful achievement. Most parents feel fortunate that their baby has survived this year, and now the sense of a new baby's vulnerability is well behind them. You will have survived the momentous changes in you and your life and are likely to feel on steadier ground.

A baby launched into the second year will be at the beginnings of walking, talking and feeding herself. She is on the move, climbing the stairs, into all the family's cupboards, able to go and get the object she wants. She will be teasing, full of passions, both reacting to her family and initiating, making things happen. She will be learning the 'rules' of what is allowed, of what is frowned on or dangerous. She will have a strong sense of her own self and may be saying her own name as well as other family names. She will be starting to understand the family routines and feel herself part of them, and perhaps be able to anticipate the next event in the day. She will be able to greet people and say goodbye and understand more than she can express in language. She will be watching her parents and others and getting an idea of the purpose of what they do by imitating some of their actions. At a year a baby has developed in body and mind. The babies who feel sure of themselves are those who have been appreciated by their parents.

We hope that you have also felt appreciated – by your baby, your families and the wider community – perhaps even by the comments in this book. We hope we have helped your confidence grow and encouraged you to face the inevitable difficulties that are part of this first year with your baby. We have commented on how normal it is to have negative feelings as well as positive ones about your baby. What we know is that these feelings are only really a threat to your baby when they are denied and pushed down. If you can be generous enough with yourself to accept these feelings, then you will be protecting your baby from any potential ill effects. We think that this 'warts and all' approach to parenting is more helpful than bland reassurance. We have also tried to show how much you can learn from observing your baby – it releases your instincts, which we have encouraged you to trust. We hope we have also made it clear that you only have to be a 'good enough' parent.

RECOMMENDED READING

Understanding babies and their behaviour

Brazelton, B. T., revised with Sparrow, J. D. (2006) *Touchpoints: Birth to Three – Your Child's Emotional and Behavioral Development*, 2nd edn, Cambridge, MA: Da Capo Press.

Brazelton, T. and Cramer, B. G. (1990) *The Earliest Relationship*, Reading, MA: Perseus Press.

Gerhardt, S. (2004) *Why Love Matters: How Affection Shapes a Baby's Brain*, Hove: Routledge.

Murray, L. (2014) *The Psychology of Babies*, London: Robinson.

Murray, L. and Cooper, P. (1999) *Postpartum Depression and Child Development*, London: Guilford Press.

Music, G. (2011) *Nurturing Natures, Attachment and Children's Emotional, Socio-cultural and Brain Development*, Hove: Psychology Press.

Nugent, K. J. et al. (2007) *Understanding Newborn Behavior and Early Relationships: The Newborn Behavioral Observations (NBO) System Handbook*, Baltimore: Brookes Publishing Co.

Reddy, V. (2008) *How Infants Know Minds*, New York: Harvard University Press.

Stern, D. (1985) *The Interpersonal World of the Infant*, New York: Basic.

Winnicott, D. W. (1964) *The Child, the Family and the Outside World*, London: Pelican.

Parenting support

Boswell, S. (2004) *Understanding Your Baby*, London: Jessica Kingsley Publishers.

Bradley, E. and Emanuel, L. (eds) (2008) *What Can the Matter Be? Therapeutic Interventions with Parents, Infants and Young Children*, London: Karnac, Tavistock Series.

Daws, D. (1993) *Through the Night: Helping Parents with Sleepless Infants*, London: Free Association Books.

Grace, A. (2007) *Gentle Sleep Solutions: Teach Yourself*, Abingdon: BookPoint. Google Andrea Grace to view short films.
Leach, P. (2010) *The Essential First Year: What Babies Need Parents to Know*, London: Dorling Kindersley.
Miller, L. (1992) *Understanding your Baby*, London: Rosendale Press.
Phillips, A. (1999) *Saying No: Why It's Important for You and Your Child*, London: Faber and Faber.
Stadlen, N. (2004) *What Mothers Do: Especially When it Looks Like Nothing*, London: Piatkus Books.

Fertility treatment

Rayner, S. (2012) *The Two Week Wait*, London: Picador/MacMillan Publishers. (A moving novel by Dilys' stepdaughter.)

Premature babies

Cohen, M. (2003) *Sent Before My Time: A Child Psychotherapist's View of Life on a NICU*, London: Karnac Books.
Jepson, J. (2006) *Born Too Early*, London: Karnac Books.
Murkoff, H. with Mazel, S. (2010) *What to Expect: The First Year*, 2nd edn, London: Simon & Schuster.

Disability

Bartram, P. (2007) *Understanding Your Child with Special Needs*, Tavistock Clinic Series. London: Jessica Kingsley Publishers.
Wyllie, R. (2012) *Loving Andrew: A fifty-two-year story of Down's Syndrome*, North Charlston, SC: CreateSpace independent publishing platform.

REFERENCES

Ainsworth, M. D. S. (1985) 'Patterns of Infant–mother attachment', *Bulletin of the New York Academy of Medicine*, 61: 771–791.

Ayers, S., Eagle, A. and Waring, H. (2006) 'The effects of childbirth-related post-traumatic stress disorder on women and their relationships: A qualitative study', *Psychology, Health & Medicine*, 11 (4): 389–398.

Baradon, T., ed. (2005) *The Practice of Psychoanalytic Parent Infant Psychotherapy: Claiming the Baby*, London: Routledge.

Bates, J. (1989) 'Concepts and measures of temperament', in Kohnstamm, G. A., Bates, J. E. and Rothbart, M. K. (eds), *Temperament in Childhood*, Chichester, UK: Wiley, pp. 321–355.

Bell, S. H. and Ainsworth, M. D. S. (1972) 'Infant crying and maternal responsiveness', *Child Development*, 43: 1171–1190.

Bion, W. R. (1956) 'Development of schizophrenic thought', *International Journal of Psyschoanalysis*, 37: 344–346; republished as W. R. Bion (1967) *Second Thoughts*. London: Karnac, pp. 36–43.

Bion, W. R. (1962) *Learning from Experience*, Lanham, MD: Rowman and Littlefield Publishers.

Bowlby, J. (1944) 'Forty-four juvenile thieves: Their character and their home', reprinted in *Attachment and Loss. Vol. 1: Attachment*, 2nd edn, London: Hogarth Press.

Bowlby, J. (1982) *Attachment and Loss. Vol. 1: Attachment*, 2nd edn, London: Hogarth Press.

Britton, R. (1991) 'The missing link: Parental sexuality in the Oedipus complex', in Britton R., Feldman, M. and O'Shaughnessy E. (eds), *The Oedipus Complex Today*, London: Karnac Books.

Brown, G. W. and Harris, T. (1978) *Social Origins of Depression*, London: Routledge.

Daly, S. and Hartmann, P. (1995) 'Infant demand and milk supply', *Journal of Human Lactation,* 11 (2): 21–37.

Daws, D. (1993) *Through the Night: Helping Parents with Sleepless Infants*, London: Free Association Books.

Douglas, M. (1966 [2002]) *Purity & Danger: An Analysis of Concepts of Pollution & Taboo*, New York: Routledge Classics.

Drabble, M. (1965) *The Millstone*, London: Penguin.
Emanuel, L. and Bradley, E. (eds) (2008) *What Can the Matter Be: Therapeutic Interventions with Parents, Infants and Young Children*, The Tavistock Clinic Series, London: Karnac Books.
Figes, K. (2008) *Life after Birth*, London: Virago Press.
Fivaz-Depeursinge, E. (2008) 'Infants in triangular communication in "two for one" versus "two against one", family triangles', *Infant Mental Health Journal*, 29 (3): 189–202.
Fivaz-Depeursinge, E. and Philip, D. A. (2014) *The Baby and the Couple: Understanding and Treating Young Familites*, London: Routledge.
Fraiberg, S. H. et al. (1980) '"Ghosts in the nursery": A psychoanalytic approach to the problem of impaired infant–mother relationships', in S. H. Fraiberg (ed.), *Clinical Studies in Infant Mental Health, the First Year of Life*, London: Tavistock Publications, pp. 164–196.
Freud, S. (1957) *On Narcissism: An Introduction*, in *Standard Edition, Vol. XIV*, London: Hogarth Press, pp. 67–102.
Genesoni, L., Curran, R. L., Huertas-Ceballos, A. and Tallandini, M. A. (2008) 'Kangaroo mother care and its effects on parenting stress and maternal post-natal attachment in cases of premature birth', *Archives of Disease in Childhood – Fetal and Neonatal Edition*, 93 (Supplement): Fa80.
Gerhardt, S. (2004) *Why Love Matters: How Affection Shapes a Baby's Brain*, Hove: Routledge.
Glover, V. (2001) 'Infant massage improves mother–infant interaction for mothers with post-natal depression', *Journal of Affective Disorders*, 63: 201–207.
Hobson, P. (2002) *The Cradle of Thought*, Oxford: Macmillan.
Hopkins, J. (1996) 'The dangers and deprivations of too-good mothering', *Journal of Child Psychotherapy*, 22: 400–422.
Karpf, A. (ed.) 'From Donald Winnicott to the naughty step', Archive on 4. Online: www.bbc.co.uk/programmes/b01s7v7b (accessed February 2014).
Kimata, H. (2007). 'Laughter elevates the levels of breast-milk melatonin', *Journal of Psychosomatic Research*, 62 (6): 699–702.
Klein, M. (1946) 'Notes on some schizoid mechanisms', *Envy and Gratitude and Other Works 1946–1963*, London: Hogarth Press and the Institute of Psycho-Analysis (published 1975).
Kraemer, S. (2005) 'Narratives of fathers and sons: "there is no such thing as a father"', in Vetere, A. and Dowling, E. (eds), *Narrative Therapies with Children and their Families: A Practitioner's Guide to Concepts and Approaches*, East Sussex: Routledge/Brunner.
Leach, P. (2009) *Child Care Today*, Cambridge: Polity Press.
Leach, P. (2010) *The Essential First Year: What Babies Need Parents to Know*, London: Dorling Kindersley.
Lewin, V. (2004) *The Twin in the Transference*, London and Philadelphia: Whurr Publishers.
Liedloff, J. (1975) *The Continuum Concept*, London: Penguin Books.

Main, M., Kaplan, N. & Cassidy, J. (1985) 'Security in infancy, childhood and adulthood: A move to the level of representation', *Monographs of the Society for Research in Child Development*, 50: 66–104.

Marks, M. (2002) 'Letting fathers in', in Etchegoyan, A. and Trowell, J. (eds), *The Importance of Fathers: A Psychoanalytic Re-evaluation*, East Sussex: Brunner/Routledge

McFayden, A. (1994) *Special Care Babies and Their Developing Relationships*, London and New York: Routledge.

McKenna, J. J. et al. (1989) 'Sleep and arousal synchrony of co-sleeping human mother–infant pairs: Implications for the study of sudden infant death syndrome (SIDS)', *American Journal of Physical Anthropology*, 78 (2): 133–161.

Meltzoff, A. N. (2007) 'The "like me" framework for recognizing and becoming an intentional agent', *Acta Psychologica*, 124: 26–43.

Mendelsohn, A. (2005) 'Recovering reverie: Using infant observation in interventions with traumatised mothers and their premature babies', *Journal of Infant Observation*, 8 (3): 195–208.

Messenger Davies, M. (1989) *The Breastfeeding Book*, London: Vintage/Elwry.

Murray, L. (2014) *The Psychology of Babies*, London: Robinson.

Murray, L. and Andrews, L. (2000) *The Social Baby,* Richmond: CP Publishing.

Murray, L. and Cooper, P. (1999) *Postpartum Depression and Child Development*, London: Guilford Press.

Murray, L. and Trevarthen, C. (1985) 'Emotional regulation of interaction between two-month olds and their mothers', in Field, T. M. and Fox, N. A. (eds), *Social Perception in Infants*, Northwood, NJ: Ablex.

Music, G. (2011) *Nurturing Natures, Attachment and Children's Emotional, Socio-cultural and Brain Development*, Hove: Psychology Press.

Nagy, E. and Molnar, P. (2004) 'Homo imitans or homo provocans? Human imprinting model of neonatal imitation', *Infant Behavior & Development*, 27: 54–63.

Pally, R. (2000) *The Mind–Brain Relationship*, London, Karnac.

Palombo, S. (1978) *Dreaming and Memory*, New York: Basic.

Parker, R. (2005) *Torn in Two: The Experience of Maternal Ambivalence*, London: Virago Press.

Patterson, C. J. and Wainright, J. L. (2007) 'Adolescents with same-sex parents: Findings from national longitudinal study of adolescent health', in Brodzinsky, D., Pertman, A. and Kunz, D. (eds), *Lesbian and Gay Adoption: A New American Reality*, New York: Oxford University Press.

Phillips, A. (1999) *Saying No: Why its Important for You and Your Child*, London: Faber and Faber.

Piontelli, A. (2004) *Twins, From Fetus to Child*, London and New York: Routledge.

Raphael-Leff, J. (1993) *Pregnancy: The Inside Story*, London: Sheldon Press.

Reddy, V. (2008) *How Infants Know Minds*, London: Harvard University Press.

Rizzolatti, G. (2005). 'The mirror neuron system and its function in humans', *Anatomy and Embryology*, 210 (5): 419–421.

Robertson, J. and Robertson, J. (1967–75) Film series *Young Children in Brief Separation*. Tavistock Institute of Human Relations, Ipswich: Concord Film Council.

Schore, A. N. (2001) 'Effects of early relational trauma on right brain development, affect regulation, and infant mental health', *Infant Mental Health Journal, Special Contributions from the Decade of the Brain to Infant Mental Health*, 1–2: 201–269.

Shakespeare, W. (1994) *The Tempest*, reprint, Hertfordshire: Wordsworth Classics.

Stadlen, N. (2004) *What Mothers Do – Especially When it Looks Like Nothing*, London: Piatkus Books.

Stern, D. (1985) *The Interpersonal World of the Infant*, New York: Basic.

Stern, D. N. (2004) *The First Relationship*, Cambridge, MA: Harvard University Press.

Stevenson, A. (1983) 'Poem to my daughter', in The Raving Beauties (eds), *In the Pink: The Raving Beauties Choose Poems from the Show and Many More*, London: Women's Press; and in A. Stevenson (1982) *Minute by Glass Minute*, Oxford University Press.

Storey, A. E., Walsh, C. J., Quinton, R. L. and Wynne-Edwards, K. E. (2000) 'Hormonal correlates of paternal responsiveness in new and expectant fathers', *Evolution and Human Behaviour*, 21 (2): 79–95.

Trevarthen, C. (2001) 'Intrinsic motives for companionship in understanding: Their origin, development, and significance for infant mental health', *Infant Mental Health Journal, Special Contributions from the Decade of the Brain to Infant Mental Health*, 1–2: 95–131.

Winnicott, D. W. (1947) reprinted in Winnicott (1964) *The Child, the Family and the Outside World*, London: Pelican.

Winnicott, D. W. (1956) 'Maternal pre-occupation', in Winnicott (1958) *Collected Papers, Through Paediatrics to Psychoanalysis*, London: Tavistock and Hogarth Press.

Winnicott, D. W. (1958) 'Transitional objects and transitional phenomena', in Winnicott, *Through Paediatrics to Psychoanalysis*, London: Tavistock and Hogarth Press.

Wyllie, R. (2012) *Loving Andrew: A Fifty-Two-Year Story of Down's Syndrome*, North Charlston, SC: CreateSpace independent publishing platform.

Zeedyk, M. S. (2006) 'From intersubjectivity to subjectivity: The transformative roles of imitation and intimacy', *Infant and Child Development*, 15 (3): 321–344.

INDEX

31901059572612